Swiss Re Rüschlikon
Centre for Global Dialogue

Marcel Meili, Markus Peter
Dieter Kienast, Günther Vogt
Hermann Czech, Adolf Krischanitz
Gilbert Bretterbauer
Günther Förg

Kunsthaus Bregenz
archiv kunst architektur
Werkdokumente 20

		006	Elisabeth von Samsonow	
		018	Beteiligte	
		020	Pläne	
		036	Kunst in Rüschlikon	
			Swiss Re Rüschlikon	
			Centre for Global Dialogue	
		038	Marcel Meili, Markus Peter	
006	Elisabeth von Samsonow			
018	Project participants	043	Dieter Kienast, Günther Vogt	
020	Views		**Das schwierige Ganze – ganz leicht**	
036	Art in Rüschlikon	048	Otto Kapfinger	
	Swiss Re Rüschlikon		**Fotos**	
	Centre for Global Dialogue	068	Margherita Spiluttini	
038	Marcel Meili, Markus Peter			
		180	Biografische Daten	
043	Dieter Kienast, Günther Vogt			
	The Complex Whole, Simply Put			
048	Otto Kapfinger			
	Photos			
068	Margherita Spiluttini			
180	Biographical Data			

Elisabeth von Samsonow

Risk

The history of mankind can also be described as the history of its eternal state of distress, as a series of those accidents from which just enough of mankind managed to come away unharmed as was required for the preservation and propagation of the species. Thus people are inherently always *survivors*, which may help us understand the tales of paradise lost. According to the concurring reports of various cultures modern-day mankind descends from a hero who survived the deluge in an ark in which he took along one pair of each species. Thus *his history of survival* also became that of all animals and plants because had it not been for the ark builder none of them would have been clever enough to ensure the survival of their species. The great calamity of ancient times was thus the deluge, the cataclysmic accident, being swept away, the abyss. To counteract the feeling of being on unstable ground, on a ship without a helmsman, man invented the stone building and made it a sacred matter, a concern for the architect-priests – who in most cases were at the same time also kings or princes like the rulers of Lagash or the Egyptian pharaohs. Building foundations became a cosmological and political gesture, which is why the great cities of the ancient world derived their strong self-image from the expense they put into their architecture. Uruk and Babylon could be seen as foundations against the hazards of the untamed waters. Here the history of human calamity enters a new stage in which the citizen is invented, a person living within the fortification walls of a city whose duty it is to believe in the fierce sentries who have been posted atop those walls for the purpose of instilling a sense of

Risiko

Die Geschichte des Menschen kann auch als die Geschichte seines ewigen Erschreckens beschrieben werden, als Serie jener Unfälle, aus denen jeweils gerade noch soviel Menschheit davonkam, wie zur Erhaltung der Art und zu ihrer Ausbreitung erforderlich war. Menschen sind also von vornherein immer schon *Überlebende,* was die Erzählungen vom verlorenen Paradies erhellt. Die jüngere Menschheit leitet sich nach übereinstimmenden Berichten verschiedener Kulturen von einem Helden her, der die Sintflut überlebt hat und in seinem »Kasten« ein Pärchen einer jeglichen Art mitnahm, sodass *seine Überlebensgeschichte* auch die der Tiere und Pflanzen wurde, wobei diese jedoch keineswegs in der Lage gewesen wären, sich ihren eigenen Fortbestand listig zu sichern wie der Archenbauer. Der Schrecken der Urzeit war also die Überschwemmung, der kataklytische Unfall, das Fortgerissenwerden, die Bodenlosigkeit. Gegen das Gefühl, sich auf einem instabilen Grund zu befinden, auf einem Schiff ohne Steuermann, half die Erfindung des Steinbaus, der deshalb eine sakrale Angelegenheit, Sache der Priesterarchitekten – in den meisten Fällen zugleich Könige oder Fürsten wie die Herrscher aus Lagasch oder die ägyptischen Pharaonen – war. Das Fundamentemachen wurde zur kosmologischen und politischen Gründungsgeste, weshalb die großen Städte der Alten Welt ihr starkes Selbstverständnis aus ihrer architektonischen Aufwendigkeit speisten. Uruk und Babylon konnten als Gründungen gegen die Gefahren der Urgewässer verstanden werden. Hier tritt die menschliche Schreckensgeschichte in ein neues Stadium, nämlich in dasjenige der Erfindung von Bürgern, die sich durch die Wachposten auf der sie umgebenden Mauer von ihrer Zugehörigkeit zu der von ihr eingeschlossenen Gruppe überzeugen lassen müssen. Die Architektur und die mit ihr verbundene Form der »Ziviltechnik«, das heißt hier:

belonging in all members of the group within those walls. Architecture and the form of "civil engineering" associated with it, meaning in this case the art of forging political communities, seem to have ended the catastrophic initial chapter of the history of mankind. The building of walls is in its primary intention a reiterative return to the Garden of Eden, the repetition of the "us-vs.-them" wall: the Neolithic walled settlements, the walls of Babylon, the walls of Jericho, the Great Wall of China, the walls of the medieval European city with its complicated and restrictive transit regulations, and the famous Berlin Wall. Being surrounded by a close boundary that simulates through architecture the universe of a stable and closed system encourages the members of a group to form a tight collective inner core. From a historical perspective the building of walls, however, is a part of an old continuum of outdated techniques to ensure large group socialisation – in our terminology: of techniques to ward off perpetual distress through "exposure" in the rough global climate – even if, as for example in the case of the Berlin Wall, every once in a while an anachronistic application occurs.

Relevant contemporary social techniques tend to rely less on the rigid integration machine (palace, temple, city) and more on the ability of groups to allow themselves to be guided by the same powerful image, the same strong imagination, i.e. to rely on the capacity to recognize within its collective imagination the same images as relevant through which they establish themselves vis-à-vis the horizon of a kind of fundamental understanding. Not in the sense that they are similar on the surface, but by virtue of the fact that their internal images match; in that people

der Kunst der Herstellung von politischen Gemeinschaften, scheinen zunächst das katastrophische Anfangskapitel der Menschheitsgeschichte beendet zu haben. Der Mauerbau repetiert in seinen primären Intentionen die Paradiesmauern des Wir: die neolithischen Wallsiedlungen, die Mauern von Babylon, die Mauern von Jericho, die chinesische Mauer, die Mauern der mittelalterlichen Stadt mit ihren komplizierten und restriktiven Durchgangsbestimmungen und die berühmte Berliner Mauer. Das Umringtsein von einem Nahehorizont, der ein in sich stabilisiertes und geschlossenes Universum mit architektonischen Mitteln simuliert, bringt die Mitglieder einer Gruppe dazu, sich in einem kollektiven Innen zu verschwistern. Historisch betrachtet gehört der Mauerbau allerdings zu einem abgeschlossenen Kontinuum älterer Techniken der Großgruppensozialisierung – in unserer Terminologie: von Techniken gegen das fortwährende Erschrecken durch »Ausgesetztsein« im rauen Weltklima – auch wenn, wie am Beispiel der Berliner Mauer zu sehen, hier und da noch eine unzeitgemäße Applikation vorliegt.

Relevante zeitgenössische Soziotechniken bauen weniger auf die steinerne Integrationsmaschine (Palast, Tempel, Stadt) als auf die Fähigkeit von Gruppen, sich durch dieselben starken Bilder, dieselben machtvollen Imaginationen leiten zu lassen, das heißt auf die Fähigkeit, in ihrem Imaginarium dieselben Bilder als maßgebliche anzuerkennen, wodurch sie sich vor dem Horizont einer Art Grund-Verständigung etablieren. Nicht dadurch, dass sie sich äußerlich ähneln, sondern dadurch, dass sich ihre inneren Bilder gleichen, durch denselben Bildbesitz nämlich werden sich Menschen verwandt und fangen an, aus ihm ähnliche Erinnerungen abzuleiten, ganz wie das natürliche Verwandte tun. In den siebziger Jahren hat die Ethnologin und bedeutende Ritualtheoretikerin Mary Douglas die These formuliert, dass ein solches starkes Bild für eine Gesellschafts- oder

possess the same pool of images, they become related and begin to derive similar memories from that pool, the same way biological relatives do. In the seventies Mary Douglas, anthropologist and prominent scholar on rituals, formulated the thesis that one example of this sort of strong image at work in the formation of a society or group is the vision of the greatest possible risk, which could occur at any given time. This potential imagined risk would act like an invisible German shepherd, herding the members of the community together. Douglas goes on to add that it seems odd to her that certain people consider the Ozone Hole – to give an example – one of the greatest hazards, while others aren't the least bit intimidated by it. The preference certain groups have for certain risks led Douglas to disregard the purely statistical and objectifiable status of risk and to start paying more attention to the operators who would present certain risks as more "fashionable" than others. Immediately she was accused of playing down the real risks and degrading them to phantasmata, i.e. of reducing the peril of existence to a mere entertaining issue of cultural social science. Nevertheless she continued studying this topic, collecting data about what clearly seems to account for a great part of the depth of human existence, and today's growing interest on the subject of risk confirms her work decades later. She believes that people have never managed to free themselves from the certainty that their existence is fraught with catastrophes, and that the impulse upon touching this perennial tenor of calamity is still able to produce powerful projections.

Gruppenbildung eine Vorstellung von dem jeweils größten Risiko sei, das jederzeit eintreffen könne. Dieses vorgestellte Risiko wirke wie eine Art unsichtbarer Schäferhund, der die Mitglieder einer Gruppe zueinander treibe. Es sei doch immerhin merkwürdig, dass bestimmte Menschen glaubten, dass – um einmal ein Beispiel zu nennen – das Ozonloch eine der größten Gefahren sei, während andere nicht im Geringsten von diesem Ozonloch zu beeindrucken seien. Die Präferenz bestimmter Risiken durch gewisse Gruppen brachte Douglas dazu, den rein statistischen und objektivierbaren Status des Risikos einzuklammern und sich für die Operatoren, die ein Risiko gegenüber dem anderen »in Mode« bringen, zu interessieren. Sie hat sich prompt die Kritik gefallen lassen müssen, die realen Risiken zu verharmlosen und sie auf Phantasmata zu reduzieren, das heißt die Gefährlichkeit der Existenz zum kurzweiligen kulturwissenschaftlichen Thema herabgewürdigt zu haben. Gleichwohl scheint sie zweifellos das, was der menschlichen Existenz zu einem wesentlichen Teil ein Relief gibt, erfasst und entfaltet zu haben, wobei das zeitgenössische wachsende Interesse am Thema Risiko ihr noch nachträglich Recht gibt. Sie ist der Meinung, dass die Menschen sich niemals aus der Evidenz, dass ihre Existenz katastophenträchtig ist, befreien haben können und der Impuls, der auf diesen perennierenden Schreckenstenor trifft, nach wie vor mächtige Projektionen hervorzurufen imstande ist.

Die philosophische Anthropologie des 20. Jahrhunderts hat nachdrücklich die »Entlastungsfunktionen« diskutiert, die zur menschlichen Schreckens- und Erschreckensgeschichte gehören, und die Erfindungen, das Freiwerden von einer unzureichenden Natur behandelt. Auch wenn man sich nicht wirklich von einem urtümlichen Aristotelismus verabschieden hat wollen, der die menschliche Findigkeit aus der Natur selbst hat hervorgehen lassen, so hat doch die Vorstellung,

Philosophical anthropology of the 20th century has discussed the long and short of the "relief functions" inherent in mankind's history of calamity and distress and examined the inventions, the liberation from an insufficient Nature. Even if one is not quite ready to depart from a classical Aristotelism that attributes human resourcefulness to Nature itself, the notion that technological history has arisen as a protest to Nature has nonetheless become more pronounced. Moreover, also gaining ground is the conviction that not just the menacing danger of risk constitutes the basis for human community, but also the effort, inventions and calculations employed to politically, technologically and economically overcome this risk, whereby the paradox is that in recent history risk and its prevention have been excised completely from the area of influence of so-called natural occurrences and must now be seen as "man-made", as genuinely human, as fundamental facts that wouldn't exist without the complex global interaction in the technological age. Ulrich Beck distinguishes clearly between the old "catastrophe community" of the early industrial social state and the modern risk society, whereby he assumes a kind of natural state for the former, since the threats to the preindustrial world, according to his view, were of an exclusively natural type ("Plague, hunger, natural catastrophes, wars, as well as magic, gods and evil spirits"[1]). In a way the third "phase", namely the risk society, is closer to the first than it is to the second phase because it undermines and goes beyond the scope of the calculations of the social state by creating its own non-calculable risks, like "nuclear, ecological and genetic engineering risks".[2] The risk situation that this societal type

dass die Technikgeschichte sich als Einspruch gegen jene formiert, an Deutlichkeit gewonnen. Die Überzeugung, nach der nicht nur das Risiko als die drohende Gefahr die Grundlage der menschlichen Gemeinschaft bilde, sondern auch die Anstrengung, die Erfindungen und das Kalkül, die unternommen werden, um dieses Risiko politisch, technisch und ökonomisch zu bewältigen, gewinnt an Boden, wobei darauf hingewiesen wird, dass paradoxerweise in der jüngsten Geschichte das Risiko und seine Abwendung vollständig aus dem Geltungsbereich eines so genannten natürlichen Geschehens herausgenommen und als »man-made«, als genuin menschliche, der komplexen globalen Interaktion im technischen Zeitalter sich verdankende Grundtatsachen angesehen werden müssen. Ulrich Beck hat zwischen der alten »Katastrophengemeinschaft«, dem frühindustriellen Vorsorgestaat und der modernen Risikogesellschaft deutlich unterschieden, wobei er für die erstere noch eine Art Naturzustand annimmt, insofern die Bedrohungen, denen die vorindustrielle Welt unterliegt, ausnahmslos natürlicher Art gewesen seien (»Pest, Hunger, Naturkatastrophen, Kriege, aber auch Magie, Götter und Dämonen«[1]). In gewisser Weise ist die dritte »Phase«, nämlich die Risikogesellschaft, der ersten näher als der zweiten, da sie das Kalkül des Vorsorgestaates durch selbst erzeugte, nicht kalkulierbare Risiken wie »atomare, ökologische und gentechnische Risiken«[2] unterläuft bzw. sprengt. Die Risikolage, die dieser Gesellschaftstypus erzeugt, ähnelt der des vorindustriellen Katastrophismus, was die Undurchsichtigkeit der Folgen und den Umfang der Kontexte, die manipuliert werden, betrifft. Es ergibt sich daraus der kuriose Umstand, dass dem modernen, in einer solchen Risikogesellschaft lebenden Individuum zugemutet werden muss, sich auf einem hohen Gefährdungsniveau einzurichten, ohne – wie es für archaische Gruppen anzunehmen ist – auf Hilfe und Beistand allerhöchster Instanzen

produces is similar to that of preindustrial catastrophism, as far as the opacity of the consequences and the range of the contexts being manipulated are concerned. What comes out of all this is the odd circumstance that a modern individual living in a risk society of this kind is expected to accept that he will be subjected to a higher level of potential danger, without – as we assume was the case in archaic groups – the hope of receiving aid or succour from high authorities, like the powerful clan deities or other relevant collective protective figures, e.g. the fourteen saints. And what's more, there is no one – not an inconstant Mount Olympus, nor an angry god, nor a well-functioning insurance company, as was the case in the social state – to be held responsible anymore. Éwald writes: "It quickly became clear to me that one of the greatest intellectual experiences of the western world was reflected in the question of risk, a question that holds within it man's entire existence: in the three dimensions time – future, chance, fortune, providence, fate –, order/disorder in Nature, the world and society, – and the existence of evil, its origin, the responsibilities it implies and the battles it provokes. Until then man had searched for the answer to these questions in divine knowledge. Now the only place left for him to look was in the current social context."[3]

When the risk zone starts to expand, when modern individuals get the impression they are dancing on a volcano or at a "suicide party" (Sloterdijk), then it's time to search for the root of whatever it is that increases risk; and paradoxically this can't be found so much in the human monstrosity, which Hölderlin referred to, as in the *play function*. Now that the security the social

wie der mächtigen Stammesgottheiten oder auch anderer einschlägig zugeordneter kollektiver Schutzherrschaften, wie etwa der Vierzehnheiligen, hoffen zu dürfen. Und nicht nur das. Es ist weder ein wankelmütiger Olymp oder eine zürnende Gottheit noch eine gut funktionierende Versicherungsgesellschaft, wie das im Vorsorgestaat geschehen konnte, zur Rechenschaft zu ziehen. Éwald schreibt: Es »wurde mir rasch klar, daß sich in der Frage des Risikos eine der großen geistigen Erfahrungen des Okzidents widerspiegelte, eine Frage, in der das gesamte Sein des Menschen enthalten ist: in den drei Dimensionen Zeit – Zukunft, Zufall, Glück, Vorsehung, Schicksal –, Ordnung – bzw. Unordnung in Natur, Welt und Gesellschaft – sowie in der der Existenz des Übels, seines Ursprungs, der Verantwortlichkeiten, die es impliziert, und der Kämpfe, die es nötig macht. Bis dahin hatte er Mensch die Antwort auf diese Fragen in der Erkenntnis Gottes gesucht. Er mußte sie jetzt allein in der Aktualität des sozialen Zusammenhangs suchen.«[3]

Wenn die Risikozone sich auszudehnen beginnt, wenn moderne Individuen den Eindruck haben, sich auf einem Vulkan oder auf einer »Selbstmörderparty« (Sloterdijk) zu befinden, dann muss die Wurzel jenes Antriebs, der auf die Erhöhung des Risikos geht, gesucht werden; und diese lässt sich paradoxerweise nicht so sehr in der menschlichen Ungeheuerlichkeit, von der Hölderlin sprach, verorten als vielmehr in der *Spielfunktion*. Nach dem Verblassen der Sicherheit, die sich der Vorsorgestaat einzurichten bemüht hatte, durch die neuen und immer neuen Risiken lässt sich vor dem Hintergrund des modernen globalisierten Risikomanagements das altmenschliche Verhältnis zum Dasein ausmachen als zarte, unscharf gewordene Skizze, in deren Linien sich auch die neuen Umstände ein wenig erhellen.

state endeavoured so hard to create has faded, we can in the face of new and ever arising newer risks and against the backdrop of modern global risk management make out the classical human relation to existence as a sketch that has become blurred, but in whose faint lines the contours of the new circumstances are slowly starting to emerge.

Homo ludens

If the risk society is at one end of the spectrum, then a "playing society" or playing community must be assumed to exist at the opposite end, whereby this means that – as in Beck's catastrophe society – contact is made with an anonymous macro agent like fate or fortune and misfortune. There is indeed an ingenious system of insurances, just as the social state fashioned itself in the likeness of Providence; the level of the incurred risks, i.e. the threshold beyond which things operate technically and economically has been raised considerably. Éwald defines: "No private insurance protection, what's more: no insurability for industrial, technological-scientific projects. This is a yardstick that society is not dependent on the sociologist or an artist to provide it with. Society itself produces this standard and measures its own development by it: beyond the insurance limit the unwanted industrial society that has mutated into the risk society through the systemically produced hazards negotiates a precarious balance."[4]

Calculating in the "macro agent", the successor of fate, draws up the over-exaggerated worst case scenario, in other words a highly speculative form of economy that draws its capital from an equally over-exaggerated willingness to assume a risk, whereby one must hope and count on the chance that this worst case *won't happen*. Certain insurance companies have been known to

Homo ludens

Komplementär zur Risikogesellschaft muss eine »Spielergesellschaft« oder Spielergemeinschaft angenommen werden, wodurch ausgedrückt wird, dass – wie in Becks Katastrophengesellschaft – mit einem anonymen Makro-Agenten wie Schicksal oder Glück und Unglück Beziehung aufgenommen wird. Es gibt zwar ein ausgeklügeltes System von Versicherungen, ganz so, wie es der Vorsorgestaat in der Nachfolge der göttlichen Vorsehung ausgebildet hatte; das Niveau der eingegangenen Risiken bzw. die Schwelle, jenseits deren in technischer und ökonomischer Hinsicht operiert wird, wird aber um ein Beträchtliches angehoben. Éwald definiert: »Fehlen des privaten Versicherungsschutzes, mehr noch: der Versicherbarkeit von industriellen, technisch-wissenschaftlichen Projekten. Dies ist eine Elle, die nicht der Soziologe oder sonst ein Künstler an die Gesellschaft von außen herantragen muß. Die Gesellschaft selbst erzeugt diesen Maßstab und bemißt daran ihre eigene Entwicklung: Jenseits der Versicherungsgrenze balanciert die ungewollte durch die systemisch erzeugten Gefahren zur Risikogesellschaft mutierte Industriegesellschaft.«[4]

Das Kalkül mit dem »Makro-Agenten«, dem Nachfolger des Schicksals, malt also den überdimensionierten Ernstfall aus, was eine hochspekulative Wirtschaftsform bedeutet, die Kapital aus einer ebenso überdimensionierten Bereitschaft ein Risiko zu übernehmen zieht, wobei gehofft – und auch kalkuliert – werden muss, dass dieser Ernstfall *eben nicht eintritt*. Gewisse Versicherungsgesellschaften hören bekanntlich auf, für unkalkulierbare Risiken Schutz anzubieten; es sind beispielsweise neun derjenigen Versicherungsgesellschaften, die in Florida und Hawaii gegen Wirbelstürme versichert hatten, in den neunziger Jahren bankrott gegangen.[5] Solche Gefahren werden nun entsichert. Es gibt also in einem zeitgemäßen *Risk Mapping* große schwarze Zonen,

stop offering protection for non-calculable risks. For example in Florida and Hawaii nine insurance companies offering cyclone insurance went bankrupt in the nineties.[5] This type of hazard is now being excluded. Thus within modern risk mapping there are large black holes that are either not covered for the aforementioned reasons or which have for non-calculable reasons escaped the social system. Moreover, now there are also insurance forms that no longer speculate with the individual risk types of the social state – e.g. accident/industrial accident, general disability – but instead have begun to play with the risk of insurance itself. In this sensitive seismographic zone of the entire insurance and "insecurity" industry the *reinsurance companies* gain significance as the last recourse for macroscopic damage claims. In a way they seem to be a kind of hero of the insurance industry, as the collective daredevil who is willing to assume the highest risk, the mother of all risks, in order to produce a new, speculative relation to risk at the same time. With reinsurances it seems that the risk society has fully transformed itself into the playing group; at least the figure of the thinker of the playing group has been aptly chosen if one considers that calculating a worst-case scenario that does not occur – in this case therefore not the occurrence but the non-occurrence – leads to a capitalisation that is comparable to the making of the "power house" in ancient cultures, i.e. the temple treasure. The temple treasure arises through a similar operation, namely through the collection of offerings intended to appease Fate or a powerful divinity that represents it. The offerings are actually stakes, which contribute to the amassing of the treasure or its accumulation as soon as the

die entweder aus den geschilderten Gründen entsichert oder aus Gründen der Nicht-Kalkulierbarkeit dem Sorge- oder Vorsorgewesen entglitten sind. Darüber hinaus gibt es nun aber Versicherungsformen, die mit den einzelnen Risikotypen des Vorsorgestaates – zum Beispiel Unfall/Arbeitsunfall, Erwerbsunfähigkeit – nicht mehr ihr Kalkül treiben, sondern mit dem Risiko der Versicherung selbst zu spielen beginnen. In der sensiblen seismographischen Zone dieses gesamten Versicherungs- und Verunsicherungswesens operieren die *Rückversicherungen,* die als letzte Instanz für die makroskopischen Schadensfälle eintreten. Sie erscheinen in gewisser Weise als eine Art heroisches Subjekt des Versicherungswesens überhaupt, als kollektiver Wagehals, der das höchste Risiko, das Risiko aller Risiken, aufzufangen sich bereit erklärt, damit zugleich aber in ein neues, spekulatives Verhältnis zum Risiko eintritt. In den Rückversicherungen erscheint die Konversion von der Risikogesellschaft zur Spielergemeinschaft vollzogen; zumindest ist die Denkfigur der Spielergemeinschaft für sie zutreffend gewählt, wenn man bedenkt, dass das Kalkül des nicht absolut eintretenden Ernstfalls – hier also nicht der Treffer, sondern das Nicht-Eintreffen – zu einer Kapitalisierung führt, die der Entstehung des »power house« in den alten Kulturen, also des Tempelschatzes, vergleichbar ist. Der Tempelschatz kommt durch eine ähnliche Operation zustande, nämlich durch das Anhäufen von Gaben, die das Schicksal oder eine für es stehende mächtige Divinität gnädig stimmen sollen. Die Gaben sind vielmehr Einsätze, die in dem Moment zur Schatzbildung oder Akkumulation führen, in dem die gefräßigen Schicksalsmächte eben nichts fordern. Diese Form der Schatzbildung ist durchaus der legitime Vorgänger der Kapitalisierungsform, von der die Versicherungsgesellschaften nach der Pronfanierung des Schicksals leben. Die Frage ist nun, was mit dem neuen Tempelschatz geschehen soll. Gewiss gibt es eine

greedy powers of Fate refrain from demanding anything. This form of amassing treasure is certainly the legitimate precursor of the form of capitalisation from which the insurance companies have lived since the secularisation of Fate. The question now is what should be done with the new temple treasure? Of course there is a responsibility to view the consolidation of capital as a thematic and existential consolidation as well, as a process of proliferation on all levels, one that must yield to the urgent wishes of the risk society in a playful, meaning above all in an aesthetic way and make them visible. From a catastrophe that doesn't occur one can siphon off the surplus, literally a *wellness reserve* that in turn should be invested in experiments for the self-improvement of a society. In this way, oddly enough the task of making evident the playful and aesthetic potential of a group has given way to a new, modern system of patronage, in fact: reinsurance has as the legitimate heir to the theological patent on potentially carrying on a dialogue with mankind's destiny even been given the task of indulging in the ornate and decorative, in beauty and adornment, in other words in the luxury of its own luxury economy. The truth of the temple treasures of ancient civilizations and the complex economy implicit in them – which lies somewhere between religious, cultural/habitual motives and a basal barter system – expresses itself in the redundant aesthetic forms that follow by architectonic means the process of treasure amassing, and furthermore also in the albeit loosely associated intellectual activity which involves a kind of existential speculation, i.e. brings back via all its circuitous routes and diversions what originally was the hope of a good

Verpflichtung, die Kapitalverdichtung auch als thematische und existenzielle Verdichtung zu lesen, als Prozess der Wucherung auf allen Ebenen, der den drängenden Wünschen der Risikogesellschaft auf spielerische, das heißt auch und vor allem auf ästhetische Weise nachzugeben hat und sie versichtbart. Aus dem Nicht-Eintreten der Katastrophe wird ein Überschuss abgeschöpft, eine buchstäbliche *Wellness-Reserve,* die ihrerseits in Experimente der Selbstverbesserung einer Gesellschaft investiert zu werden hat. Merkwürdigerweise geht so der Auftrag, die spielerischen und ästhetischen Potenzen einer Gruppe manifest werden zu lassen, in ein neues, zeitgemäßes Mäzenatentum über, ja mehr noch als das: die Rückversicherung hat als legitime Erbin des theologischen Patents auf eine Dialogmöglichkeit mit dem menschheitlichen Schicksalshaften die Aufgabe, dem Ornat und dem Dekorum, dem Schönen und dem Schmuck, also dem Überfluss aus der eigenen Überflusswirtschaft heraus Raum zu geben. Die Wahrheit der Tempelschätze der alten Kulturen und der ihnen impliziten komplexen Ökonomie – die sich zwischen religiösen, kulturellen/habituellen Motiven und einer basalen Tauschökonomie ausmachen lässt – drückt sich in den redundanten ästhetischen Formen aus, die den Prozess der Schatzbildung mit architektonischen Mitteln nachzeichnen, ferner in der an diese, wenn auch lose, angebundenen geistigen Aktivität, die eine Art existenzieller Spekulation betreibt, das heißt, wieder in alle ihre Zirkelgänge und Zerstreuungen zurückführt, was ursprüngliche Hoffnung auf ein gutes Dasein war. Dazu gehören natürlich die Zusammenkünfte des oberen Risikomanagements, das heißt die »Kastenbildung« als Effekt einer intensiven Verständigung. Die Qualität oder der Reichtum des Tempels beruhte auf seiner Fähigkeit, ein äußerst einleuchtendes Bild eines Risikos und einen Vorschlag für seine Abwendung zu vermitteln. Aus diesem Grund war

existence. This of course also entails the coming together of the upper echelons of risk management, i.e. the formation of a "caste system" as the result of intensive communication. The quality or affluence of the temple depended on its ability to communicate an extremely transparent picture of a risk and a convincing proposal of how to avert it. For this reason the ancient treasuries practically always to some degree employed an oracle, for example in Delphi. Within the horizon of an old-new risk society this oracle tradition can be seen in a new light: converging on the symbolic *bridge* are the people who have been trying to predict the course of – to use Buckminster Fuller's imagery – "spaceship Earth", which has been without a captain since Noah's day, and who at the same time from within their elitist groups make decisions about the possibilities of the future course of Earth. The ambivalence of this imagery suggests a virtual world, the possible, open world to come.

Corporation and architecture

From here it becomes clear why a modern reinsurance company far removed from big modern office buildings has made room for this "oracle work", i.e. for future-oriented research activity aimed at examining the basic trends of society's developmental potentials. An enterprise like this is also a consequence of Éwald's hypothesis that the theological concept of Providence has shifted to include all levels of complex social interaction, which means that we have to explore the body of opinions, knowledge, convictions and prognoses from the different and ever changing constellations of opinion leaders from all areas of society. But for reasons of the characteristic identity of a reinsurance company the concentration of

für die alten Schatzhäuser eine gewisse Orakeltätigkeit, wie etwa in Delphi, so gut wie die Regel. Das Orakelwesen zeigt sich vor dem Horizont einer alt-neuen Risikogesellschaft in einem neuen Licht: Ganz vorne, in einem symbolträchtigen *Cockpit*, treten diejenigen zusammen, die den Kurs des seit Noah steuerlosen »Raumschiffs Erde« – um eine Bezeichnung von Buckminster Fuller zu gebrauchen – vorauszusagen versuchen und sich zugleich mit ihren Voraussagen auf einer elitären Ebene über die Möglichkeiten des zukünftigen Kurses verabreden. Die Ambivalenz der Sprüche deutet in eine virtuelle Welt, in die mögliche, offene, die kommt.

Körperschaft und Architektur

Von hier aus wird einsichtig, weshalb sich eine moderne Rückversicherungsgesellschaft, abseits der großen modernen Bürokasernen, einen Raum für diese »Orakelpraxis«, das heißt für eine zukunftsgerichtete Forschungstätigkeit, die die Grundtendenzen der gesellschaftlichen Entwicklungspotenziale ausmachen soll, erobert. Eine solche Unternehmung ist auch eine Konsequenz aus Éwalds Annahme, dass sich der theologische Begriff der Vorsehung auf die Ebene der komplexen sozialen Interaktion verschoben hat, was bedeutet, dass die Konstellationen von Meinungen, Wissen, Überzeugungen und Prognosen auszuloten sind, die sich aus den Äußerungen verschiedener und wechselnder Gruppen von *Opinion Leaders* aus allen Bereichen der Gesellschaft ergeben. Die intellektuelle Anstrengung, die sich auf einen solchen Ort konzentrieren soll, ist jedoch aus Gründen der charakteristischen Identität einer Rückversicherung nicht ohne die Betätigung der Spielfunktion denkbar, weshalb besonders im vorliegenden Fall, für das Zentrum in Zürich-Rüschlikon, erstens ein eminent hoher Anspruch auf seine zeitgenössische künstlerische Qualität gefordert und zweitens nicht-formelle Gesprächs-, nicht-formelle Begegnungs- und Kommunikationsformen favorisiert worden waren.

intellectual energy to converge at a venue like this would be entirely inconceivable without an element of the play function. This is why, particularly in the case of the centre in Zürich-Rüschlikon, first of all, eminently high standards have been placed on the contemporary artistic quality and secondly, non-formal forms of dialogue, meeting and communication have been favoured. Rüschlikon is therefore not only an intellectual but also above all a social laboratory with the sophisticated architectonic forms of a "long Moderne", which rely not on the irony of Postmodernism but on the affirmative perfection of the principles of proportion based on the transparency, lightness, truth of the construction and the quality of the materials. The "training" that is to take place here favours not only speculative dimensions but practical ones too, and the improvement of certain professional skills, however the main emphasis of the centre – this can be easily decoded from the dramatic sequence and structural significance of the restaurant, teahouse, bar and sauna – has been placed on interaction. For the interested visitor the Swiss Re building will translate into a concentrated modern version of a Roman thermal bath, which became the headquarters of the Mithra warrior religion. By visiting the thermal baths and indulging in the collectivised rituals of hygienic – and gastronomic – incorporation, the distilled thought or essence can be achieved more easily and later shared in the great, public presentation rooms. Thermal baths would also allow a similar revitalization of the oligarchic idea of the strengthening and understanding of society's best men, as one can witness in the revival among the neoconservative elite classes of a global culture.

Rüschlikon ist also nicht nur ein intellektuelles, sondern auch im Besonderen ein soziales Labor, das mit den ausgereiften architektonischen Formen einer »langen Moderne«, die anstatt auf die Ironie der Postmoderne auf die affirmative Vollendung des auf Transparenz, Leichtigkeit, Wahrheit der Konstruktion und Qualität des Materials gegründeten Kanons setzt. Die »Ausbildung«, die dort stattfinden soll, privilegiert neben der spekulativen Dimension auch diejenige des Trainings und der Vertiefung gewisser professioneller Fertigkeiten, wobei der Hauptzweck des Zentrums – das lässt sich leicht in der dramatischen Abfolge und strukturellen Bedeutung von Restaurant, Teehaus, Bar und Sauna dechiffrieren – in die Interaktion verlegt ist. Für den interessierten Besucher wird sich das Haus der Swiss Re in Rüschlikon als konzentrierte moderne Fassung eines römischen Thermenbaus dechiffrieren, der zur Zentrale der Kriegerreligion des Mithras geworden war. Im Durchgang durch das Schwitzbad und in der Kollektivisierung der Rituale hygienischer – auch gastronomischer – Inkorporierung wird jenes Destillat oder jene Sublimierung leichter erreicht, die dann für den Auftritt in den großen öffentlichen Präsentationsräumen qualifiziert. Die Thermen erlaubten im Übrigen eine ähnliche Belebung einer oligarchischen Idee der Stärkung und Verständigung der Besten, wie sie in den neokonservativen Eliten einer globalen Kultur auflebt. Eine Einsicht in die vielfältigen Bedingungen der Möglichkeit des *Knowledge Transfer* legte ein bauliches Konzept nahe, das die schizoide Planung von Schulungs- und Seminarräumen einerseits und von Ruhe-, Rekreations- und Begegnungsorten andererseits aufhebt und beide Raumtypen auf geheimnisvolle Weise ineinander verschränkt. Man sieht aus der Synthese das Bild des in der »Architektur des Lernens« oft verloren gegangenen »ganzen Menschen« antiker Prägung emergieren, der, wie man weiß, seine besten Ideen zwangsläufig nicht

Insight into the multifarious conditions of the potential of knowledge transfer suggests a building concept that does away with the schizoid planning of training and seminar rooms, on the one hand, and rest, recreation and meeting spaces, on the other, and allows both types of space to cross over back and forth in a mystical way. From this synthesis one can see emerging from the "Architecture of Learning" the image of the "whole person" of classical times who we have often lost sight of, who, as we know, is not capable of coming up with his best ideas sitting still in a lecture, but inside the gym as a place of athletic and artistic activity. Meili, Peter's major architectonic image is that of an *agon,* a classic arena or stage for nice games and contests upon which they superimpose the ideal type of a cloister: thus the spacious atrium, which has been chosen as the basic form, determined more or less by the position of the historical villa, i.e. this emptiness is seen as a connection between Sky and Earth, as the column of all columns or the absolute vertical from which all architecture originates. Leading around this green square is a path that is partially open, partially a continuation of the historicistic peristyle, a peripatos, i.e. a walk with no definite course, similar to the ones that served the Aristotelian philosopher (the Peripatetic, one who walks from place to place) as an essential source of inspiration.

1   Ulrich Beck: "Risikogesellschaft und Vorsorgestaat – Zwischenbilanz einer Diskussion", in: François Éwald: *Der Vorsorgestaat* (orig. *L'Etat Providence,* Paris 1986), translated from French by W. Bayer and H. Kocyba, Frankfurt/Main 1993, page 539 (English by the translator of this text).
2   Ibid. page 541
3   F. Éwald, loc. cit. page 10
4   Ibid. page 541
5   See ibid. page 541, footnote 6

während des Stillsitzens anlässlich eines Kolloquiums produziert, sondern in der Nähe eines Gymnasiums als sportlich und künstlerisch verstandenen Ort. Das architektonische Leitbild von Meili, Peter ist dasjenige eines *Agon,* also eines klassischen Kampf- oder Schauplatzes für schöne Spiele und Wettkämpfe, über das der Idealtypus eines Klosters gelegt ist: Man sieht die Bevorzugung des geräumigen Atriums als Grundform, die gewissermaßen durch die Platzierung der historistischen Villa vorgegeben ist, das heißt der Leere als Verbindung zwischen Himmel und Erde, als der Säule aller Säulen oder absoluten Senkrechten, aus der sich die Architektur überhaupt herleitet. Um dieses grüne Viereck herum führt ein zum Teil offener, zum Teil als Fortsetzung des historizistischen Peristyls angelegter Weg, ein *Peripatos,* ein Wandelgang, ähnlich demjenigen, der für die aristotelischen Philosophen (die Peripatetiker, die Herumwandelnden) wesentliche Inspirationsquelle war.

1   Ulrich Beck: Risikogesellschaft und Vorsorgestaat – Zwischenbilanz einer Diskussion, in: François Éwald: *Der Vorsorgestaat* (orig. *L'État Providence,* Paris 1986), aus dem Französischen von W. Bayer und H. Kocyba, Frankfurt/Main 1993, Seite 539
2   ebenda, Seite 541
3   F. Éwald, a.a.O., Seite 10
4   ebenda, Seite 541
5   ebenda, Seite 541, Fußnote 6

Beteiligte
Project participants

Projektsteuerungsausschuss Swiss Re
Project steering committee Swiss Re
Peter Huegle (Leitung | Management) | Ulrich Bremi | Walter B. Kielholz | Walter Anderau | Otto Kern | Giovanni Olgiati | Fritz Gutbrodt

Projektmanagement | Bauherrenvertretung
Project management | representation of client
Otto Kern (Leitung | Management) | Rolf Keller

Architektur
Architecture
Marcel Meili, Markus Peter Architekten | Zürich
•
Detlef Schulz | Tobias Wieser (Projektleitung | Project manager) | Martin Aerne | Maria Aström | Aita Flury | Samuel Gäumann | Carole Iselin | Adrian Kast | Nadja Keller | Christian Penzel | Patrick Sidler | Jürg Spaar | Katharina Stehrenberger | Othmar Villiger | Adrian Weber (Mitarbeiterinnen und Mitarbeiter | Collaborators)

Projektmanagement und Bauleitung
General contractor
Karl Steiner AG | Zürich
•
Rolf Hirschi (Projektleitung | Project manager) | Hans Bossi | Willi Kummer | Romina Pierandozzi | Adolf Spruit | Max Stahel | Rainer Ziesemer

Landschaftsarchitektur
Landscape architecture
Kienast Vogt Partner | Zürich
•
Klaus Müller (Projektleitung | Project manager)

Innenarchitektur
Interior design
Hermann Czech | Wien
Adolf Krischanitz | Wien
•
Zeljiko Ivosevic | Werner Neuwirth | Thomas Roth

Textilkunst
Textile design
Gilbert Bretterbauer | Wien

Kunstprojekt Villa
Art project, villa
Günther Förg | Areuse

Lichtplanung
Lighting
Moser Sidler | Zürich

Grafik
Graphic design
WBG
Weiersmüller Bosshard Grüninger | Zürich

Bauingenieure
Civil engineers
Fietz AG | Zürich
Conzett, Bronzini, Gartmann AG | Chur

Fassadenplanung
External envelope
Emmer Pfenninger Partner AG | Münchenstein

HLK-Planung
Heating, plumbing, ventilation
Meierhans + Partner | Fällanden

Sanitärplanung
Sanitary facilities
Walter Müller AG | Zürich

Elektroplanung
Electrical installations
Ernst Baseler + Partner | Zürich

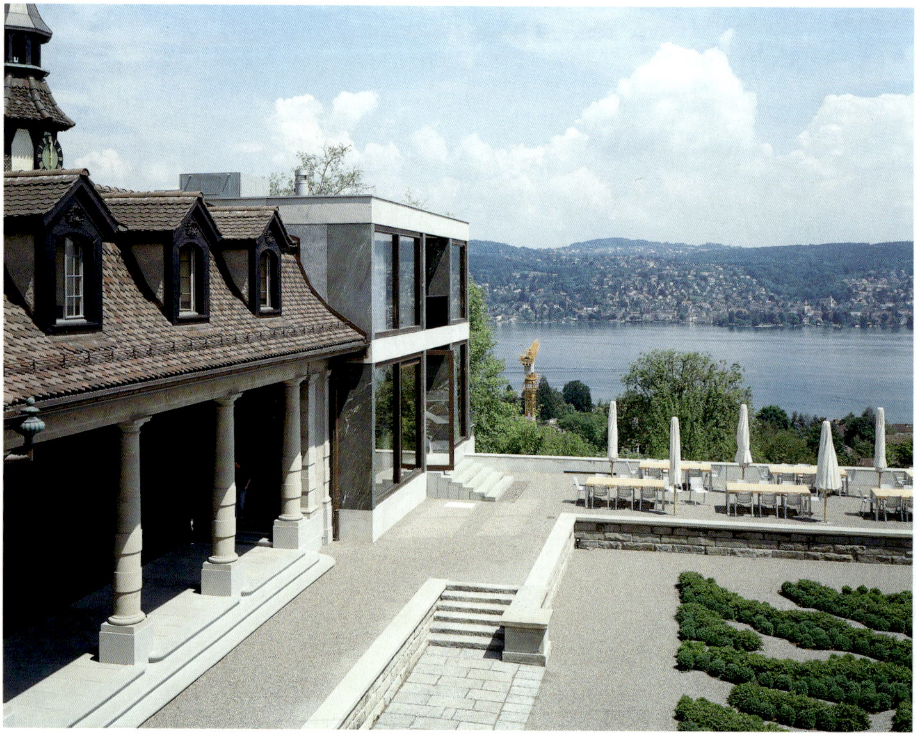

In der Mitte die Ebene des geometrischen Gartens,
darum herum der Landschaftsgarten
At the center, the strict geometric park
surrounded by the natural garden

1. Seminargebäude | Seminar building
2. Gärtnerhaus mit Czech-Bar | Gardender's house with Czech bar
3. Villa | Villa
4. Restaurant | Dining Room
5. Teehaus | Tee house
6. Skulptur, Sol LeWitt | Sculpture, Sol LeWitt
7. Baptistenkirche der Gemeinde Rüschlikon | Baptist church of the municipality of Rüschlikon

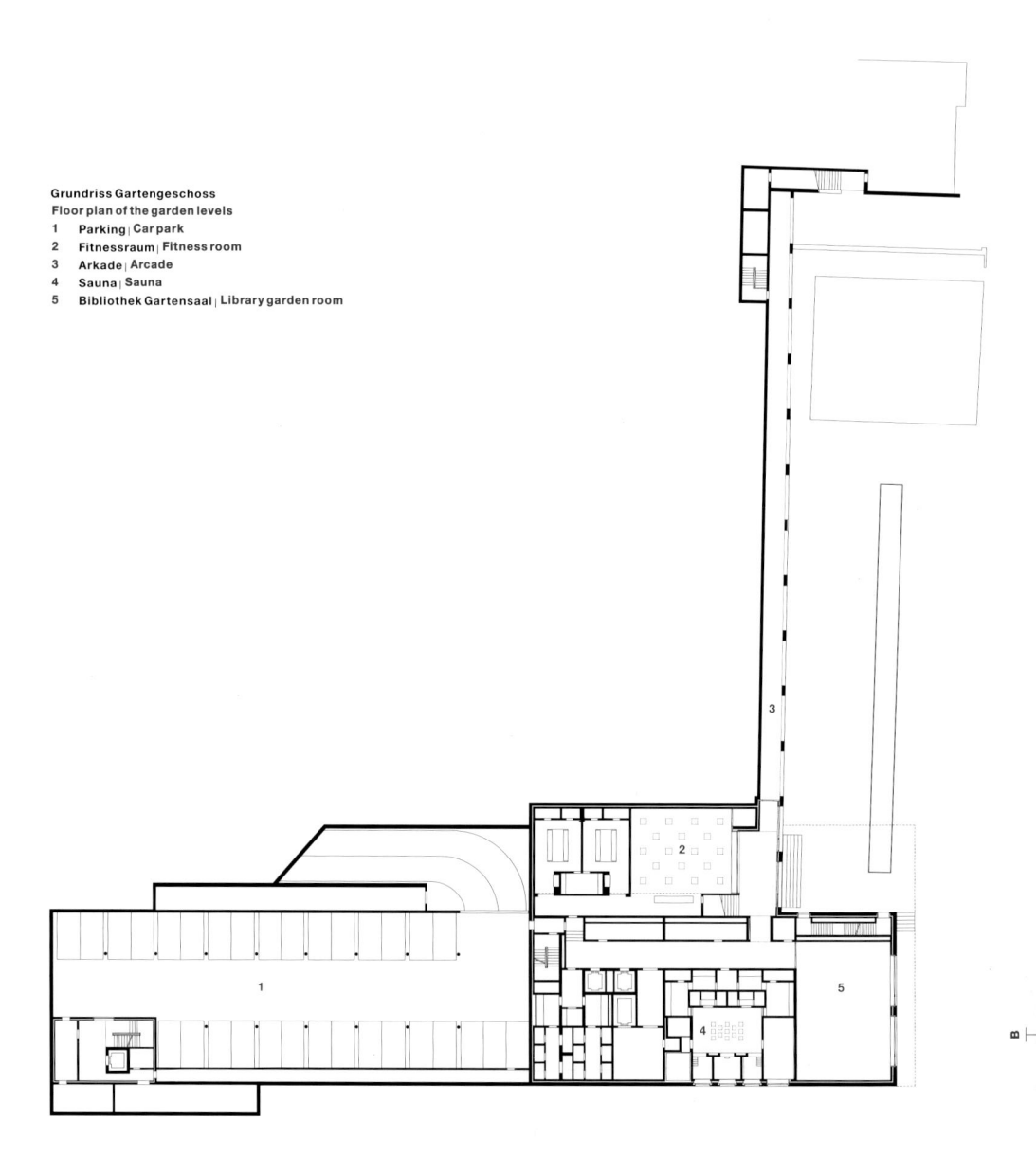

Grundriss Gartengeschoss
Floor plan of the garden levels
1 Parking | Car park
2 Fitnessraum | Fitness room
3 Arkade | Arcade
4 Sauna | Sauna
5 Bibliothek Gartensaal | Library garden room

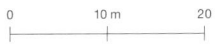

0 10 m 20

Grundriss Saalgeschoss
Floor plan of the auditorium
1 Parking | Car park
2 Forumsfoyer | Forum | foyer
3 Forum | Saal | Forum | auditorium

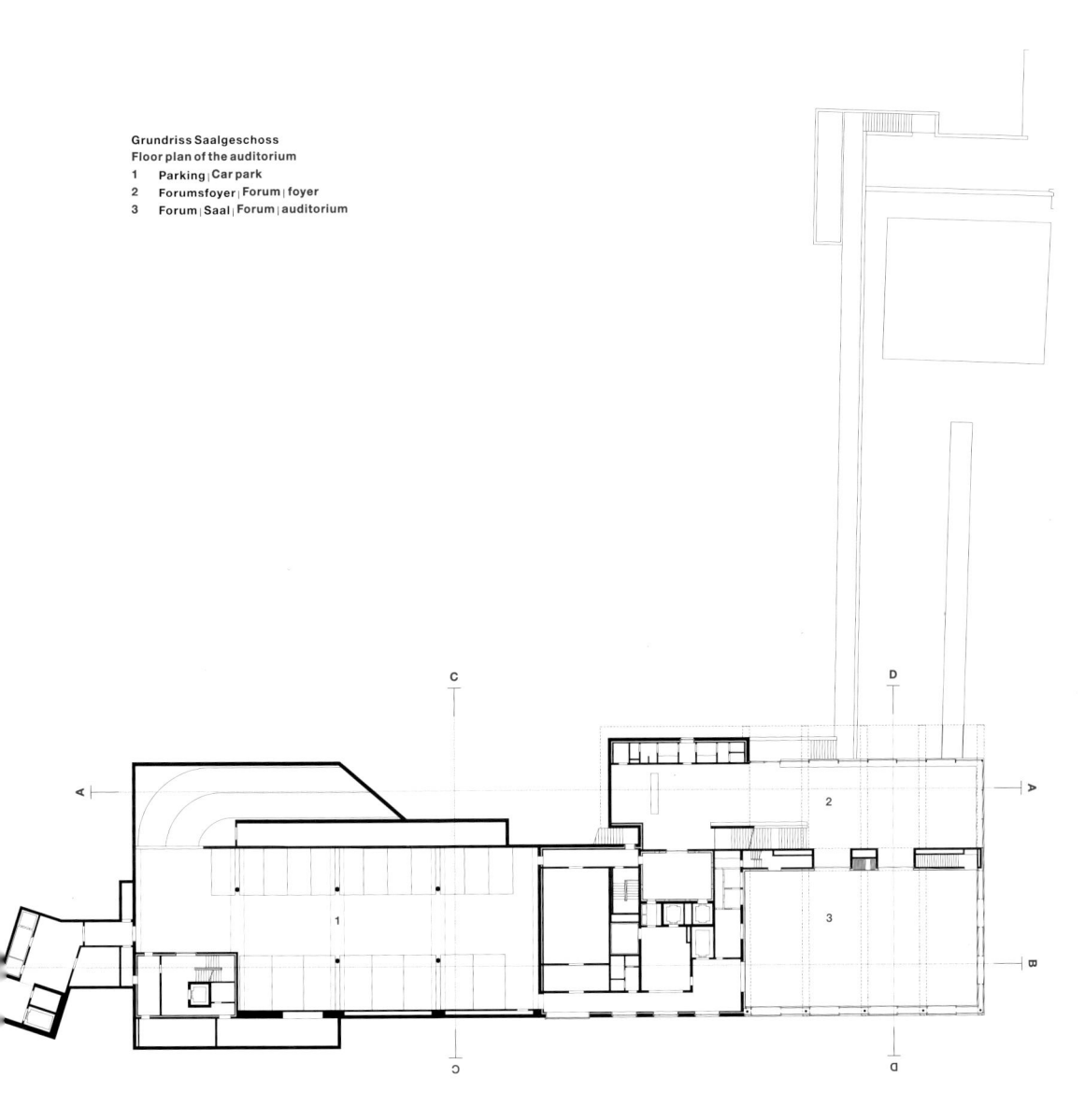

0   10 m   20

Grundriss Hotelgeschoss
Floor plan of the guest area
1   Nordzimmer | Guestroom north
2   Südzimmer | Guestroom south
3   Ecksuite | Corner suite

Grundriss Eingangsgeschoss
Floor plan of the entrance area
1   Gärtnerhaus mit Czech-Bar | Gardener's house with Czech bar
2   Eingang Seminargebäude | Entrance to the seminar building
3   Seminarfoyer | Seminar foyer
4   Seminarräume | Seminar rooms
5   Cafeteria | Cafeteria

1

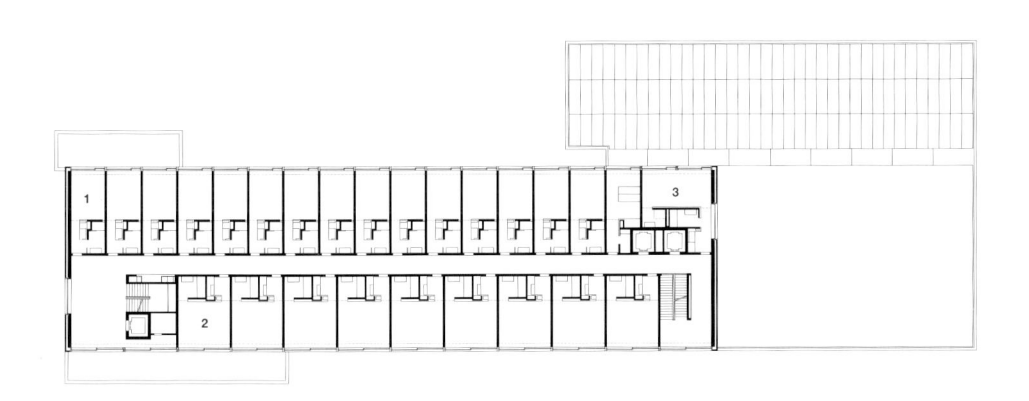

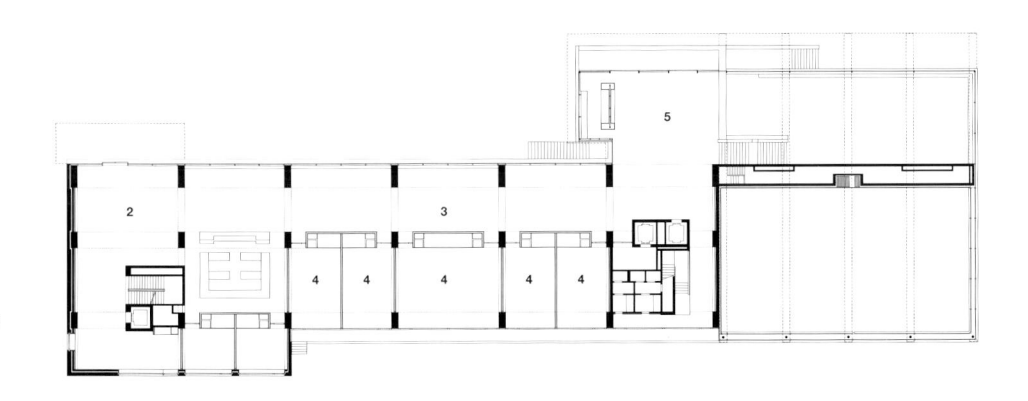

0   10 m   20

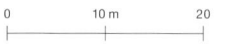

Schnitt A – A
Section A – A

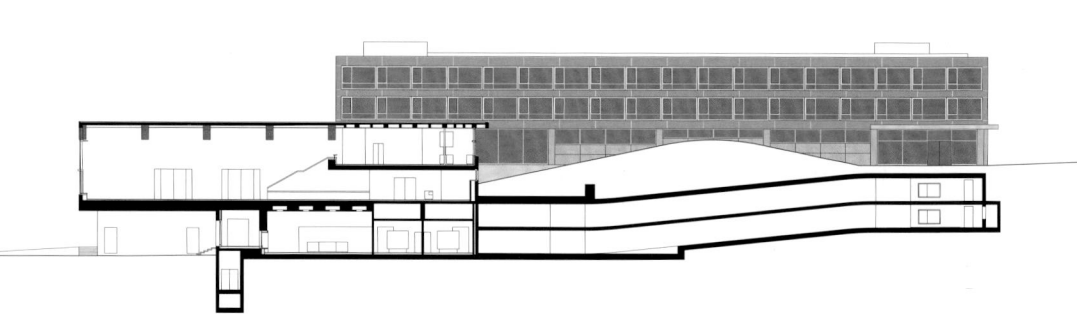

Südfassade
South façade

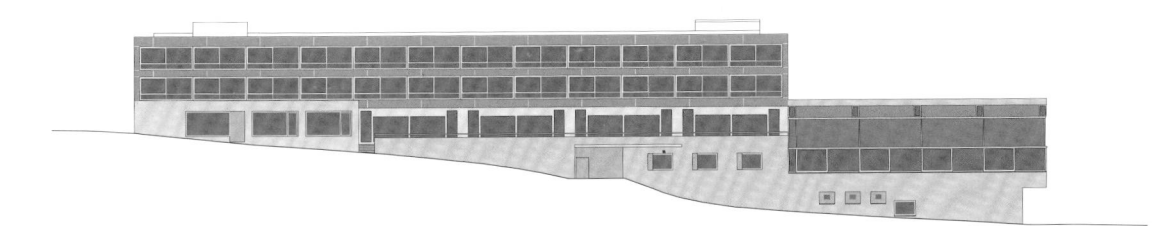

Schnitt B – B
Section B – B

0 5 m 10

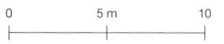

Schnitt D
Section D

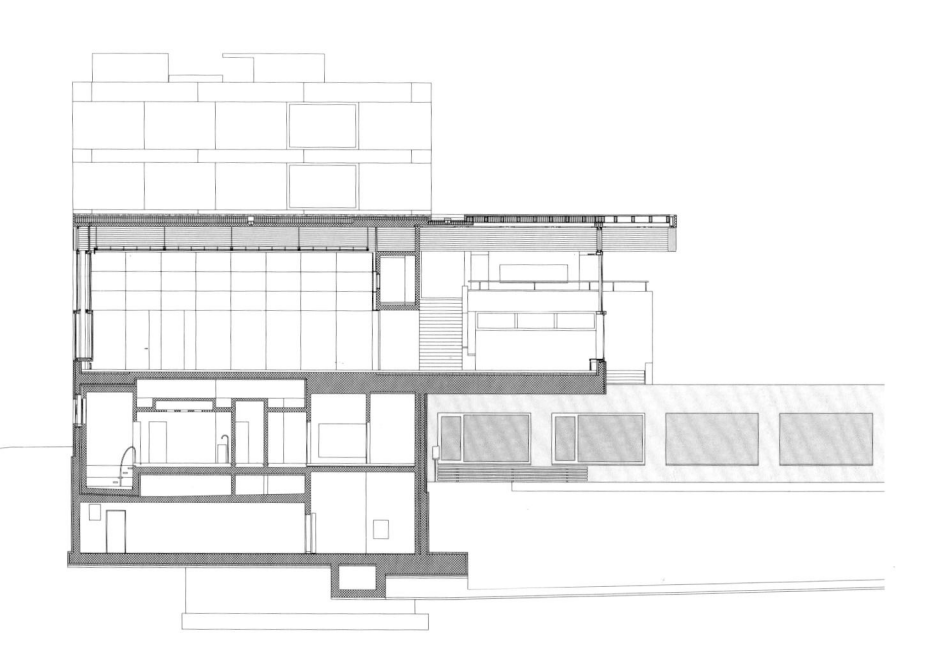

Ostfassade und Arkade
East façade and arcade

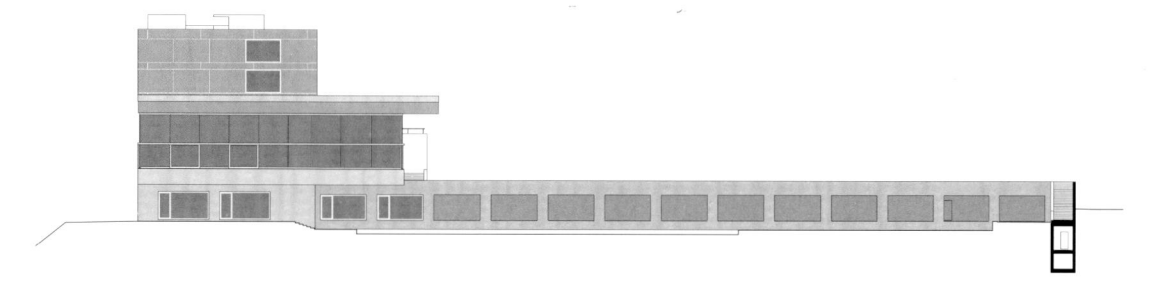

Grundriss Erdgeschoss Villa Restaurant
Floor plan of the ground floor villa restaurant
1 **Clubzimmer** | club room
2 **Halle** | Hall
3 **Sitzungszimmer** | Meeting rooms
4 **Küche** | Kitchen
5 **Peristyl** | Peristyle
6 **Salon | Bar** | Lounge | bar
7 **Restaurant** | Dining room

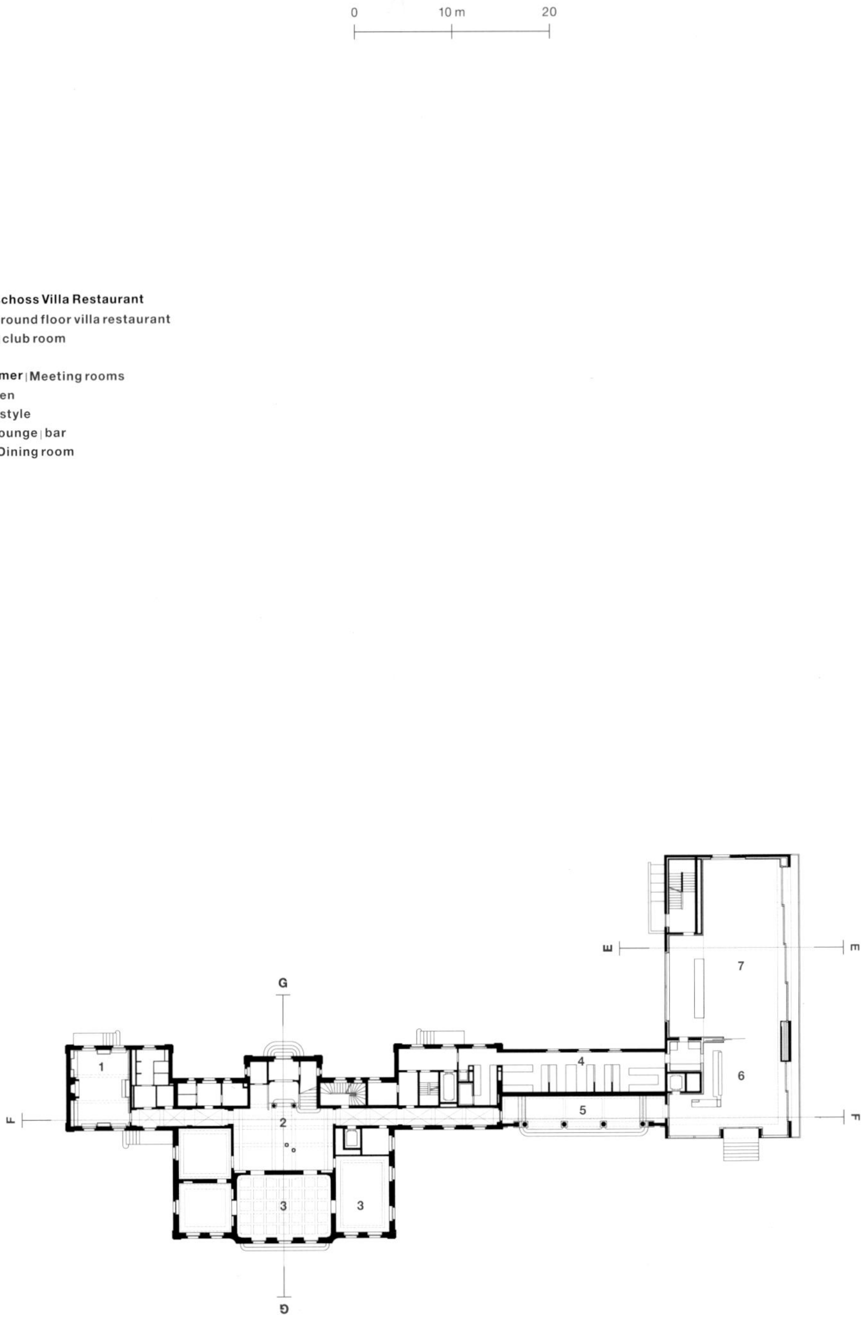

Grundriss Dachgeschoss Villa
Floor plan of the top floor of the villa

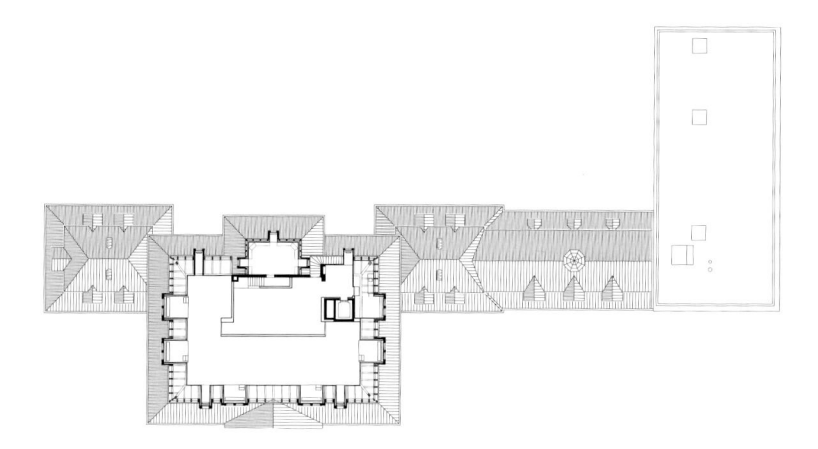

Grundriss Obergeschoss Villa | Suiten
Floor plan of the villa | suites
1 **Sitzungszimmer** | Meeting rooms
2 **Personalrestaurant** | Staff dining room
3 **Suiten** | Suites

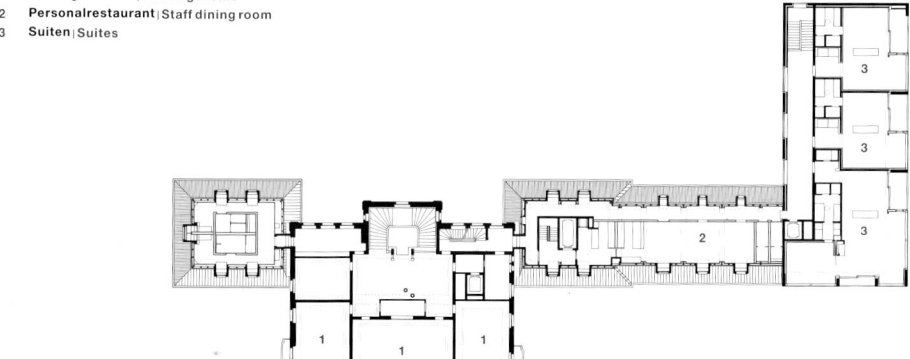

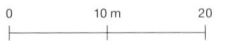

Schnitt E – E
Section E – E

Gartenfassade Villa
The villa's garden façade

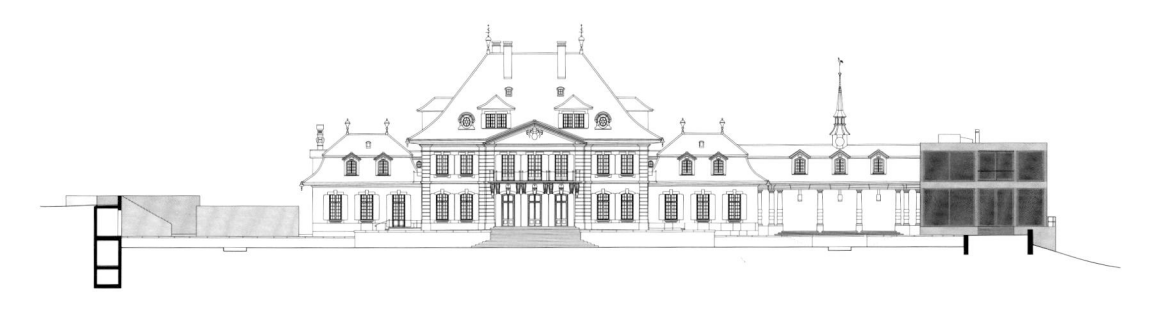

Schnitt F–F
Section F–F

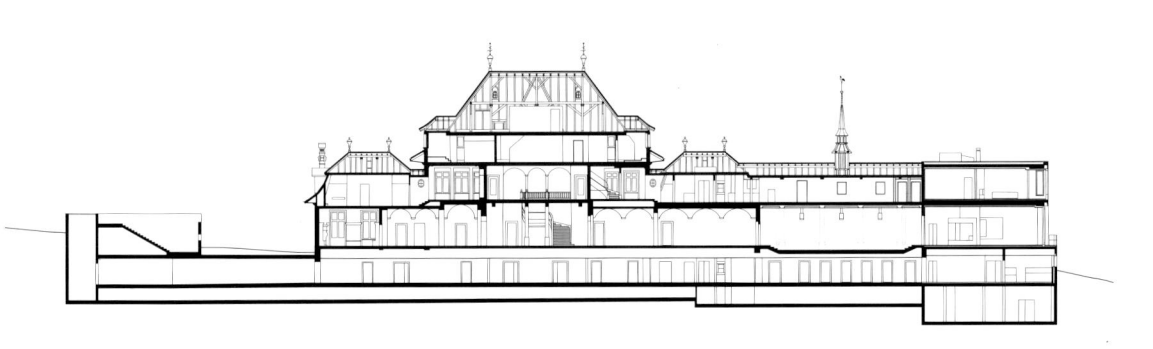

0　　5 m　　10

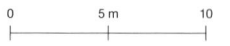

Schnitt G–G
Section G–G

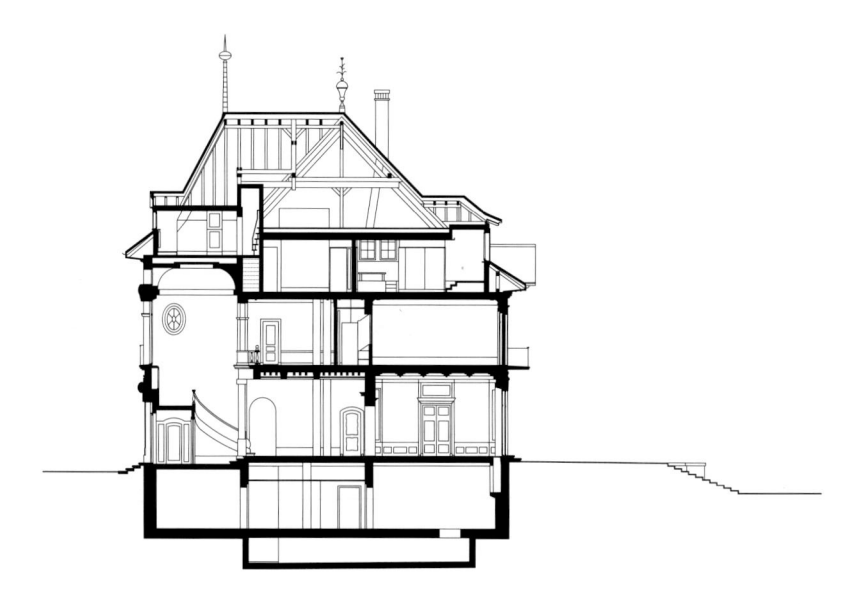

Fassade Restaurantanbau
Façade of the restaurant extension

Günther Förg
Sol LeWitt
Ulrich Rückriem

Nobuyoshi Araki
John M. Armleder
Silvia Bächli
Louise Bourgeois
Olaf Breuning
Angela Bulloch
Jean-Marc Bustamante
Martin Disler
Peter Doig
Olafur Eliasson
Helmut Federle
Urs Fischer
Franz Gertsch
Karen Klimnik
Sherrie Levine
Richard Long
Olivier Mosset
Meret Oppenheim
Blinky Palermo
Jorge Pardo
Markus Rätz
Gerwald Rockenschaub
Ed Ruscha
Christoph Rüttiman
Adrian Schiess
Albrecht Schnider
Nicola Tyson
Bernhard Voita
Christopher Wool

Kunst in Rüschlikon
Art in Rüschlikon

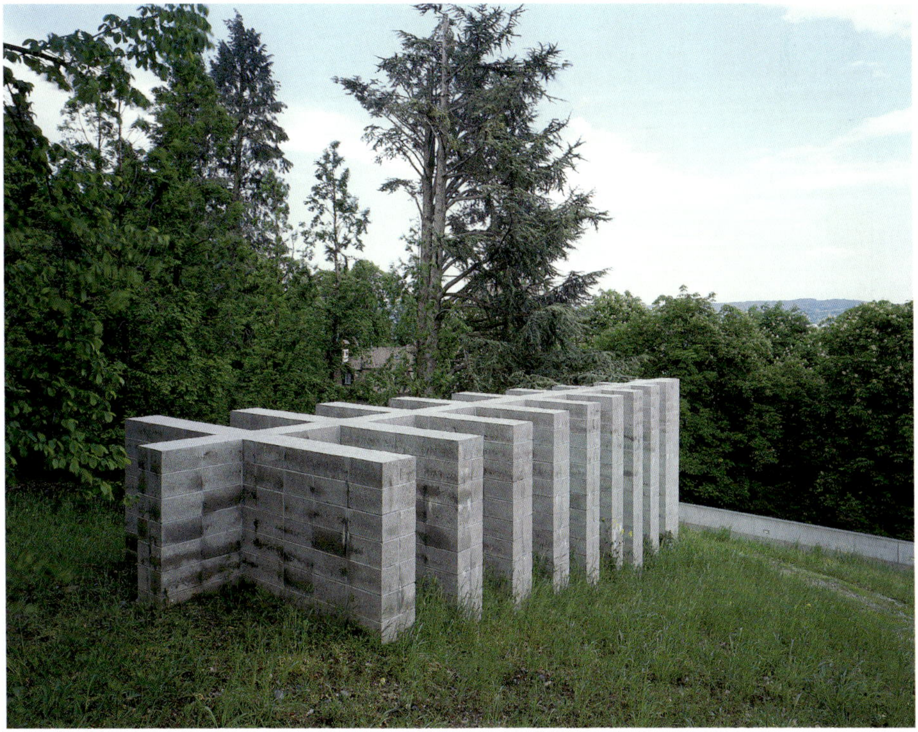

Swiss Re Rüschlikon
Centre for Global Dialogue
Marcel Meili, Markus Peter

Essentially the new location in Rüschlikon is a sort of retreat from today's secular, global society: a think tank, a platform for dialogue and a training center for one of the largest reinsurance companies in the world. It is here that professionals will meet in the future to ponder, discuss, and lecture on some of the most complex risks of contemporary society. Thus the perfect choice seemed to be a park possessing the irresistible power of meditative suggestion, even without the presence of a building…

Sixty years ago the design for a villa transformed this site high above Lake Zürich into a fantastical garden setting. Here classical and landscape elements converge in an odd, indefinable relationship, and the unusual refusal to recognize the rest of the surroundings and the lake lend the complex an extraordinary, somewhat aloof charm. Although the villa, a neo-Baroque construct, has been classified a historical monument, it is of but mediocre architectural quality. Therefore its relevance today lies not so much in its architectonic appeal as in the geometric power it commands to order, focus, and hold together the different parts of the park.

Even today the density and picturesque character of these images still dominate one's perception of this site and they have influenced the design process from the start. To avoid robbing the villa of its ordering power we positioned the much larger seminar building as far away as possible. In doing so we have made the empty space of the French park into the most important space of the entire complex: we wanted all the building units, irrespective of their tremendous differences in size, to be placed comfortably along this empty green

Im Grunde ist der neue Ort in Rüschlikon eine Art Klause der profanen, globalen Gesellschaft: ein Denklabor, eine Dialogplattform und ein Ausbildungsort für eine der größten Rückversicherungs-Gesellschaften der Welt. An diesem Ort wird in Zukunft über die schwierigsten Risiken der modernen Gesellschaft nachgedacht, gesprochen und gelehrt werden. Deswegen fiel die Wahl auf einen Park, dessen meditativer Suggestion man sich kaum entziehen kann, selbst wenn dort kein Haus stehen würde…

Vor sechzig Jahren hat der Entwurf für eine Villa diesen Ort hoch über dem Zürichsee in eine phantastische Gartenlandschaft verwandelt. Klassische und landschaftliche Teile stehen in skurrilen, unscharfen Beziehungen und eine seltsame Missachtung der weiteren Umgebung und des Sees verleiht der Anlage einen eigenartigen, etwas abgehobenen Charme. Die Villa selbst, ein neubarockes Konstrukt von mäßiger Qualität, steht unter Denkmalschutz. Ihr heutiges Gewicht liegt deshalb weniger in ihrer architektonischen Ausstrahlung als vielmehr in der geometrischen Kraft, mit der sie die verschiedenen Teile des Parkes ordnet, zentriert und zusammenhält.

Die Dichte und der malerische Charakter dieser Bilder beherrschen auch heute noch die Wahrnehmung dieses Ortes und sie haben von Beginn weg den Entwurf geprägt. Um der Villa ihr Gewicht als ordnender Schwerpunkt der Anlage nicht zu rauben, haben wir das viel größere Seminargebäude so weit wie möglich von ihr weggeschoben. Mit dieser Geste haben wir die Leere des französischen Parks zum bedeutendsten Raum der Anlage ausgebaut: Wir wollten, dass alle Körper, unbesehen von ihren enormen Größenunterschieden, mit größtmöglicher Gelassenheit an diesem leeren, grünen Platz stehen sollten wie die Häuser in einer Stadt. Deshalb haben wir in der Gestalt

space just like the buildings of a city. Thus in the layout of this open space we tried to negotiate a kind of equilibrium between marked contrasts. At opposite ends of the longest diagonal the new restaurant and the glass hall face each other in asymmetrical tension, while the villa keeps the modest symmetrical axis of the Baroque complex in check.

In its eccentric location the seminar building seems to slice into the terrain with almost brute force, tearing away one side of the hill of the natural garden. Crouched at the foot of the artificial hill it draws the visitor in from the street, pushes past the mound toward the lake, rises in a counter-movement of a monumental cantilever thrust into the chestnut trees. This building, which combines many different functions, is constructed like a large ship with a single uniform width, but with the load-bearing elements in different positions. Only the wing containing the lobby juts out into the park, thus creating a glass veranda at the height of the treetops. An "endless ribbon" of glass and concrete stretches in the form of a low wall from the villa, through the arcade, and up to the main entrance, overcoming thus the contrasts in the landscape. Unlike the villa, the entire top part of the building is glazed: the glass reflects the gorgeous old trees, forming a kind of "green wall" for the various rooms.

Vis-à-vis is the villa. The fact that it has been declared a historical monument presented a serious challenge for the designer. Precisely because the villa is not consistent we had to treat it very carefully as a "monument" in order to keep it from appearing ridiculous. This was particularly true also of the old rhythm of

dieses Raumes eine Art Gleichgewicht zwischen sehr Verschiedenem gesucht. In der weitesten Diagonale stehen sich das neue Restaurant und der gläserne Saal in einer asymmetrischen Dehnung gegenüber, während die Villa die verhaltene Symmetrie-Achse der barocken Anlage kontrolliert.

In seiner exzentrischen Lage ist das Seminargebäude mit beinahe brachialer Kraft seitlich des künstlichen Hügels im Landschaftsgarten in das Terrain eingeschnitten. In gedruckter Haltung empfängt es den Besucher an der Straße, schiebt sich am Erdreich vorbei Richtung See, um sich in der Gegenbewegung einer monumentalen Auskragung zwischen den Kastanien des Parks aufzuwerfen. Dieses Gebäude, das sehr viele unterschiedliche Funktionen beherbergt, ist wie ein großes Schiff mit einer einzigen durchgehenden Gebäudeweite, aber mit wechselnder Stellung der Tragelemente aufgebaut. Einzig der Foyerflügel kragt seitlich in den Park hinein und schafft damit eine gläserne Veranda auf der Höhe der Baukronen. Ein ›endloses Band‹ aus Glasbeton zieht sich als Sockelmauer von der Villa über die Arkade hoch bis zum Haupteingang und bewältigt auf diese Art die Sprünge in der Landschaft. Darüber ist das ganze Gebäude, als Gegensatz zur Villa, gläsern: im Glas spiegeln sich die wunderschönen Bäume und diese Bäume bilden auch eine Art ›grüne Wand‹ der verschiedenen Räume.

Vis-à-vis davon steht die Villa: deren Denkmalschutz stellte eine beträchtliche entwerferische Herausforderung dar. Gerade weil die Villa nicht sonderlich konsistent ist, mussten wir sie als ›Denkmal‹ besonders vorsichtig behandeln, um sie schließlich nicht der Lächerlichkeit preiszugeben. In besonderem Maße galt diese Aufmerksamkeit dem alten Rhythmus von Volumen und Räumen. Auf der Seeseite haben wir die alte, zwischenzeitlich zerstörte Säulenhalle wieder

volumes and spaces. On the side facing the lake we rebuilt the former portico that had been torn down. Adjacent to it, where the former garden hall had been, we erected a restaurant and guest wing, which we enlarged in respect to the garden hall. In this way we closed off the Great Court towards the lake, thus presenting an "obstructed view" to anyone approaching the villa: the view of the lake is now revealed only on a scenic stroll through the grounds. Likewise, the restaurant wing is closed off at the back by a wall, while the sides are built of huge, load-bearing stone slabs like a house of cards so as to open up the spaces towards the lake.

The ensemble is supplemented by two small buildings, light-hearted like *divertimenti*. In the former gardener's house Hermann Czech established a kind of garage bar, and the teahouse on the side facing the lake, which is really a kind of open-air terrace with huge awnings that can be spread out as necessary, does not fit the vocabulary of the rest of the architecture, rather like a pagoda in an English garden: it is concealed, curved not rectilinear, and oriented straight at the loveliest view of the lake.

The easy balance with which these buildings merge into the landscape of the park is the premise for the underlying architectonic theme of the new complex: movement. The contemplative or light-hearted distracting movement dominates the visitor's overall sense of being. Use of the site invites a stroll through the garden, demands frequent walks between the different yet equal buildings.

But what inspired these movements more than the park itself were the insights into the unusual world of corporate dialogue and

hergestellt. Anschließend daran errichteten wir dort, wo einst die Gartenhalle gestanden hat, einen Restaurant- und Gästetrakt. Diesen Flügel haben wir gegenüber der Fassung der Gartenhalle vergrößert. Damit haben wir den Ehrenhof gegen den See hin abgeschlossen und dem Ankommenden einen ›verstellten Blick‹ verschafft: die Aussicht auf den See erschließt er sich nun erst in einem szenischen Gang durch die Anlage. Der Restaurantflügel ist deshalb auch im rückwärtigen Teil durch eine Mauer verschlossen, während die Aussichtsseiten wie ein Kartenhaus aus riesigen, tragenden Steinplatten aufgebaut sind, um die Räume zu See zu öffnen.

Ergänzt wird das Ensemble durch zwei kleine Bauwerke, die wie Divertimenti wirken in dieser großen Anlage. Im alten Gärtnerhaus hat Hermann Czech eine Art Garagen-Bar eingerichtet; und das Teehaus auf der Seeseite, eigentlich eher eine Aperoterrasse mit riesigen, ausfahrbaren Sonnensegeln, entzieht sich der Sprache der restlichen Architekturen fast wie eine Pagode im englischen Garten: Sie ist verborgen, geschwungen und genau auf die schönste Blickachse des Seeraumes ausgerichtet.

Das unangestrengte Gleichgewicht, wie sich diese Häuser in die Landschaft des Parkes einfügen, ist die Voraussetzung für das unterschwellige, architektonische Thema der neuen Anlage: die Bewegung. Die kontemplative oder divertierende Bewegung beherrscht die Grundbefindlichkeit der Besucher. Der Gebrauch des Ortes legt den Wandel durch den Garten nahe und verlangt die häufigen Spaziergänge zwischen den verschiedenen, aber gleichwertigen Häusern.

Mehr noch als der Park haben aber die Einblicke in die eigenartige Welt des ›corporate dialogue‹ und der ›kommunikativen Ausbildung‹ zu den Bewegungen angeregt. Denn bemerkens-

communicative training. For, remarkably, the most important and inscrutable elements of these events are the spaces and times in between, informal phases of free, speculative conversation, unhindered debate and unofficial remarks away from flipcharts, PowerPoint or video … For this reason we envisioned this place as a quiet, sensual stage for a different kind of dialogue, an antithesis to the world of ringing cell phones and lists of e-mails on computer screens.

In Rüschlikon we made room in this dialogue for movement: the relaxed strolling of a person, perhaps lost in thought, or group of persons conversing. Basically, therefore, the entire layout of the building complex is that of an agora, a space where reflection, dialogue and movement converge. Thus the largest spaces are the corridors and halls, and the free movement through them is encouraged by the flow of spaces that is hardly obstructed by doors.

The circulation through these halls and into the rooms is characterised by an austere geometry, but also by an almost scenographic sequence of materials treated in unusual ways and by colours whose nuances change almost imperceptibly as one walks along, the whole experience being framed by sometimes odd constructions. However, this completely abstract sequence of images and spatial moods achieves its effect through the gradual perception of its contrast to the spatial experience of the world of modern office buildings. Hardly a room has been determined merely by its purpose, and the sensual impressions emanate from the rooms themselves.

werterweise scheint der wichtigste und abgründigste Teil dieser Veranstaltungen der Zwischenraum oder die Zwischenzeit zu sein, jene informelle Phase des freien, spekulativen Gesprächs, der unbehinderten Debatte oder der inoffiziellen Bemerkung, abseits von Flipcharts und Powerpoint oder Video… Wir dachten uns deshalb, dass dieser Ort ruhig und voller sinnlicher Anreize sein müsste, eine stille Bühne für einen anderen Dialog, eine Art Antithese zur Kommunikation des klingelnden Handy und der Liste von E-Mails auf den Bildschirmen.

In Rüschlikon haben wir diesem Dialog die Bewegung zugeordnet: der entspannte, zuweilen gedankenverlorene Wandel einer Person oder einer Gruppe im Gespräch. Im Grunde ist deshalb das Zentrum aufgebaut wie eine Agora, ein Raum, der Reflexion, Dialog und Bewegung miteinander verbindet. Die größten und weitläufigsten Räume sind deshalb die Gänge und Wandelhallen, und die freie Bewegung darin wird durch den Fluss der Räume provoziert und durch kaum eine Türe behindert.

Der Gang entlang dieser Wege und in die Räume hinein wird von einer strengen Geometrie, aber von einer beinahe szenografischen Folge von eigenwillig behandelten Materialien und kaum merklich wechselnden Farbtönen begleitet, und er wird von zuweilen ungewöhnlichen Konstruktionen gefasst. Diese abstrakte Folge von Bildern und Raumstimmungen entfaltet ihre Wirkung erst mit der Zeit, im langsam erkennbaren Kontrast zur räumlichen Erfahrung in der Welt von modernen Bürobauten. Kaum ein Raum verdankt seine Gestalt unmittelbar einem Zweck, und der sinnliche Eindruck bleibt sich selber überlassen.

Diese schwebende, vom Gebrauch gelöste Stimmung verdankt die Anlage dem Privileg einer unmittelbaren Zweckarmut: Da ein Dialog in fast jeder Form fast an jedem Ort stattfinden

This weightless atmosphere that comes from not being bound by immediate purpose would not have this privilege if it weren't for the layout of the complex: since dialogue can take place in any form and anywhere, the architecture does not in any way emphasize a functional formulation of the activities at the center. The perception and mood of the architecture at Rüschlikon reveal less about a practical task than about the potential for the compositional interplay of new and old assembly architecture, of contemplative spaces, of light and proportions in a remarkable setting…

An important element in the atmosphere has been the contributions by friends: furniture and textile designers as well as artists. We imagined it would be interesting to have the quiet and austere rooms interpreted by other architects who designed the furnishings according to their own ideas. Hermann Czech, Adolf Krischanitz and Gilbert Bretterbauer have given some of the rooms quite unexpected emanations. The individuality of their contributions has filled some spaces with the unique exciting life of a room that is subsequently occupied by a new owner with the curiosity of a discoverer.

Even greater independence is achieved by Günther Förg's contribution. By his use of colour, remakes of furniture, and the fake pair of columns by Plečnik, the German artist exposes the villa as a historical forgery. Leaving aside the villa's historical monument status, he creates a subversive atmosphere, which lets the viewer decide if this is a surreal, ironic, or free reconstruction. In Förg's designs the authorship gradually blurs, just as the times and spaces in the entire complex merge together.

kann, unterdrückt die Architektur weitgehend eine funktionelle Fassung der Tätigkeiten im Zentrum. Im Grunde geben deshalb die Wahrnehmung und die Stimmung der Architektur in Rüschlikon weniger über eine praktische Aufgabe Auskunft als vielmehr über die Möglichkeiten des kompositorischen Zusammenspiels von neuen und alten Architekturen für eine Zusammenkunft, von kontemplativen Räumen, von Licht und Proportionen in einer bemerkenswerten Umgebung…

Einen bedeutenden Beitrag zu dieser Atmosphäre stellen die Beiträge der befreundeten Schöpfer von Möbeln und Textilien sowie zur Kunst dar. Wir haben uns vorgestellt, dass es interessant sein müsste, die ruhigen, strengen Räume durch andere Architekten und Künstler interpretieren zu lassen, indem diese selbstständig Einrichtungen entwerfen würden. Hermann Czech, Adolf Krischanitz und Gilbert Bretterbauer haben den Räumen zum Teil unerwartete Schwingungen gegeben. Die Unabhängigkeit ihres Beitrages verleiht manchen Orten jenes eigenartige, aufregende Leben eines Raumes, der später durch einen neuen Eigentümer mit der Neugierde eines Entdeckers bezogen worden ist.

Eine noch wesentlich größere Eigenständigkeit erreicht der Beitrag des deutschen Künstlers Günther Förg in der Villa. Mit Farben, Remakes von Möbeln und mit dem falschen Säulenpaar Plečniks qualifiziert er diese Villa selber als historische Fälschung. An der Denkmalpflege vorbei schafft er eine subversive Atmosphäre, welche offen lässt, ob sie als surreal, ironisch oder frei rekonstruktiv wahrzunehmen ist. In diesen Entwürfen verschleift sich die Autorschaft langsam, so wie sich in der ganzen Anlage die Zeiten und die Räume verschleifen.

Dieter Kienast, Günther Vogt

Villa Bodmer was built during the 1920s high above Lake Zürich. This advantageous location of the Training Centre of Swiss Re at Rüschlikon makes for charming views of the surrounding countryside as well as a sublime view of the distant Glarner Alps.

The gardens of Villa Bodmer were laid out as a typical upper middle class park of its time. Within its grounds the two essential garden concepts, the formal French garden and the "natural" English type, were combined and the original layout has been preserved to a remarkable extent to this day.

Together with the buildings, valuable old trees planted in the early years of the park, now thinned out wherever necessary and supplemented by newly planted trees, create the spatial structure of the entire grounds. The interrelationship between architecture and gardens which was already part of the original historic concept has been further refined in the course of the renovation. The subtle and precise co-ordination results in an aesthetic interpenetration of interior and exterior spaces, an interplay of proximity and distance.

This interesting juxtaposition of the two contrasting garden typologies – the centrally located, geometrically laid out part and the natural, landscaped area framing it – has been maintained and reinterpreted after the renovation. Although the dividing line between the two parts of the park is obvious, visual relationships constantly provide interesting connections between the two. The simultaneous perception of both parts enhances their individual autonomous identities.

Die Villa Bodmer wurde während der zwanziger Jahre des letzten Jahrhunderts oberhalb des Zürichsees erbaut. Dieser begünstigten Lage verdankt das Seminarzentrum der Schweizer Rück in Rüschlikon die reizvollen Ausblicke in die nahe Landschaft und eine erhabene Fernsicht auf die Glarner Alpen.

Der Garten der Villa Bodmer wurde als typisch großbürgerlicher Park der damaligen Zeit angelegt. Die zwei wesentlichen Gartenkonzeptionen, der französische und der englische Typus, wurden innerhalb einer Anlage vereint und befinden sich in einem bemerkenswert originalen Zustand.

Ein wertvoller Baumbestand, gepflanzt in den Entstehungsjahren der Parkanlage, durch Neupflanzungen ergänzt und mittels Rodungen gelichtet, schafft in Zusammenhang mit den Gebäuden das räumliche Gerüst der Anlage. Die Wechselbeziehungen von Architektur und Garten sind schon im historischen Konzept angelegt und wurden im Rahmen der Neugestaltung weiter präzisiert. Die feine und exakte Abstimmung führt zu einer ästhetischen Durchdringung von Innen- und Außenraum, einem Wechselspiel von Nähe und Distanz.

Die Neugestaltung der Parkanlage behält die reizvolle Gegenüberstellung der zwei kontrastierenden Gartentypologien bei – des zentral gelegenen, geometrisch architektonischen Teils und eines landschaftlich frei gestalteten Rahmens –, schreibt diese Stile fort und interpretiert sie neu. Obwohl die Grenzen zwischen beiden Gartenteilen klar erkennbar sind, lassen Sichtbeziehungen beide in spannungsreiche Beziehungen zueinander treten. Durch die Gleichzeitigkeit der Wahrnehmung steigern sich die eigenständigen Identitäten gegenseitig in ihrer Wirkung.

The geometric part of the gardens is characterised by precise, pronounced surfaces, volumes and proportions in a monochrome play of iridescent nuances of green. Thus the original structure of the two boxwood parterres has been preserved, even though they are now filled with green leafy textures instead of flowers while the latter have been "restaged" in the form of 400 000 crocuses on the nearby lawn. Surprising views of the surrounding landscape provide a link with the adjacent parts of the park.

The natural landscaped outer area is composed of individual images that suggest a precise landscape that can be walked through, consisting of spaces reminiscent of stage sets and continuous spatial sequences of varying density and transparency. A gently shaped terrain planted with strange and bizarre trees alternates with seemingly natural areas created by gardeners in combination with noble cultivated forms. In the course of the seasons a carefully composed interplay of colours of blossoms, leaves and autumn colours, fragrant aromas and fruits, leaf textures and bark structures and the effect of light and shadow evoke changing moods.

The spatial and atmospheric contrasts and tensions of the park cannot be experienced in their entirety from any one standpoint, but only by walking around. In this way the park invites its visitors to stroll through it in contemplative leisure – just as it did at the time it was first laid out.

Der geometrische Gartenteil zeichnet sich durch präzise, kräftige Flächen, Volumen und Proportionen im monochromen Spiel changierender Grünnuancen aus. So bleibt die Struktur der beiden Buchsparterre erhalten, ihre Füllung mit Blumenschmuck aber wandelt sich in grüne Blatttexturen und wird stattdessen auf der angrenzenden Rasenfläche in Form von 400 000 Krokussen neu inszeniert. Überraschende Ausblicke in die Landschaft und Einblicke leiten über in die angrenzenden Parkteile.

Der landschaftliche Rahmen setzt sich aus verschiedenen Einzelbildern zusammen, die eine begehbare exakte Landschaft suggerieren. Raumbildende Kulissen und kontinuierliche Raumfolgen in unterschiedlicher Dichte und Transparenz entstehen. Sanfte Erdmodellierungen in Verbindung mit fremd und bizarr wirkenden Baumcharakteren wechseln mit gärtnerischen Inszenierungen aus natürlich wirkenden Bereichen in Kombination mit edlen Zuchtformen. Ein abgestimmtes Spiel von Blüten-, Blatt- und Herbstfärbungen, von Düften und Früchten, Blatttexturen und Rindenstrukturen, der Wirkung von Licht und Schatten ruft wechselnde Stimmungen im Verlauf der Jahreszeiten hervor.

Die räumlich-atmosphärischen Spannungen lassen sich von keinem Standort in ihrer Gesamtheit erleben, vielmehr muss die Anlage dazu begangen werden. Damit lädt der Park seine Besucher zur Lustwandelung und betrachtenden Muße ein – wie dazumal, zur Zeit seiner ersten Entstehung.

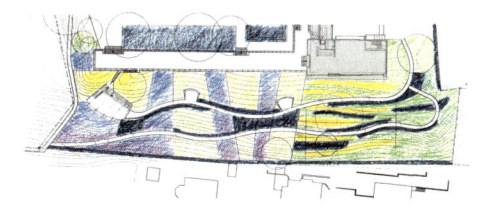

Hangpartie zum See
Frühling-Aspekt Bodenschicht
Slope facing the lake
Spring view with lawn

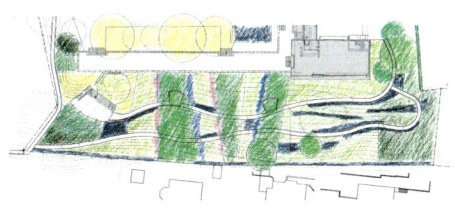

Frühling-Aspekt Strauchschicht
Spring view with shrubs

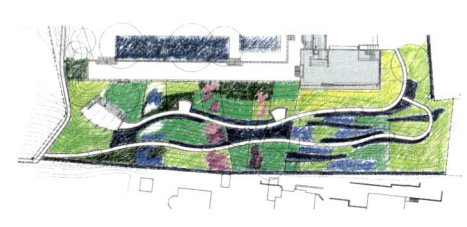

Sommer-Aspekt Bodenschicht
Summer view with lawn

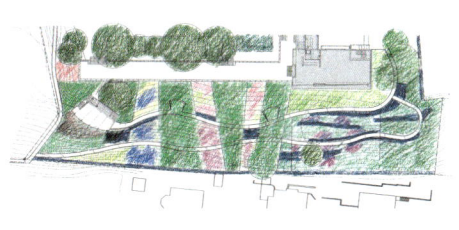

Sommer-Aspekt Strauchschicht
Summer view with shrubs

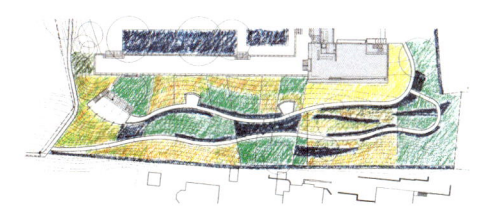

Herbst-Aspekt Bodenschicht
Fall view with lawn

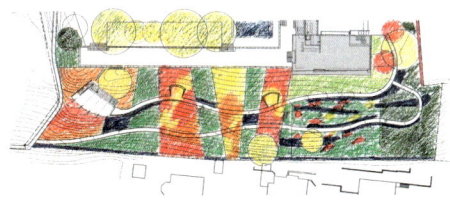

Herbst-Aspekt Strauchschicht
Fall view with shrubs

Das schwierige Ganze – ganz leicht
The Complex Whole, Simply Put
Otto Kapfinger

Meili, Peter Architekten is not a commercial name. Nor do these architects produce commercial architecture. The fact that their work nonetheless does possess commercial value derives from a stance that clearly distances itself from what has popularly come to be seen as the image of this trade in the postmodern age. The environment in which this stance evolved was the Swiss architecture scene in the 1980s. Here, on the one hand, one witnessed the fading of the typology and urban discussion that had been an essential part of the seventies and the Tessin "Tendenza" – i.e. the departure from Aldo Rossi's theory (not his sensibility). At the same time there emerged, on the other hand, a profound criticism of the re-semantisation of architecture and of the star status of the postmodern architect who in a subjective and virtuoso manner believes he has the power to collectively determine images and signs, whether they be the images of everyday life, of history, of the future or utopia.

In Switzerland "Learning from Las Vegas", Robert Venturi's distinctly Pop Art approach, received much more intensive and critical attention than elsewhere. And it was out of the multi-polar search for an authenticity that the medium architecture might still be able to present in our consumer and information society that Switzerland brought forth the so-called "semantic turn" that Martin Steinmann has used to define the phenomenon of the newer architecture of western Switzerland. At the time, in reaction to formalistic or constructivistic attempts to give architecture stronger imagery and more powerful

Meili, Peter Architekten ist kein Markenname. Diese Architekten produzieren auch keine Marken-Architektur. Dass ihre Arbeit inzwischen dennoch Marktwert hat, resultiert aus einer Haltung, die sich klar von dem in der Postmoderne populär gewordenen Berufsbild der Branche distanziert. Das Umfeld für die Entwicklung dieser Haltung bildete die Schweizer Architekturszene der neunzehnachtziger Jahre. Hier zeigte sich einerseits das Verblassen der für die siebziger Jahre und die Tessiner »Tendenza« essenziellen Typologie- und Stadtdiskussion – also die Loslösung von der Theorie (nicht der Sensibilität) Aldo Rossis. Zugleich entstand eine profunde Kritik an der Re-Semantisierung von Architektur und am Star-Status des nachmodernen Baukünstlers, der subjektiv und virtuos über die kollektive Setzung von Bildern und Zeichen zu verfügen meint, sei es nun über die Images des Alltags, der Geschichte, oder solche der Zukunft, der Utopie.

In der Schweiz wurde damals auch Robert Venturis der Pop Art verpflichteter Ansatz – »Learning from Las Vegas« – intensiver und kritischer rezipiert als anderswo. Und gerade aus der mehrpoligen Recherche nach einer Authentizität, die das Medium Architektur innerhalb der Konsum- und Informationsgesellschaft überhaupt noch darstellen konnte, entstand in der Schweiz jener »semantic turn«, mit dem Martin Steinmann das Phänomen der neueren Architektur der Westschweiz definierte. Entgegen formalistischen oder konstruktivistischen Versuchen, die Baukunst für eine breitere Akzeptanz oder für ihren Anspruch als Leitkunst der Epoche wieder bildmächtig und symbolkräftig zu machen, verlagerten damals etliche Architekten dieser Region ihr Interesse von den Dingen als Bedeutung – dem Thema der Pop Art – zurück zu den Dingen als unvermittelte Erfahrung. Und primär auf dieser strukturellen

symbolism in the hopes that it would gain broader acceptance or live up to its claim to being the main art form of the age, a great many architects from this region shifted their interest from objects as meaning – the theme of Pop Art – back to objects as direct experience. And it was primarily this structural level, and not the surface of "simple forms" that constituted the basis of its parallel to Minimal Art.

One of the conditions that brought about the de-ideologizing of high-brow building was the discovery of the urban peripheries as the scenes and changing faces of today's life cycles. The periphery eludes the planning patterns of the classical Moderne; it produces what might be referred to in the academic sense as "non sites", but which have long since been recognized and employed by photography, cinema and literature as *the* quintessential backdrops of postindustrial quotidian life. In the periphery debate of the late eighties Marcel Meili formulated one of his first, lucid texts to receive international attention. Venturi, before him, had already looked at the "strip" with unbiased eyes, though his view, of course, included few motifs and was limited to the dialectics of signs and objects. Meili, by contrast, saw in the "chaotic", mute spaces of the European urban peripheries not formal problems, but structural conditions, saw new modes of operation unaffected by the controls of "design" that allowed him to mix opposites or realities teeming with vitality. He called this a "precarious balance" marked by the flux of permanent construction and by an "anonymous character that rendered the repertoire of modern architecture ineffectual".

Ebene, und nicht auf der Oberfläche »einfacher Formen«, basierte die Parallelität zur Minimal Art.

Einen Hintergrund für diese Entideologisierung des avancierten Bauens brachte die Entdeckung der urbanen Peripherien als Schauplätze und Aggregatzustände heutiger Lebenszyklen. Die Peripherie entzieht sich den Planungsmustern der klassischen Moderne; sie erzeugt »Nicht-Orte« in akademischem Sinne, die aber von Fotografie, Film und Literatur längst als die Folien des postindustriellen Alltags erkannt und bearbeitet wurden. In der Peripherie-Debatte der späten achtziger Jahre formulierte Marcel Meili einen seiner ersten, luziden Texte, der auch internationale Beachtung fand. Schon Venturi hatte den »Strip« mit unvoreingenommenen Augen gesehen. Sein Blick war freilich motivisch und auf die Dialektik von Zeichen und Objekten begrenzt. Meili dagegen sah in den »chaotischen«, stummen Räumen der europäischen Stadtränder nicht Formprobleme, sondern strukturelle Zustände, neue Wirkungsweisen der Mischung von Gegensätzen, von vitalen Realitäten, außerhalb jeder Kontrolle durch »Design«. Er nannte dies ein »unstabiles Gleichgewicht«, geprägt vom Fluss permanenter Konstruktion und von einem »anonymen Charakter, der das Repertoire moderner Architektur außer Kraft setzt«.

Die oft »brutale« Überlagerung von Einfamilienhaus- und Siedlungsclustern mit großen technischen Infrastrukturen, durch Bahn- und Straßenanlagen, Industriehallen und Shoppingcenters mit ihren instrumentellen Leitsystemen und den dazwischen verbleibenden Resten rural gestalteter Natur, das Nebeneinander von ungleichzeitigen Zuständen, von alten und neuen, schnellen und langsamen Partikeln – all das führte Meili im Gegensatz zu vielen anderen nicht zur Diagnose einer

The oftentimes "callous" layering of clusters of single-family dwellings and housing tracts with their large engineering infrastructures, of rail and road facilities, large industrial buildings, and shopping centres replete with their instrumental governing systems and the remnants of rurally designed nature, the coexistence of non-simultaneous states, of old and new, fast and slow – all this led Meili, unlike many others, not to the diagnosis of an aesthetics of the collage or the fragment. Rather, in his view there was in the phenomenon of the heterogeneity of such spaces a fundamental tendency towards abstraction, a disappearance of the classical levels of symbol and meaning, a dominance of the vague and unspecific, of lapidary constructions, and thus a greater elasticity to allow for changes or distortions than one finds in the conventional, meticulously designed and regulated urban areas.

With this analysis Meili departed from the bathos of the Avant-Garde and from the moralising bathos of Functionalism, too. He embarked on the search for a "new actuality" beyond subjective, architectural gestures, applied a mode of intervention to complement the city or given environment in a subtle, undramatic way rather than imposing manifestos of the "new". But it wasn't the establishing of images, whether old or new, that allowed the city to inscribe new meanings for itself. Smaller, structural changes that permitted multiple interpretations were more likely to achieve this. The many-layered aspect, the "complex whole" of the urban state, whether central or peripheral, was perhaps attractive for its

Ästhetik der Collage oder des Fragments. Er konstatierte vielmehr im Phänomen der Heterogenität solcher Räume eine Grundtendenz zur Abstraktion, ein Verschwinden der klassischen Symbol- und Bedeutungsebenen, ein Dominieren des Undifferenzierten, der lapidaren Konstruktionen und: eine größere Elastizität, um Veränderungen oder Verformungen aufzunehmen, als in konventionell durchgestalteten und regulierten Stadtbereichen.

Mit dieser Analyse verabschiedete sich Meili vom Pathos der Avantgarde, auch vom moralisierenden Pathos des Funktionalismus, und begab sich auf die Suche nach einer »neuen Eigentlichkeit« jenseits von subjektiven, baukünstlerischen Gesten, nach einem Modus des Eingreifens, um die Stadt bzw. die jeweilige Umgebung subtil, undramatisch zu ergänzen, nicht um Manifeste des »Neuen« aufzupflanzen. Nicht die Setzung von Bildern, ob alt oder neu, vermochte der Stadt neue Bedeutungen einzuschreiben. Dies konnten eher kleinere, strukturelle Veränderungen, die mehrfache Interpretationen erlaubten. Das vielschichtige, das »schwierige Ganze« des urbanen Zustandes, ob zentral oder peripher, konnte mit spektakulären »Architektur-Würfen« an Schauwerten vielleicht gewinnen, an lebbaren Dimensionen und Komplexitäten in der Regel aber nur verlieren.

Meili, Peter verlagerten folglich ihre Recherche – wie einige andere auch, und nicht nur in Basel und Zürich – von der Grammatik der Zeichen auf die Grammatik der Materialien und die Robustheit der Raumangebote. Eine spezifische Färbung und damit Unterscheidung etwa von Herzog & de Meuron, von Peter Zumthor oder Gigon & Guyer erhielt ihre Arbeit durch die intensive Kooperation mit hochkarätigen Ingenieuren, im Besonderen mit Jürg Conzett – nicht zum naiven Zweck der Erfindung avantgardisti-

spectacular "architectural masterpieces", but in general in its practical-life dimensions and complexities it had little to offer.

Thus Meili, Peter shifted their systematic search – like others as well, and not just in Basel and Zürich – from the grammar of signs to that of materials and the robustness of the available spaces. Their work began to take on a delicate nuance of difference to that of Herzog & de Meuron, Peter Zumthor or Gigon & Guyer, for example, in that theirs cultivated intensive co-operation with prominent engineers, in particular with Jürg Conzett – not for the naive purpose of inventing Avant-Garde constructions, but for their quite conscious, analytical approach of bringing out the potential that sets contemporary building materials and technologies in their syntax, tectonics and spatial character apart from those dictated by tradition.

The building designed for Swiss Re remains true to this concept, from the general approach right down to the small details and in its choice of the other contributing artists. Even without this background knowledge the complex achieves its effect through its use. Form and materials have, as mentioned earlier, been abstracted, de-problematized, and de-subjectified to such an extent that the technical and sensual purposes of building – meaning situations offering visual, haptic and proportionally pleasing aspects and moods – reveal themselves as concretely and matter-of-factly as possible. For an examination that goes beyond casual, indifferent perception, a frame of reference for appreciation is important, especially where the complexity of the design

scher Konstruktionen, sondern zur sehr bewussten, analytischen Durcharbeitung des Potenzials, das zeitgenössische Werkstoffe und Technologien in ihrer Syntax, in Tektonik und Raumcharakter vom Tradierten unterscheidet.

Der Bau für Swiss Re steht vom generellen Ansatz bis zum Detail und zur Wahl der Kooperationspartner in diesem konzeptionellen Zusammenhang. Natürlich entfaltet er auch ohne die Kenntnis solcher Hintergründe im Gebrauch seine Wirkung. Form und Stoff sind ja, wie gesagt, soweit abstrahiert, entproblematisiert und entsubjektiviert, dass die sachlichen und sinnlichen Zwecke des Bauens – die Definition von Situationen mit visuellen, haptischen und proportionalen Angeboten und Stimmungen – sich möglichst konkret und selbstverständlich darbieten. Für eine Rezension, die über beiläufige, interesselose Wahrnehmung hinausgeht, sind Verständnishilfen jedoch gerade dort wichtig, wo die Entwurfskomplexität sich nicht zur Schau stellt, wo die Architektur – wie etwa ein perfektes Service bei Tisch – offenbar kaum auffällt und dennoch die faktischen und atmosphärischen Ansprüche vollendet erfüllt.

»Das beste Detail ist kein Detail« – ein Satz von Benedikt Loderer zu Swiss Re – bringt es paradox auf den Punkt. Die Details – von den Fugen, den Profilen und Oberflächen bis zu den Beschlägen, Stößen und Gelenken – sind hier nicht zelebriert, wie etwa bei Carlo Scarpa. Die Feinformen der Raumfügung sind eher soweit wie möglich weggeschliffen, sind zugunsten der »undifferenzierten«, elementaren Gestalt reduziert, homogenisiert. Die Anzahl verschiedener Materialien ist möglichst knapp gehalten. Dafür sind ihre Qualität, ihr Finish und ihr Zusammenwirken ungemein sorgfältig bearbeitet. Meili, Peter vermeiden die »Duftmarken« einer individuellen, gestalterischen Handschrift.

doesn't stand out, where architecture – like perfect service at the table – hardly draws any ostensible notice, yet fulfils the actual and subjective demands of the situation entirely.

"The best detail is no detail," commented Benedikt Loderer to Swiss Re, using paradox to make his point. The details – from the seams, sections, and surfaces to the mounts, joints, and hinges – don't get the same kind of attention they do with Carlo Scarpa. The delicate forms that hold this space together have been whittled away as much as possible, reduced in favour of the "unspecific", elemental form, homogenized. The number of different materials used has been kept to a minimum. Whereas great care has been taken with their quality, their finish, and the way they interact with each other. Meili, Peter sought to avoid leaving the "mark" of a single, creative signature. Their will to abstraction, however, does not dematerialise materiality as the "white" architectural works of the young Le Corbusier or a Richard Meier did. In the sense of what was mentioned earlier, the main intention here is to keep the building as lapidary and as "untainted" by subjectivisms as possible, while at the same time to use this abstraction to ensure that the intensity of the materials be highly autonomous and concrete.

What can be said here about detail applies even more fundamentally to the general approach of the plan. Meili, Peter designed the overall spatial plan with the stipulation that this peculiar "old" villa and the unique position to its nearby and more remote surroundings were to remain intact as components, as actors in the new complex. Moreover, the best quality

Ihr Wille zur Abstraktion entstofflicht aber nicht die Materialität, wie es etwa die »weißen« Architekturen des frühen Le Corbusier oder eines Richard Meier demonstrieren. Im Sinne des eingangs Gesagten geht es darum, den Bau möglichst lapidar, von Subjektivismen »unverschmutzt« zu halten, durch diese Abstraktion aber zugleich die Intensität der Materialien jeweils möglichst autonom und konkret zu machen.

Was hier zur Feinform gesagt werden kann, betrifft grundsätzlicher noch den generellen Entwurfsansatz. Meili, Peter organisierten das große Raumprogramm unter dem Aspekt, dass diese eigenartige »alte« Villa und ihre ungewöhnliche Stellung zum näheren und weiteren landschaftlichen Umraum als Komponenten, als Mitspieler des neuen Ganzen intakt blieben. Mehr noch, die beste Qualität der vorgefundenen Situation – die Beziehung zwischen Bau, streng manikürtem Gartenparterre, pittoreskem »Natur«-Park als Kulisse auf Mitteldistanz und dem See-Panorama als Fernperspektive abseits der Hauptachse –, diese Qualität wurde zum Angelpunkt der Disposition der Neubauten. Sie wurde neu gefasst, in ihrer latenten Dialektik bestärkt und ins Gegenwärtige gesteigert. Wir erinnern uns an die Stichworte von vorhin: subtil, undramatisch ergänzen, Images nicht mit oder gegen den Strich des Vorhandenen bürsten, eher strukturell analysieren, mit Veränderungen strukturell und dosiert reagieren, weitertreiben des »schwierigen Ganzen« usw.

Allein die Neuorganisation des Grundstückes, die Balance zwischen Altbau, Neubauten und dem Frei- bzw. Naturraum, die Verwandlung des Gartens als Relais aller anderen Komponenten in eine neue, komplexere Mitte als zuvor, die Behandlung der Bauteile als Vektoren, die nicht bloß sich selbst inszenieren, sondern über sich hinaus einen Ort »jenseits

of this original constellation – the relation between the building, the austerely manicured garden, the picturesque "natural" park as the scene at centre stage, and the panorama of the lake as the backdrop off from the main axis – this quality became the pivotal point determining the layout of the new buildings. It was reformulated, its latent dialectics reinforced, and thus remade it was brought into the present with fresh élan. Let us once again call to mind the key concepts mentioned earlier: complementing in a subtle, undramatic way, not creating images to go with or against the grain of the already existing, analysing in a more structural way, responding to changes in a structural and moderate way, extending and elaborating the "complex whole", etc.

The re-organization of the grounds alone, the balance between the old building, the new buildings, and nature i.e. the open spaces, the transformation of the garden as a relay point between all other components into a new, more complex hub or centre, the treatment of the building units as vectors that do not play their own isolated roles, but swell in a synergy of tension to create a place "beyond architecture" – these general features alone produce a logical, masterful arrangement, the essence of the whole plan and what ultimately won the competition for Meili, Peter.

Just as the garden is the open centre of the new complex, the large seminar wing also has its focal point where the relations of all physical and visual movement culminate: the large lobby between the wide open hallways and the forum of the new main building. Here Meili, Peter push their strong but imperturbable

von Architektur« aufspannen, allein diese generellen Merkmale ergeben eine schlüssige, meisterhafte Disposition – die Essenz der gesamten Planung, die auch das Wettbewerbsverfahren zugunsten von Meili, Peter entschied.

So wie das Gartenparterre die offene Mitte der neuen Komposition ist, so hat auch der große Seminartrakt einen Fokus, in dem die Relationen aller körperlichen und visuellen Bewegungen kulminieren. Es ist das große Foyer zwischen dem Wandelgang und dem Forum des neuen Hauptgebäudes. Meili, Peter treiben da ihre ebenso starke wie gelassene Reaktion auf den Kontext in eine Intensität, wo die Verschiebung des Erzählerischen vom Objekt auf dessen Zusammenhang in einen monumentalen Maßstab springt. Der kompakte, in den Hügel geschnittene Riegel ist hier in der Höhe um zwei Geschoße abgetreppt, bricht dafür seitlich aus den bündigen Baulinien aus und schiebt eine respektable Auskragung zwischen die Bäume hinein. Nachdem die Zugänge keine Aussicht auf Garten und See erlauben und im Wandelgang der Park nur in schmalen Ausschnitten und teilweise in Untersichten präsent ist, bringt das Foyer die überraschende vertikale und diagonale Öffnung nach außen – die Totale.

Das Hinuntersteigen vom oberen Sitzbereich in den doppelt so hohen, völlig verglasten Foyerbereich intensiviert noch die Erscheinung der riesigen Kronen der Kastanienbäume, die mitten im Binnenraum zu stehen scheinen und die zwischen sich nun den unvermuteten Prospekt von Villa und See präsentieren. Oberes und unteres Foyer werden von derselben, über die Glasfassaden auskragenden Dachplatte überdeckt. Im Bereich des unteren Foyers und des anschließenden Forums, des großen Saales, wird die Decke jedoch von mächtigen Holz-Leimbindern

reaction to context to a degree of intensity that provokes a monumental shift in the narrative from the object to its surroundings. The compact, elongated block is stepped back two stories at the point where it cuts into the hill, it then juts out to the side from the straight line of the building and cantilevers out impressively into the trees. The entrances do not afford a view of the garden or the lake, and from the wide hallways the park is only visible in narrow segments or from a lower angle. By contrast it is the lobby that throws open to us the surprising vertical and diagonal gateway to the outside – the extreme long shot.

Descending from the upper sitting area to the lobby with its ceilings twice as high and its fully glazed walls intensifies even more the impression one has looking out at the tops of the gigantic chestnut trees. They seem to be right in the middle of the interior space, and through them we glimpse in the background the unexpected view of the villa and the lake. Both the upper and lower lobbies are covered by the same roof plate, which cantilevers out over the glazed façade. The ceiling in the area of the lower lobby and the adjacent forum, the Great Hall, is supported by mighty composite lumber trusses, which jut out unsupported, with their uniform cross sections extending past the glass walls into the open space beyond.

Standing in the lobby looking out, one sees earth, gravel, rock, grass, foliage, trunks, branches, water, air. The lobby itself is composed essentially of the engineered transformation of these materials: terrazzo, concrete, glass and – plywood. More than the other

getragen, die ohne Unterstützung und mit gleichbleibendem Querschnitt über die Glaswände hinweg in den Außenraum vorstoßen.

Was man vom Foyer aus sieht ist Erde, Kies, Stein, Gras, Laub, Stämme, Äste, Wasser, Luft. Das Foyer selbst ist im Wesentlichen aus der technischen Transformation dieser Stoffe gebaut: Terrazzo, Beton, Glas und – Schichtholz. Vor allem diese mächtigen Träger sind nun keineswegs selbstverständlich. Der besondere Ort rechtfertigt aber das gestalterische Extrem, dessen konstruktive Komplexität hintergründig bleibt, da sie dem Erreichen einer spezifischen, dem Konstruktiven übergeordneten Wirkung dient. Die Träger überspannen wie gesagt nur die hohen Räume – unteres Foyer und Forum; diese funktionell zentralen Bereiche liegen beiderseits einer raumhältigen Betonwand, die das statische Rückgrat des ganzen Seminartraktes bildet. Im niedrigeren Annex, dem oberen Foyer, wäre zwar dieselbe Spannweite der Auskragung gegeben. Hohe Träger hätten dort aber die Raumproportion erdrückt. Zudem liegen in diesem Abschnitt auf der anderen Seite der Beton-Achse nur untergeordnete, kleinteilige Räume. Das obere Foyer hat generell eine andere, weniger dynamische Wechselwirkung mit dem Park, auch die Glasteilung (und Möblierung) ist hier anders als im unteren Foyer, das sozusagen in voller Höhe und über Eck den Dialog zwischen Innen und Außen exklusiv inszeniert. Die großen Balken geben dort dem hohen, der Weite des Umraums voll ausgesetzten Raum den entsprechenden Rhythmus und Halt. Sie bilden ein Gegengewicht zum dunklen Beton-Monolith der Mittelwand, sie erzeugen einen mächtigen horizontalen Sog zwischen Drinnen und Draußen und ermöglichen die fast entmaterialisierte, stützenfreie Glaswand und Glasecke. Die vorgespannten Holzbalken erstrecken sich in einem Stück

elements the mighty trusses are by no means a natural matter-of-fact. Yet this unique site justifies the extreme design. Its constructive complexity remains unobtrusive because it serves a specific purpose, one that transcends the mere constructive aspect. The trusses only span the high-ceilinged rooms – the lower lobby and forum; these functionally important areas are situated on either side of a concrete wall, which forms the load-carrying backbone of the whole seminar wing. In the low-ceilinged annex, the upper lobby, the cantilevers might have called for the same span as in the lower rooms; high trusses, however, would have overpowered the room's proportions. Moreover, in this section on the other side of the concrete axis there are only small secondary rooms. In general the upper lobby's communication with the park is different and less dynamic, even the glass boundary (and furnishings) differ from those in the lower lobby, which is like a stage affording an exclusive ceiling-to-floor, trans-corner dialogue between interior and exterior. The large beams give this high room, which is exposed to the full expanse of its surroundings, the proper rhythm and stability. They provide a counterweight to the dark concrete mono-lith of the axial wall, they produce a strong horizontal pull between inside and outside and make it possible to erect this virtually dematerialised, mullionless glazed wall and corner. The wooden trusses span the forum and lobby in one continuous piece, rest on the axial wall and cantilever out 13 m beyond the lobby, whereby here the profiles of the glazed surface in the form of long vertical edges fasten the whole construction to the ground,

über Forum und Foyer, liegen auf der Mittelwand auf, kragen am Foyer 13 m weit aus, wobei hier die Profile der Verglasung als Zugbänder das Ganze wieder nach unten verspannen, während beim Forum runde Stahlstützen im Luftraum der dort zweischaligen Verglasung die Balken abspannen, dort aber auch Druckkräfte aufnehmen können.

Das Ganze wäre wohl prinzipiell auch in Beton denkbar gewesen. Warum also Holz? Auch wenn Holz größere Dimensionen erfordert, wirkt es optisch leichter – und Masse war bei dieser Raumkonstellation kein Nachteil, sondern gestalterisch erwünscht; die Holzträger belassen auch die Beton-Rückwand und den mit Zement gebundenen Terrazzo des Bodens in ihrer jeweiligen Autonomie, schaffen ein lebhaftes Spiel zwischen den unterschiedlichen statischen Primärelementen, zwischen vertikal und horizontal, zwischen Wand und Balken, zwischen dem isotrop Gegossenen und dem homogen Geschichteten, zwischen dem ruhig Stehenden und dem gespannt Darübergelegten; weiters war mit Holz der thermische Übergang beim Vordach viel einfacher und eleganter lösbar und konnten die Balkenuntersichten im Saal akustisch und optisch pur in dem dort noch anspruchsvolleren Raumcharakter mit-spielen; und schließlich – Veranden zum Garten sind im kollektiven Gedächtnis immer noch als Holzvorbauten mit großen Glasfenstern abgespeichert. Meili, Peter rühren vielleicht an diese Erinnerung. Der Typus ist jedoch voll-kommen neu dargestellt und unsentimental in die Wirkung modernster Holzbautechnologie übergeführt, wo flächige Schichtungen, Vor-fertigung enormer Teile und statische Ausrei-zung mit Vorspannung und dergleichen eine ganz neue Grammatik des Materials und seiner Ausstrahlung erzeugen. Und zu allerletzt – im Hinblick auf die vorhin erwähnte asymmetrische

whereas in the forum round steel columns in the space between the double-layered glazed wall support the beams while also absorbing the forces bearing down upon them.

In principle the whole thing would certainly also have been conceivable in concrete. Why then in wood? Even if lumber requires constructions of greater dimensions, optically it still appears lighter – and with this spatial constellation mass was not a disadvantage, in fact it was even a desired part of the design; moreover, the wooden trusses do not interfere with the autonomous planes of the concrete back wall and the terrazzo floor and even create a playful exchange between different static primary elements, between the vertical and the horizontal, between wall and beam, between the isotropic poured and the homogeneous layered, between the stable standing members and the tense members spanning those supports; furthermore, wood facilitated the thermal transition at the awning and made it more elegant, and the undersides of the beams could be incorporated acoustically and optically more purely into the sophisticated spatial character of the hall; and finally – verandas opening out onto gardens have been stored in the collective memory throughout time as wooden structures with large glass windows. Meili, Peter are perhaps toying with this image. A traditional building type, but with a brand-new face, transformed to incorporate in an unsentimental way the fruits of modern wood engineering and construction technology. Layered surfaces, huge prefabricated parts and the use of prestressed components to push the static bounds of technology, etc. produces

Spiegelung der Stofflichkeit zwischen Umraum und Veranda: Wäre nicht auch denkbar, die großen Holzträger als das stofflich entsprechende, technisch und tektonische transformierte Rahmenwerk für das damit aufbereitete Bild der mächtigen Kastanienstämme zu verstehen?

Wir sehen an diesem Punkt, wie eine lakonische, auf den ersten Blick undifferenzierte Architektur einen ganzen Kosmos an Begründungsschichten und Interpretationen auftut und in Bewegung setzt, wenn sie befragt wird. Man könnte eine solche Analyse natürlich um weitere Facetten vertiefen, man könnte auf diesem Niveau das ganze Gebäude durchchecken und würde dann auch an scheinbar beiläufigen Zonen eine Konsequenz wahrnehmen, die eben nicht auf designhafte Einheitlichkeit oder universalistische Isotropie von Stoff, Konstruktion und Raum abstellt (wie etwa die späten Bauten von Mies van der Rohe). Man würde zum Beispiel gerade im Bereich unter dem auskragenden Foyer, der zu dem, was sich darüber tut, seltsam unambitioniert erscheint, jene gestalterische Logik verstehen, die sich nicht am harmonisch Durchgehaltenen klassischer Planstrategien orientiert, sondern an Brüchen und Tempowechsel der Peripherie, die ja deshalb elastisch, spannend und offen wirkt, weil da jede Behauptung, jede Systematik, jedes Pathos sogleich auf die Leere des Kontextes trifft oder am Widerspruch benachbarter, konträrer Wirklichkeit unvermittelt abprallt.

Meili, Peter arbeiten daran, das »schwierige Ganze«, wie Steinmann es nannte, so einfach und so profund wie möglich zu realisieren – eine Häufung von Paradoxien, gewiss. Jedenfalls verbinden sie erfolgreich die »Anonymität« ingenieurhaften Planens mit der Sensibilität von Gestaltern, die auch sozusagen unarchitektonische oder banale Situationen wahrnehmen und auf sie reagieren können. Der Auftrag für

a whole new grammar of building materials and the images they present. And last but not least, in respect to the abovementioned asymmetrical mirroring of the materiality between the environment and the veranda: might it not also be conceivable to view the great wooden trusses, fashioned indeed from an appropriate material and technically and tectonically transformed, as the framework for the image of the mighty chestnut trees it has been created to reflect?

We see at this point how when prodded with a question an example of laconic, at first glance unspecific architecture will unfold a whole universe of reasons and interpretations and set them in motion. One could, of course, delve deeper into this analysis and explore further facets, one could on this level examine the entire building and would then perceive in seemingly arbitrary zones a constancy that didn't concentrate on design uniformity or a universal isotropy of material, construction and space (e.g. the later buildings by Mies van der Rohe). And precisely in the area beneath the cantilever lobby, which compared to what is going on above seems oddly ambitionless, one would for example understand the logic of the designer that doesn't orient itself on that which is harmoniously traditional in classical plan strategies, but on the breaks and changes in momentum of a periphery that is elastic and seems exciting and open precisely because every claim, every systematic idea, every bathos immediately encounters the emptiness of the context or clashes directly with the contradiction of nearby, opposing reality.

Swiss Re konfrontierte sie mit einer Sphäre, die ihrem kritischen Realismus sicher nicht so direkt entgegenkam wie der periphere Kontext in Biel, wo sie kürzlich den viel beachteten Neubau der Schweizerischen Hochschule für Holzwirtschaft realisierten. Formelles Understatement mit sachlicher Perfektion und einem weiten Horizont für aktuelle Entwicklungen zu verbinden, gehört freilich auch für Swiss Re zu den Maximen, ebenso wie ein pointierter Zugang zur aktuellen Kunst und die Kooperation mit hochrangigen Planern wie Kienast Vogt Partner, die auch für Rüschlikon beigezogen wurden. Diese verfuhren mit den Naturräumen der Villa Bodmer ganz analog wie die Architekten mit dem baulichen Ensemble, forcierten vorhandene Substanz, indem sie diese mit neuen Qualitäten überlagerten: Auch hier kein Hang zur großen Einheit oder zum exzessiven Statement, sondern das Aufmischen eines neuen, heterogenen Ganzen mit analytisch erarbeiteten, strukturellen Eingriffen.

Eine heikle Entscheidung betraf die innere Ausstattung und Möblierung der Gebäude. Die Selbstverständlichkeit von durchgängigen Ensembles, wie sie noch im Historismus gang und gäbe war, ist nach dem Schnitt der Moderne nicht mehr möglich. Dem schwierigen, additiven und »unkünstlerischen« Prinzip des Adolf Loos steht da nach wie vor nur die stilistische, hermetische Obsession »Gesamtkunstwerk« gegenüber, die mit Olbrich, Mackintosh und Hoffmann begann und vielleicht mit Philippe Starck endet. Die besten Innen- und Wohnräume von Frank Lloyd Wright sind übrigens jene, die Rudolph Schindler »subversiv« möblierte, indem er die maßlichen Module des Meisters akzeptierte, die virtuose Zwanghaftigkeit der Wrightschen Räume aber mit legeren, unprätentösen Ausstattungen entschärfte.

Meili, Peter's work attempts to realise the "complex whole", as Steinmann called it, in as simple and as profound a way as possible – quite paradoxical, to be sure. In any case they successfully bring together the "anonymity" of the engineer's plan and the sensibility of designers who are also able to perceive nonarchitectonic or commonplace situations and respond to them. The work commissioned by Swiss Re put them face to face with a sphere that certainly did not correspond as directly to their critical realism as the peripheral context in Biel, where they recently completed the highly acclaimed new building for the Swiss Timber Engineering University. To be able to combine formal understatement with technical perfection and an open mind for current developments is also without a doubt a part of Swiss Re's philosophy, along with a keen approach to contemporary art and co-operation with prominent planners like Kienast Vogt Partner, who were also called in to work on Rüschlikon. They proceeded with natural spaces of the Bodmer Villa grounds in a manner analogous to the way the architects did with the building ensemble, emphasized the existing substance by superimposing new qualities onto it: here again no trend towards overall uniformity or towards some kind of excessive statement, but rather the concocting of a new, heterogeneous whole with analytically planned structural interventions.

One of the most critical decisions about this project concerned the interior design and furnishing of the building. The clear assumption of the ensemble as was common in Historicism has ceased to be viable since the advent of Meili, Peter entschieden auch hier gegen das Stilprinzip und für ein schwieriges Ganzes. Aufgrund einer internationalen Ausschreibung, mit der sie nach Partnern für die Raumgestaltung suchten, wurden die Wiener Architekten Hermann Czech und Adolf Krischanitz ausgewählt, die sich gemeinsam beworben hatten. Beide, insbesondere Czech, konnten auf einschlägige Realisierungen hinweisen und vertreten eine unspektakuläre, aber nicht unsinnige Linie, die – analog zur Haltung von Meili, Peter – nicht auf subjektive Erfindung aus ist, sondern die lakonische, sensitive Durcharbeitung des Alltäglichen betreibt. Für alle Beteiligten bedeutete dieses Unternehmen logistisches Neuland. Denn für sämtliche festen und mobilen Einrichtungen, Bestuhlungen, Tische, Beleuchtungskörper für Konferenz-, Seminarräume und Appartements bis zur Ausstattung von Restaurant, Bar und Rekreationsbereichen wurden in Abstimmung mit Swiss Re spezifische Lösungen erarbeitet. Für Vorhänge und Teppiche wurde noch der Wiener Maler und Textilkünstler Gilbert Bretterbauer beigezogen.

Czech vertritt wie schon Loos, Frank und andere die Auffassung, dass die von der klassischen Moderne gesuchte stilistische Kohärenz zwischen Architektur und Mobiliar ein Trugschluss war, der den direkten Körperbezug speziell von Sitzmöbeln zugunsten formaler Innovationen vernachlässigte. Kritisch gegenüber allen vordergründigen Moden und Formen, »die nicht Gedanke sind«, propagiert Czech »Architektur als Hintergrund« und schuf private und öffentliche Interieurs als Mischungen von alten und neuen Elementen in der Gewissheit, dass nur solche Räume komfortabel sind, die so wirken, als wären sie immer schon so gewesen, und die zudem imstande sind, Irreguläres und auch Banales zu integrieren.

Modernism. All there is to counteract Adolf Loos' complex, additive and "inartistic" principle is still only the stylistic, hermetic "Gesamtkunstwerk", an obsession which began with Olbrich, Mackintosh and Hoffmann and ended perhaps with Philippe Starck. The best interiors and living spaces by Frank Lloyd Wright are incidentally the ones that Rudolph Schindler furnished "subversively" by accepting the proportional modules of his master, the virtuoso obsession of the Wrightian spaces, which he however mellowed with casual, unpretentious appointments.

Here too Meili, Peter decided against the stylistic principle and for a complex whole. Through an international competition intended to find partners to design the interiors the architects chose the Viennese interior designers Hermann Czech and Adolf Krischanitz, who had submitted a joint project. Both, particularly Czech, were able to refer to relevant completed projects. Also their approach followed an unspectacular but not unsensual course that is – analogous to Meili, Peter's own stance – not aimed at subjective invention, but at the laconic, sensitive processing of the quotidian. All artists involved in this project were about to enter new logistic territory, for in co-operation with Swiss Re they would be elaborating specific designs for all the stationary and mobile facilities, chairs, tables, lamps and light fixtures to be used in the conference and seminar rooms and the apartments, not to mention all the appointments for the restaurant, bar and recreational areas. The curtains and carpets were to be designed by the Viennese painter and textile artist Gilbert Bretterbauer.

Im Zentrum des Denkens von Adolf Loos stand die Auffassung, dass bewährte Formen nur dann verändert werden sollten, wenn damit eine Verbesserung einhergeht. In diesem Sinn hat Czech beispielsweise für das Wiener MAK-Café Sessel und Armlehnsessel in der klassischen Bugholztechnik entworfen. Die berühmten Thonet-Sessel waren Produkte, bei denen Technologie und Form, Material und Zweck, anonyme Typhaftigkeit des Seriellen und Emotionalität der organhaften Form vollendet im Gleichgewicht standen. Es waren Möbel, so leicht wie nie zuvor, so billig wie nie zuvor, mit körperhafter, vitaler Anmutung und mit grafisch-abstraktem Ausdruck; handwarm, durchsichtig etc. Und trotzdem die Problematik: Kann man so etwas heute noch einmal machen? Ist das nicht schon Geschichte? Kann man das weiterdenken? Man kann es, wenn man es konsequent genug tut. Das Manko der Thonetsessel war und ist, dass sie relativ unbequem sind. Sie sind nicht ergonomisch, sie haben beispielsweise eine horizontale Sitzfläche, sie haben keinen Körperschluss. Wenn auch Loos dann, wie Hevesi sagte, das Bugholz so gebogen wie möglich machte, sein Bugholzsessel war zwar leichter und dünner als jeder andere, aber nicht bequemer. Und genau da hat Czech eingehakt.

Seine Verbesserung einer scheinbar längst ausgereizten Form besteht darin, ihr Potenzial in Richtung dieses Mankos noch einmal zu durchdenken und weiterzutreiben, die Kurven wirklich so weit zu biegen, dass plötzlich ein tatsächlich bequemeres Möbel entsteht. Eine ergonomische, körperschlüssige, vitale Form – unverkennbar aus den neunziger Jahren und dennoch klassisch Thonet. Czech würde vermutlich dazu sagen: Das latente Potenzial dieser Möbel ist hier mit gutem Grund über die klassische Grenze hinaus in eine manieristische Vollendung getrieben.

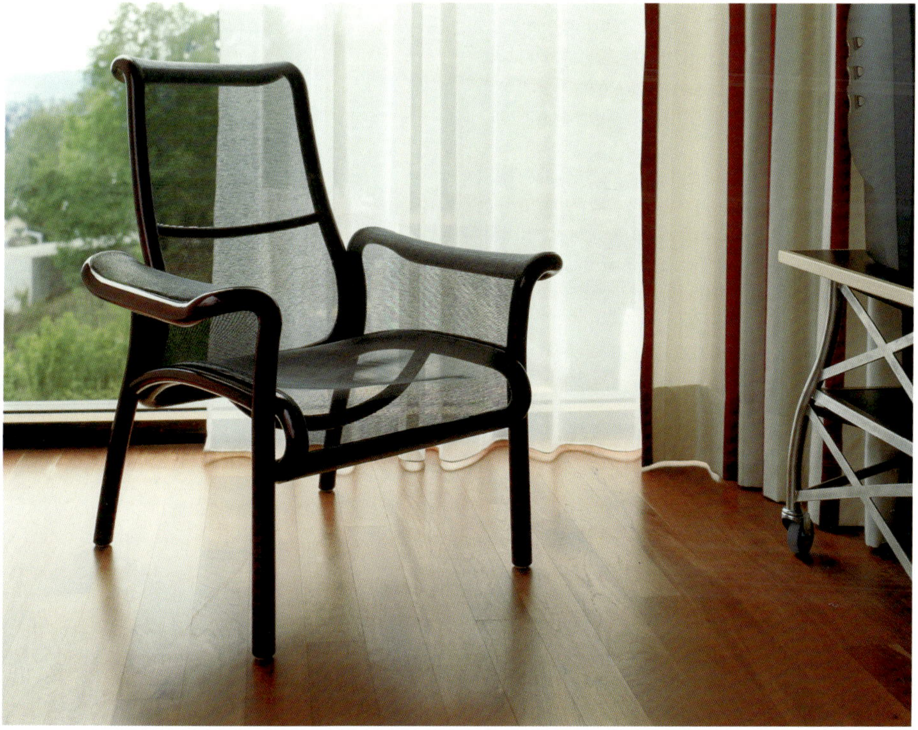

Czech believes, like Loos, Frank and others, that classical modernism's search for the stylistic coherence between architecture and its appointments was a fallacy that neglected the direct relationship to the body, particularly in the case of chairs, in favour of formal innovation. Czech who is critical of all ostensible fashions and forms "that aren't themselves thought" supports an "architecture as backdrop". He created private and public interiors as mixes of old and new elements, certain that the only comfortable room was one that gave the impression of always having been that way and which was also capable of integrating irregular and even commonplace elements.

At the centre of Adolf Loos' philosophy was the view that well-tried forms should only be changed if this would bring about an improvement. In this sense Czech, for example, used the classic bentwood technique to design the chairs and armchairs for the MAK Café in Vienna. The famous Thonet chairs were products in which technology and form, material and purpose, anonymous typification of a serial product and emotional attachment to the organic form came together in perfect harmony. Furniture lighter than ever before, cheaper than ever before, with physical, lively grace and with graphically abstract expression; pleasant, transparent, etc. And still there was the dilemma: Is it possible to make something like this again today? Isn't it already history? Can one go on and develop it further? It is possible if one is consistent enough about it. The Thonet chairs' weakness was and is that they are relatively uncomfortable.

Hier zeigt sich der große Unterschied etwa zu Philippe Starck, der vor allem am erotisch-vitalen Ausdruck konventioneller Möbel als Form-Bild arbeitet, also am bildhaften Mehrwert der Produkte, während bei Czech solcher Mehrwert nicht das Ziel ist, sondern das Resultat einer konkreten, gebrauchsorientierten Konsequenz.

Für Swiss Re hat Czech nun etliche Typen seiner Kollektion weiterbearbeitet: die Clubfauteuils in grünem Leder, die er in Fortführung der anthropomorphen Modelle von John Soane schon für Bar und Restaurant Schwarzenberg entwickelt hatte; die erwähnten MAK-Sessel; die Ohren-Fauteuils und Rittlings-Sessel mit gepolstertem Lehnenbrett aus dem Wiener Theatercafé. Hinzu kamen neue Typen wie die Paraphrase auf die Design-Ikonen »Grand Comfort LC 2 und LC3« – historische Schulbeispiele der Aufpfropfung architektonischer Formkonzepte auf das körpernahe Gerät, deren mangelnden Sitzkomfort und inkonsistente Konstruktion (Mischung von Rund- und Flachstahl, stumpfe Schweißungsverbindung, keine Griffzone für die Hände zum Schwungholen beim Aufstehen) Czech mit subtilen Veränderungen korrigierte; als Lehnsessel für die Vorstandssuite ein Versuch, die von Charles und Ray Eames mit Metallrahmen kombinierten Netze so auf ein Traggestell zu spannen, dass der gestützte Körper im Idealfall nur an Netzflächen, und nicht, wie bei den Eames, auch ans Traggestell stößt; die Vollendung der anonymen Kugelleuchte durch Integration von Spots für gerichtetes Up-Light und Down-Light; stapelbare Blechhocker mit Rundrohren und fragile Beistelltischchen aus Metall.

Czechs Interventionen sind am dichtesten im Restaurant und in der dem alten Gärtnerhaus eingepflanzten Bar gegeben. Beim Restaurant wurde die Position der Leuchtkugeln auf

They aren't ergonomic, they have horizontal seats, they don't correspond well to the body's contours. And as Hevesi commented, when Loos took the bentwood technique to its most bent extreme, his chair was lighter than the others and its proportions thinner, but it still wasn't any less uncomfortable. And that was precisely Czech's point of departure.

His improvement of a seemingly long exhausted form consisted in focusing on its weakness, rethinking it and getting the most out of the design's potential, in taking those curves and really bending them until he'd suddenly made a truly more comfortable piece of furniture. An ergonomic, body-friendly, spirited form – unmistakably nineties and yet classically Thonet. Czech would probably comment: The latent potential of this piece of furniture has not without good reason been forced to transcend its classical limitations and become a work of Mannerist perfection.

Here we see the big difference in contrast to someone like Philippe Starck, who is concerned above all with the erotic-vital expression of conventional furniture as a form-image, i.e. with the value added to the product through its imagery, whereas with Czech value added is not the goal, but the result of a concrete utilitarian consequence.

Czech has taken a number of furniture types from his collection and adapted them for Swiss Re: the club armchairs in green leather, which he had already designed in a continuation of the anthropomorphic models by John Soane for the Schwarzenberg bar and restaurant; the already mentioned MAK chair; the armchairs and straddle chair

wechselbare Tischstellungen abgestimmt und korrespondiert »zufällig« mit den wechselnden Rhythmen der Fensterteilungen und der nicht-gerasterten Deckenteilung von Meili, Peter; die Größe der Tische wurde in peniblen Versuchsserien mit verschiedenen Tellermaßen, Gläseranordnungen und Besteck-Garnituren minimiert und auf Bistro-Atmosphäre optimiert; die Bar mit dem bei Czech obligaten Venezianischen Luster präsentiert im Kontrast zur Sachlichkeit des Übrigen jene frivole, gemischte Alltäglichkeit, die spontan anregt und einstimmt, und dennoch Hintergrund bleibt.

Den Part der korporativen Möblierungen übernahm Krischanitz: die dunklen Fauteuils für Wandelgang, unteres Foyer und Zimmer, die Leuchtstelen mit zweischaligen Glashüllen, die durch innen und außen versetzte Ätzstreifen auf raffiniert einfache Weise eine blendfreie Lichtwirkung zeigen; Tische und Stapelstühle für die Schulungsbereiche (an dem sehr leichten und stabilen Stuhl mit gepresster, durch Spanten verstärkter Holzschale wurde ein Jahr lang mit dem Hersteller getüftelt). Die vielfältigsten Anforderungen stellte das Forum, das mit möglichst wenig Stauraum für Bankett, Schulung, Diskussion, Vortrag oder Konzert jeweils maßgeschneiderte Ausrüstungen erhalten sollte. Zusätzlich zum Stapelstuhl hat Krischanitz deshalb gepolsterte, für die Lagerung leicht zerlegbare Fauteuils entwickelt, weiters stapelbare Paravents zur Abschirmung von Arbeitsinseln, gebaut aus gekurvten Holzgestellen, bespannt mit drei Schichten Plexiglas und Stoff – nicht mehr durchsichtig und doch noch durchscheinend. Die Kurvenvarianten wurden hier durch verschieden gelegte Schnitte aus einer amorphen, geschlossenen Grundform gewonnen.

Forum und Zimmer des Seminartraktes wurden komplett von Krischanitz ausgestattet, in anderen Bereichen gibt es Mischungen

with the cushioned backrest from the Vienna Theatercafé. In addition he also developed new types like his versions of the design icons "Grand Comfort LC2 and LC3" – historical academic examples of the grafting of architectonic concepts of form onto the object intended to come in contact with the body but whose lack of a comfort-affording design and inconsistent construction (a mix of steel round and flat bars, course welding seams, absence of handrests to facilitate standing up) were corrected by Czech with subtle alterations; an attempt at an armchair for the executive suite, by taking the metal-frame and fabric construction by Charles and Ray Eames and drawing the material over the frame in such a way that the body would ideally only make contact with the fabric and not, as with Eames' design, knock against the frame as well; the perfecting of the anonymous hanging globe lamp by integrating spotlights to direct the beam up or downwards; the stackable metal stools made of steel round bar; the fragile metal side tables.

Most of Czech's interventions can be found in the restaurant and in the bar located in what was formerly the gardener's house. In the restaurant the position of the light fixtures was set to accommodate changing table positions and corresponds "coincidentally" to the changing rhythms of the window divisions and the non-grid pattern of the ceiling divisions by Meili, Peter; the table size was reduced through a series of meticulous experimentation with different plate sizes, glass arrangements and silverware settings and is now optimised for a bistro atmosphere; in contrast to the matter-of-fact austerity of the rest of the rooms, the

mit Czech (Wandelgang, Bibliothek, Foyer), wobei der Kontrast von massigen und filigranen Elementen bewusst eingesetzt ist. Im Seminartrakt kamen Deckensysteme und Deckenleuchten von Meili, Peter hinzu. In der Bibliothek wechselte Krischanitz in Czechs Reviere und gestaltete die Stehlampen mit den lose fallenden Seidenschirmen, die blauen Sitzbänke sind eine Gemeinschaftsarbeit.

Für Probemöblierungen wurden, während der Bau noch in den Fundamenten steckte, 1:1 Modellräume gebaut und dabei auch Ensembles mit Möbelklassikern von Le Corbusier, Charles und Ray Eames und anderen ausprobiert. Erst nachdem alle Beteiligten sich darauf geeinigt hatten, dass diese Ikonen heute schon klischeehaft wirken und auch nicht zum Duktus der Architektur passen würden, auch nicht als sinnreicher Widerspruch oder Kontrast, erst dann entschloss man sich, auf diese Standards ganz zu verzichten und alles selbst zu machen – mit der Maxime, eine eher anonyme, durchaus heterogene Möblierung zu schaffen, die nicht modisch, aber auch nicht charakterlos sein sollte, den hohen Ansprüchen genügend, und zugleich beiläufig, leger: keine Designer-Stimmung, aber auch nicht die Austauschbarkeit üblicher Objektmöblierungen. Die Kooperation der beiden Wiener mit den Schweizern, ihre internen Positionswechsel zwischen »modern« und »nicht-modern«, zwischen retrospektiver Akribie und prospektiver Ironie, bedeutete für alle Beteiligten eine primäre Erfahrung. Das Resultat fügt der Architektur von Meili, Peter eine wichtige Klangfarbe hinzu: Wirkungen, die man nicht auf Abruf kalkulieren, sondern nur in sachlicher Teamarbeit erzielen kann. Dieses Konzept ergänzte im Textilbereich Gilbert Bretterbauer, ein Maler und Textilgestalter, der sich seit den achtziger Jahren mit den ornamentalen Parametern der durch Muster

bar with the for Czech obligatory Venetian chandeliers creates a frivolous, mixed quotidian atmosphere that spontaneously attracts and sets the mood and yet remains unobtrusive.

Krischanitz took over the role of designing the corporate furnishings: the dark armchairs for the wide hallways, the lower lobby and rooms, the lamps with their double glass walls that have a staggered pattern of etched lines on both panes to produce an ingeniously simple glarefree lighting effect; tables and stackable chairs for the areas designated for the training courses (it took a year of brainstorming and working with the manufacturer to come up with this extremely light and stable chair made of a laminated wood shell reinforced by a vertical frame). A challenging task was the forum, which disposed of little storage space but was at the same time supposed to receive custom-made furnishings for its diverse functions of banquet, training, discussion, lecture or concert hall. Thus in addition to the stackable chair, Krischanitz also designed armchairs that could be easily assembled and disassembled, moreover there were also partitions for sectioning off workspaces. Made of curved wooden frames, into which three layers of Plexiglas and fabric were fitted – no longer transparent but yet still translucent – they could be pushed together to take up as little space as possible when not in use to. The curve variations were taken from different cross-sections of a solid, amorphous basic form.

The interiors of the forum and the rooms in the seminar wing were designed exclusively by Krischanitz; in other areas furnishings

und Farben konstituierten Flächen-, Web- und Wirkstrukturen auseinandersetzt und für Rüschlikon eine serielle Sequenz von Teppichen und Stoffen gestaltete.

Die denkmalgeschützte Villa erforderte eindeutig eine nochmals separierte Behandlung, und Günther Förg war zweifellos die beste Wahl, um diese unzeitgemäße, der intendierten Illusion von Anfang an nicht gewachsene Kulisse durch künstlerische Re-Inszenierung flott zu machen und in die Gegenwart zu holen. Seine Eingriffe mit kräftigen, neuen Wandfarben, mit echten Stilmöbeln, dem Vergolden der Fensterrahmen, mit Remakes moderner Möbel und Tische aus dem Baujahr der Villa, mit dem obskuren Säulenpaar im Stiegenhaus – einem von Förg in allen Abgründen und Metaphern wiederholt behandelten Sujet – und mit Plexiglaslustern scharf neben allen Raumachsen bringen das totgelaufene Spiel dieser alten Inszenierung wieder in Gang. Sie bewältigen die prekäre Situation der nachträglichen Kunstwerdung von Kitsch, indem nun ein neues Netz von Referenzen über das Alte gelegt ist, das exakt die Mechanik der Referenzialität selbst thematisiert –»falsch« und »richtig« spielen da keine Rolle mehr, tauschen die Plätze –, indem Förg den Nutzern alles bietet was dazugehört, sie und sich selbst aber auf grandiose, elegante Weise aus diesem Spiel distanziert.

Das schwierige Ganze – ganz leicht: Rüschlikon ist kein Werk der Avantgarde im kanonischen Sinn, obwohl auch Kunstwerke der Avantgarde – Sol LeWitt, Louise Bourgeois unter anderen – an gut gewählten Stellen integriert wurden. Rüschlikon bietet das außergewöhnliche Beispiel einer Planung, die Alt- und Neubauten, Landschafts- und Raumgestaltung, Möbeldetail und künstlerische Intervention zu einem vielfältigen Ganzen fügt: eine souveräne,

are a mix of his and Czech's work (wide hallways, library, lobby), whereby the contrast between massive and delicate elements was intentional. In the seminar wing, however, the ceiling system and ceiling lighting were done by Meili, Peter. In the library Krischanitz switched to Czech's territory and designed the floor lamps with the undulating silk shades; the blue couches are joint project.

To test the furniture, 1:1-scale model rooms were set up while the building itself was still in its early stages of construction. Here ensembles with classic designs by Le Corbusier, Charles and Ray Eames and others were tested. Eventually everyone agreed that these icons seemed cliché today and that they didn't go with the style of the architecture, not even as an ingenious contradiction or contrast – it wasn't until then that these standards were abandoned completely and the decision made to design everything from scratch, based on the principle of creating furnishings that tended to be anonymous and altogether heterogeneous; not distinctly stylish, but not lacking character either; designed to meet high standardsand at the same time ostensibly casual, as if only in passing: a non-designer atmosphere, but without the interchangeability of common furnishings. The co-operation between the two Viennese and the Swiss, their internal shift in position between "modern" and "not modern", between retrospective meticulousness and prospective irony, was a primary experience for everyone involved. The result lends Meili, Peter's architecture an important timbre: effects that can't be calculated or produced by pushing a button, but which can only be achieved through sober teamwork. This concept was also realized in the textiles created for the project by Gilbert Bretterbauer, a painter and textile designer who has since the eighties worked intensively with the ornamental parameters of patterns and colours in flat, woven and knitted structures. Bretterbauer designed a series of carpets and fabrics for Rüschlikon.

The villa, which has been classified as a historical monument, clearly required a separate approach, and Günther Förg was undoubtedly the man to put some pep into this old-fashioned building that from the outset never lived up to its original intentions. If there was an artist who could give it a new face and bring it up to date, it was Förg. His interventions, for example walls repainted in bold colours, real period furniture, gilded window frames, remakes of modern furniture and tables from the same year the villa itself was actually built, the strange twin columns in front of the staircase – a theme repeatedly addressed by Förg metaphorically and in its darkest aspects – and the Plexiglas lampshades running along the room axes, albeit positioned off-centre, breathe life into this dreary setting. They successfully negotiate this precarious situation in which what was kitsch becomes art. Förg achieves this by placing a new network of references over the old one, a system that itself directly addresses the mechanics of referentiality – "true" and "false" are no longer important here, they swap roles – in so doing, Förg offers the user everything, fulfils all his expectations, while at the same time distancing both the user and

himself in a grandiose and elegant manner from the scene.

The complex whole – simply put: Rüschlikon is not a work of Avant-Garde in the classical sense, although Avant-Garde artworks – Sol LeWitt, Louise Bourgeois, among others – have been integrated into the complex at specially selected places. Rüschlikon is an extraordinary example of a design that brings together old and new buildings, landscape and interior design, furniture details and artistic intervention in a heterogeneous whole: an unperturbed, contemporary rendering, a forceful and at the same time calm presence; no new "Gesamtkunstwerk cast in one piece", but rather the structural concurrence of different stances, which are both autonomous and also capable of engaging in a dialogue, converging in an exciting and at the same time undramatic ensemble; not a manifesto of any particular style, but the logical interpretation of this specific place and its programmatic vision.

zeitgenössische Setzung, eine starke und zugleich unaufgeregte Präsenz; kein neues »Gesamtkunstwerk aus einem Guss«, sondern die strukturelle Konkordanz verschiedener autonomer, gleichwohl dialogfähiger Haltungen zu einem spannungsreichen und zugleich undramatischen Ensemble; kein Manifest irgendeines Stils, sondern die schlüssige Interpretation des konkreten Ortes und seiner programmatischen Vision.

Margherita Spiluttini

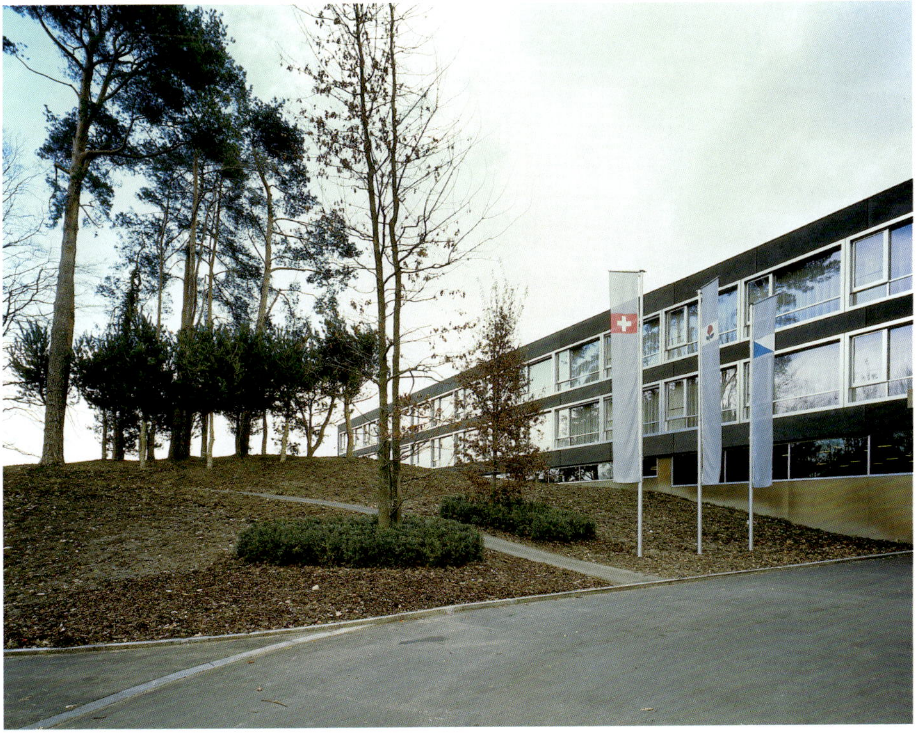

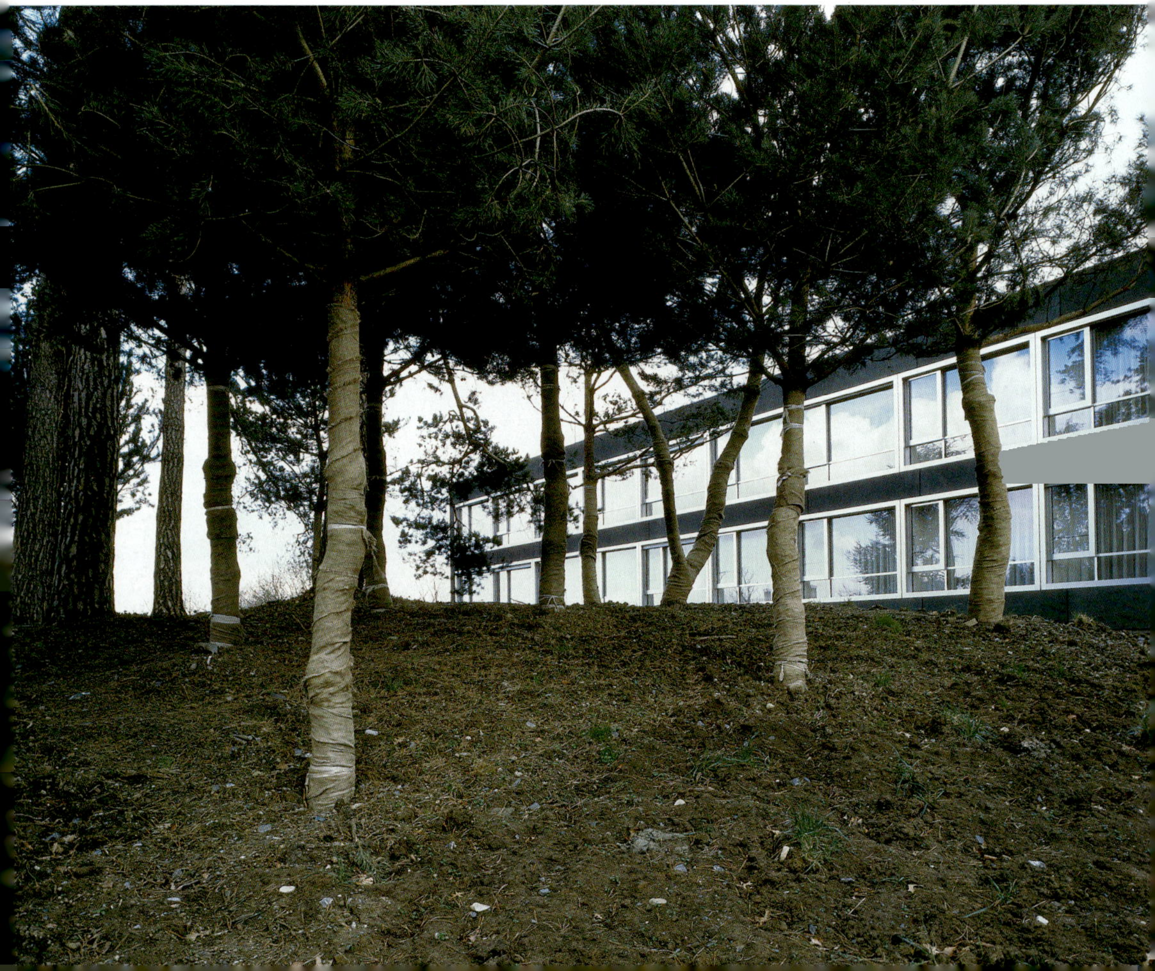

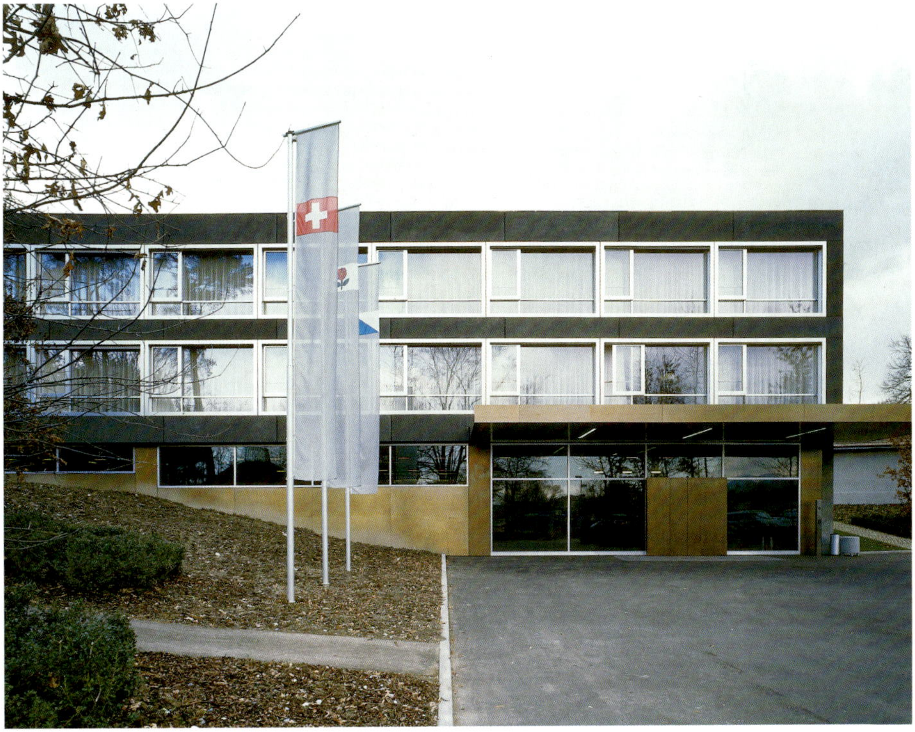

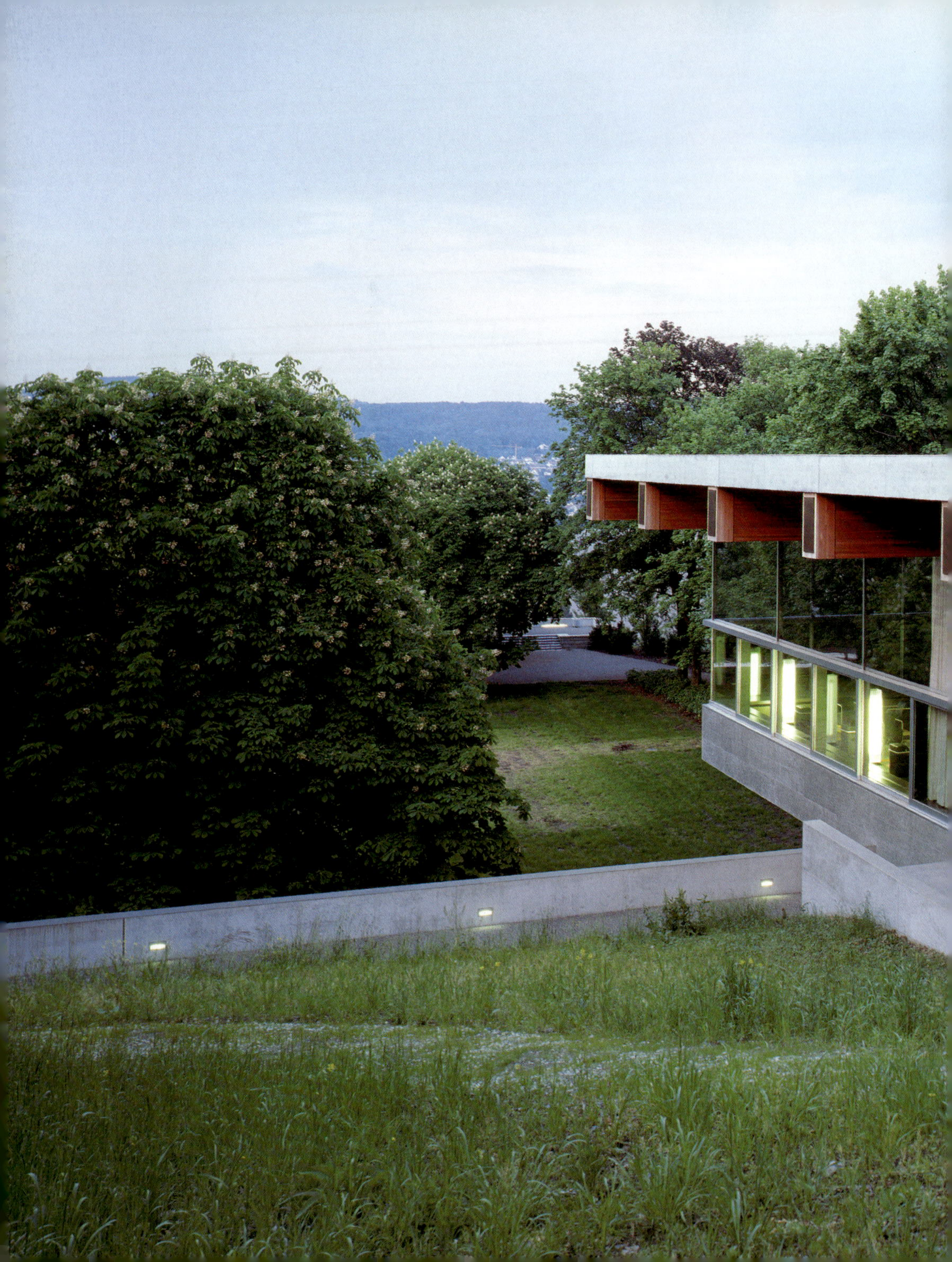

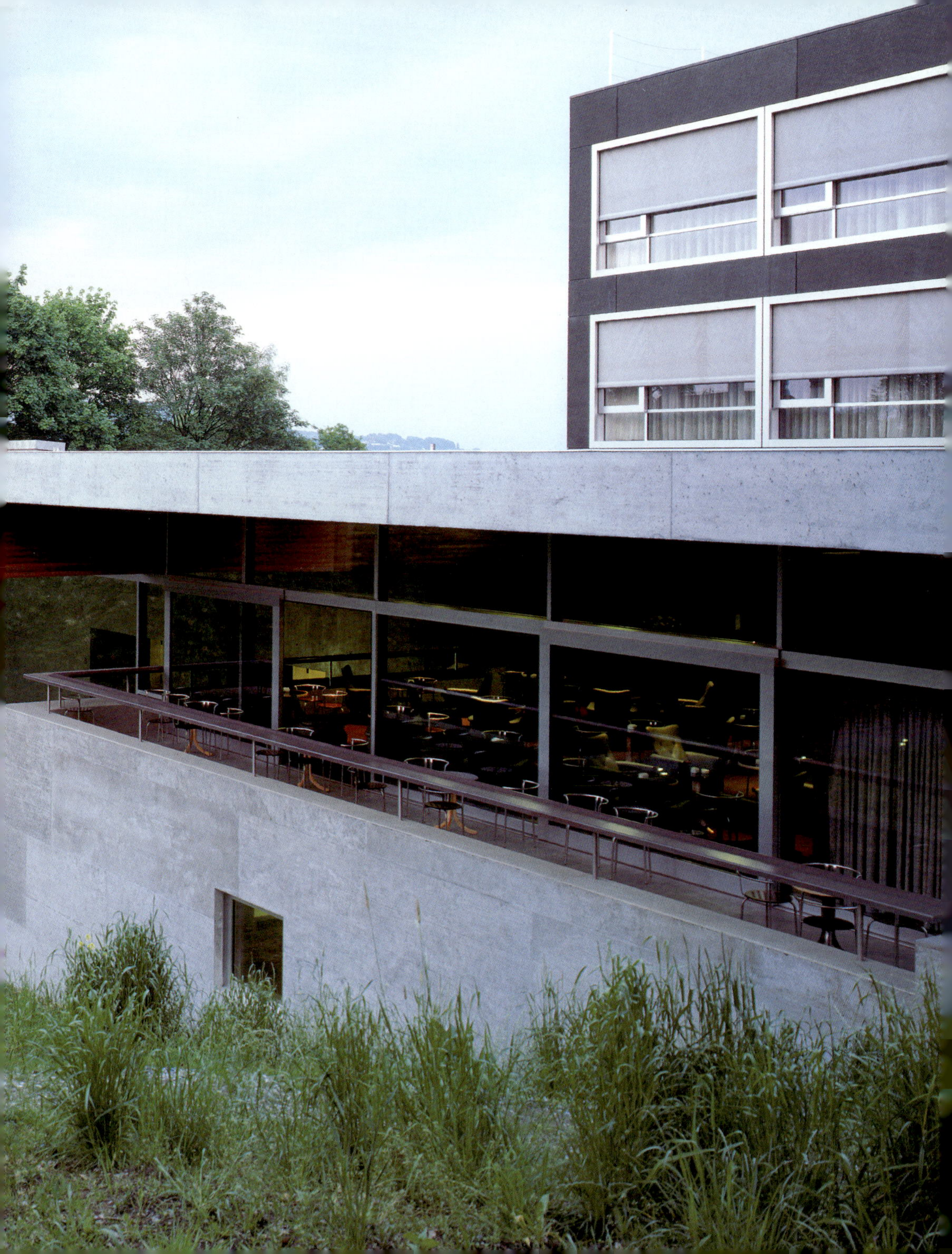

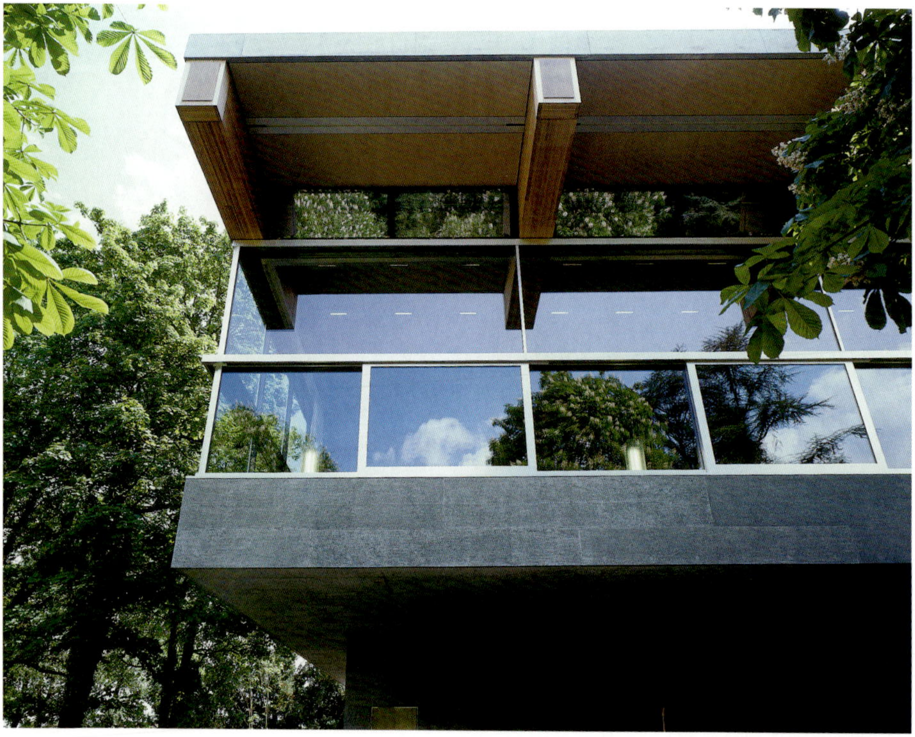

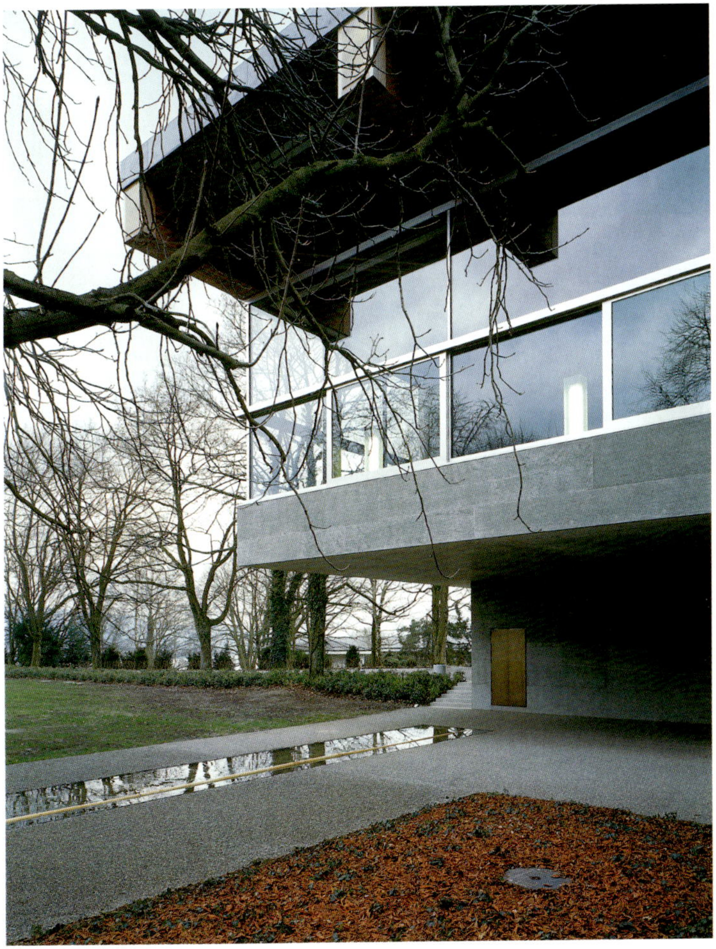

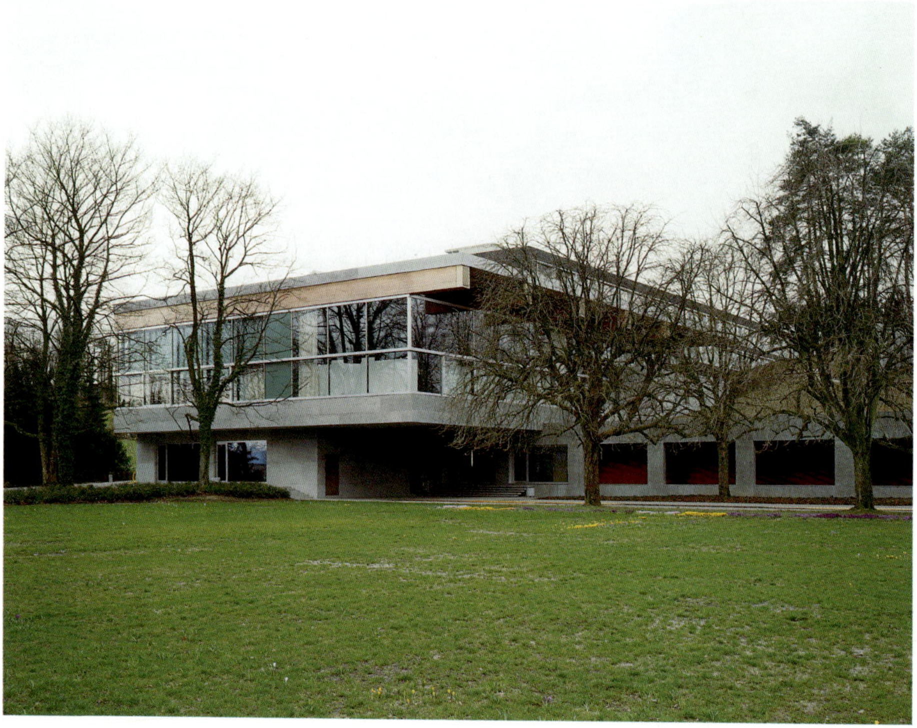

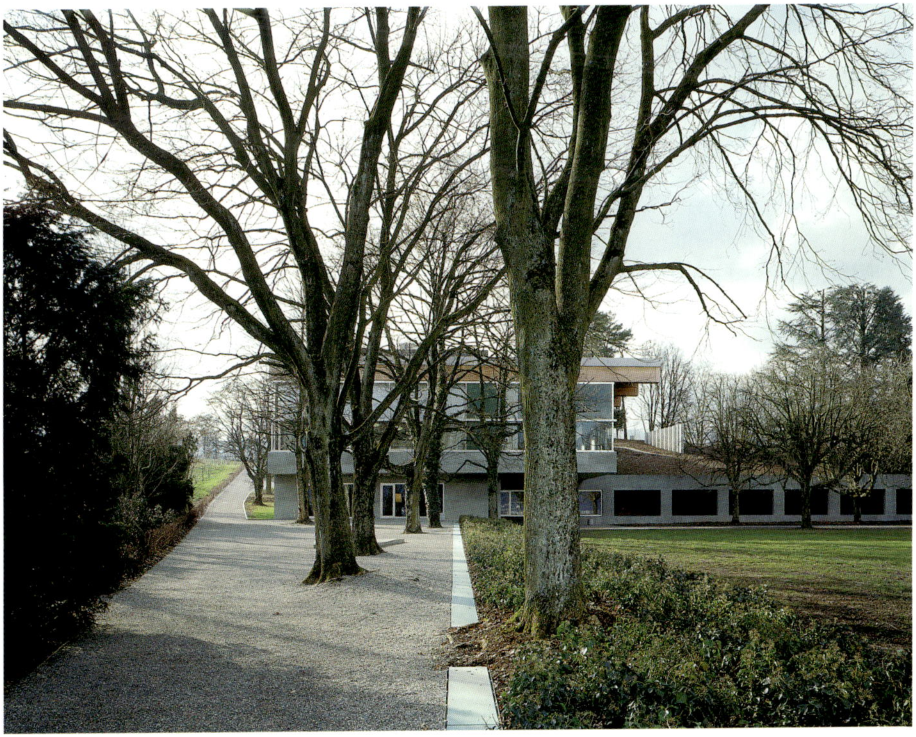

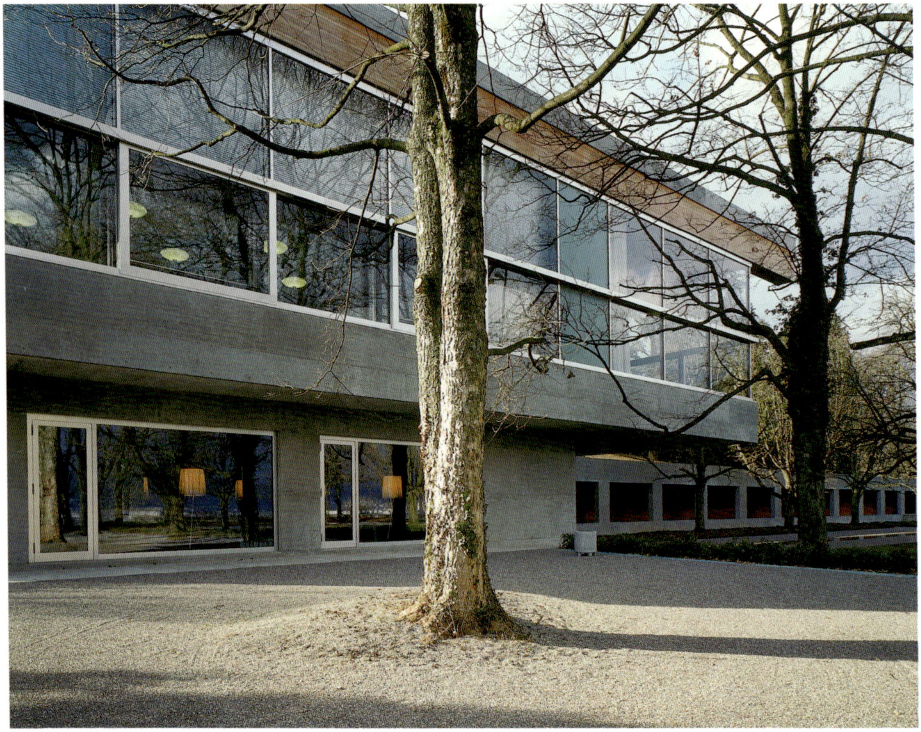

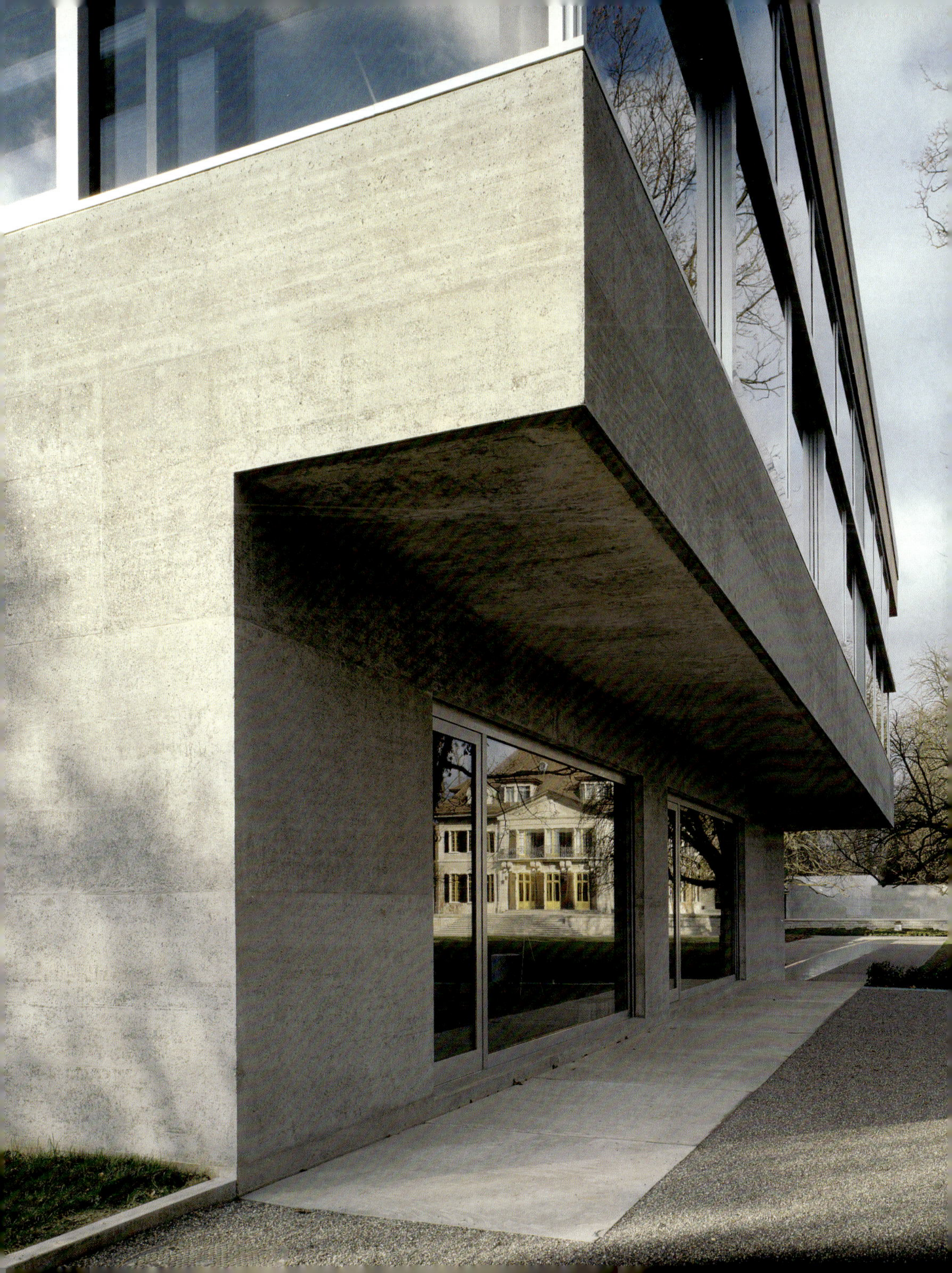

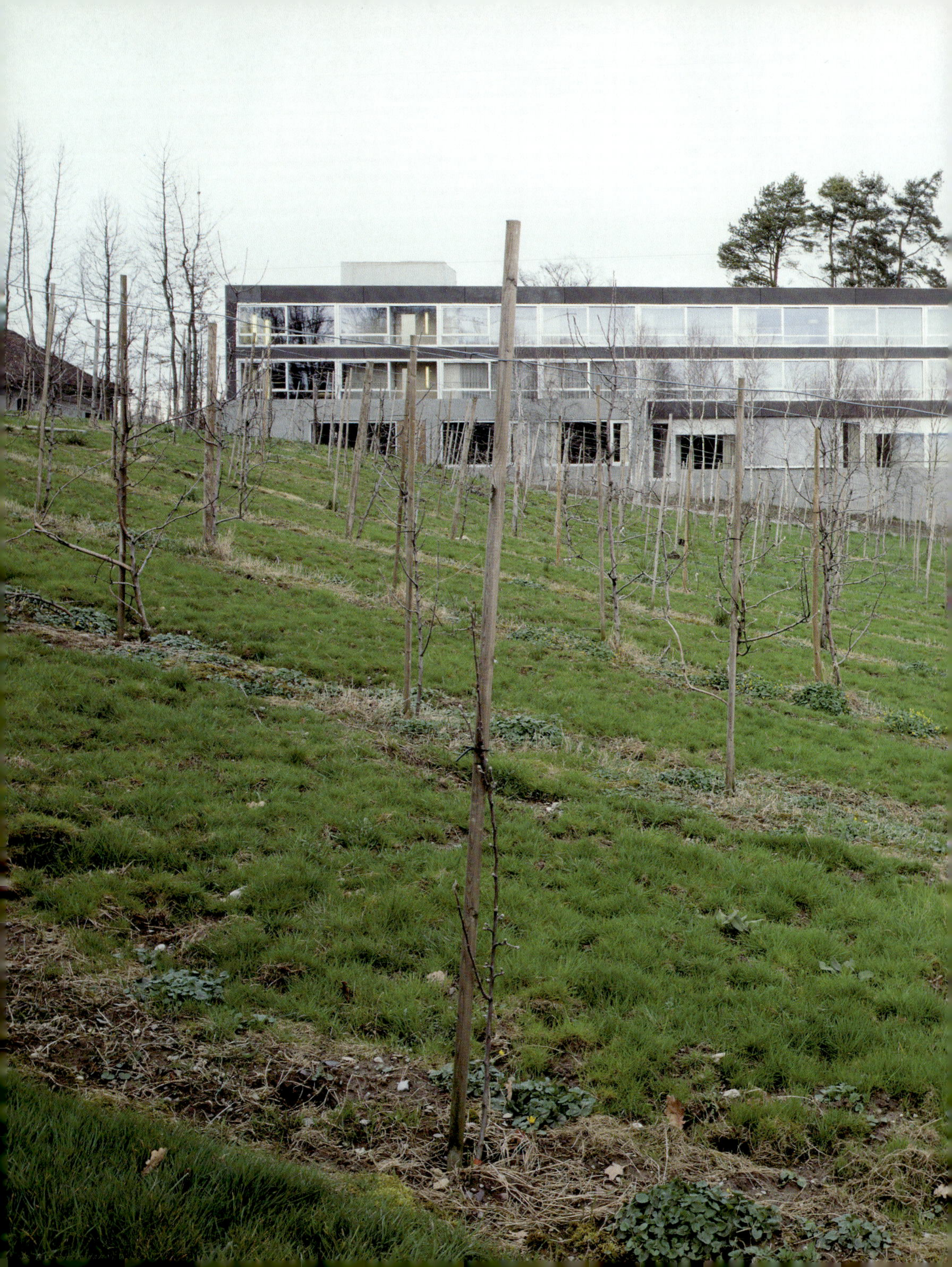

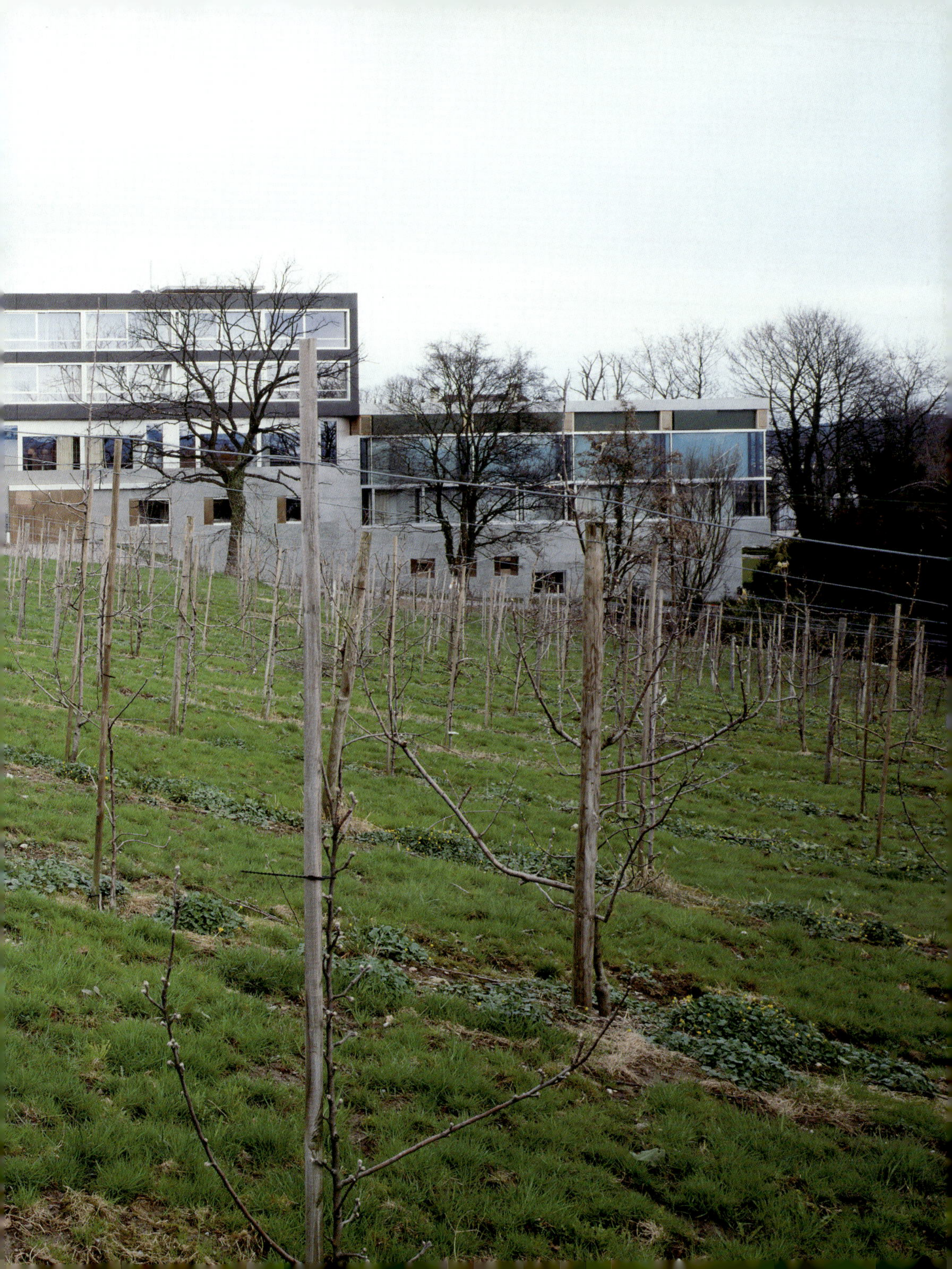

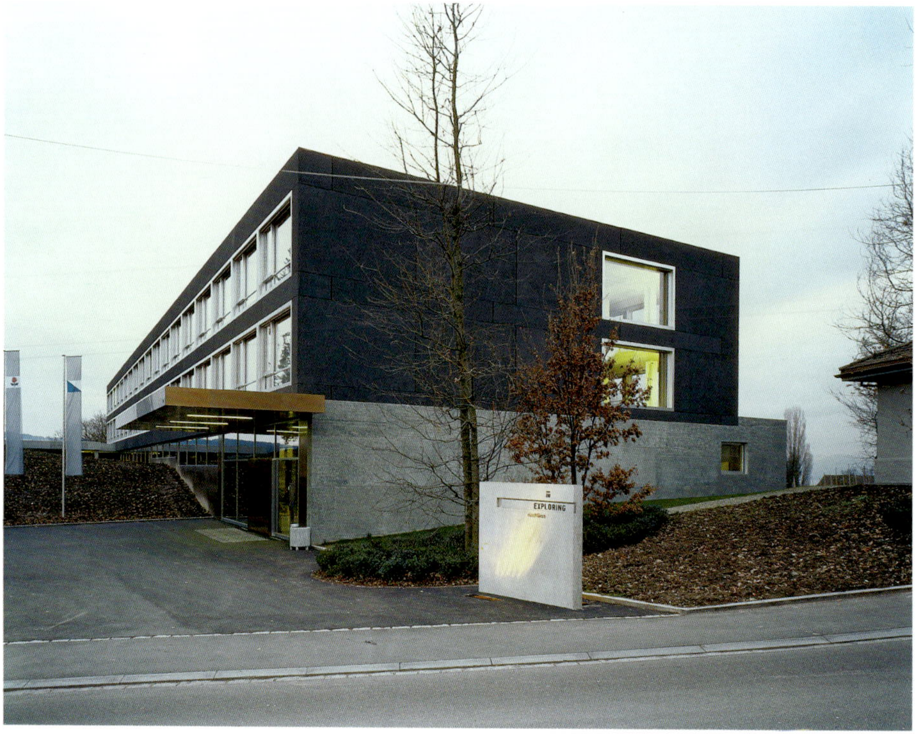
EXPLORING

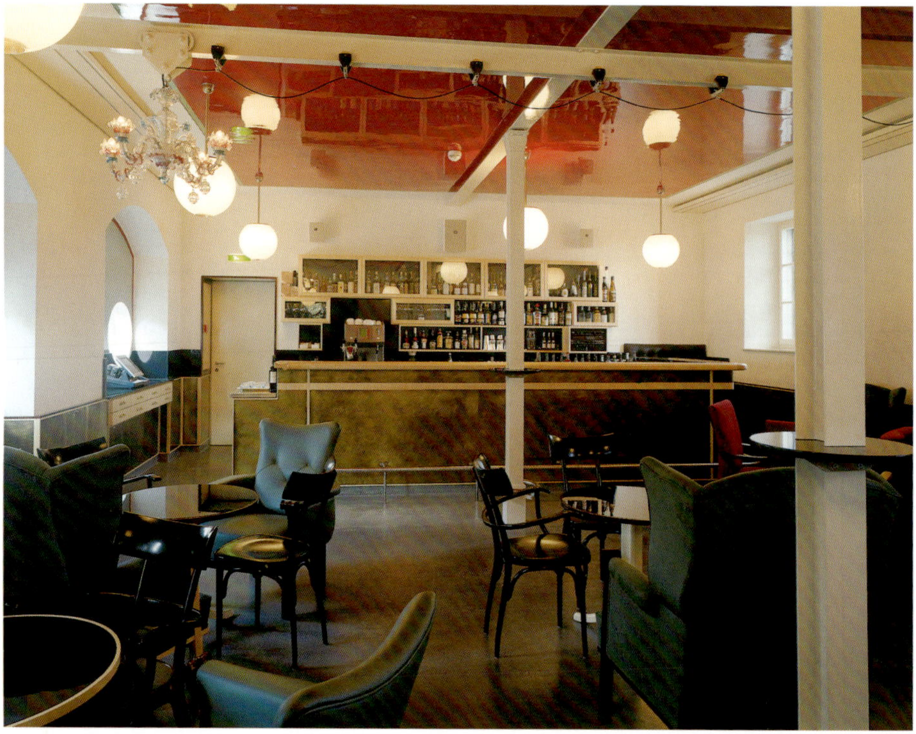

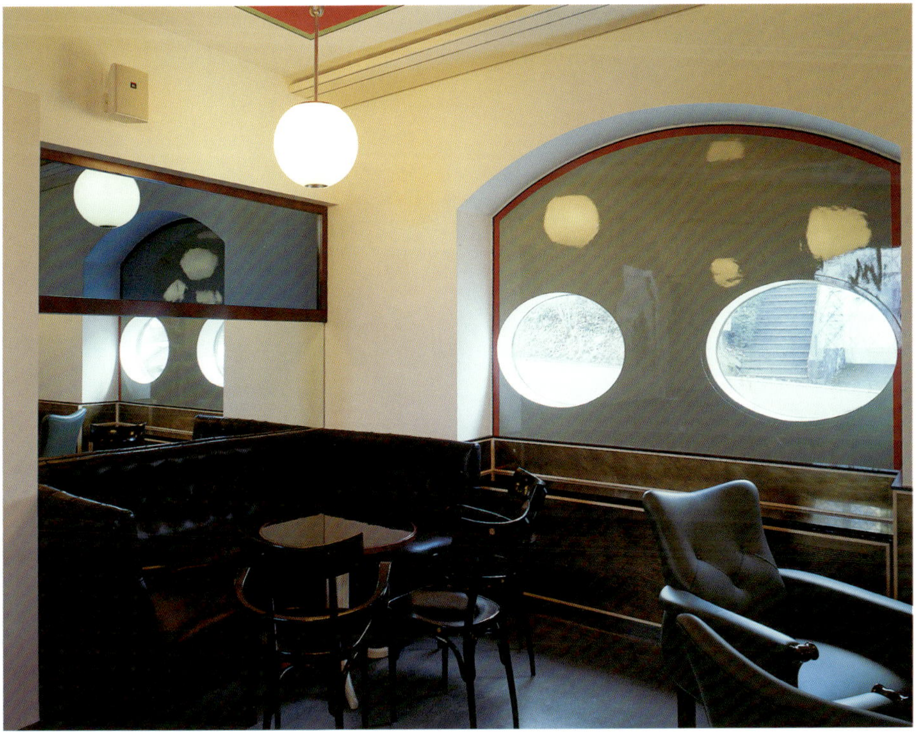

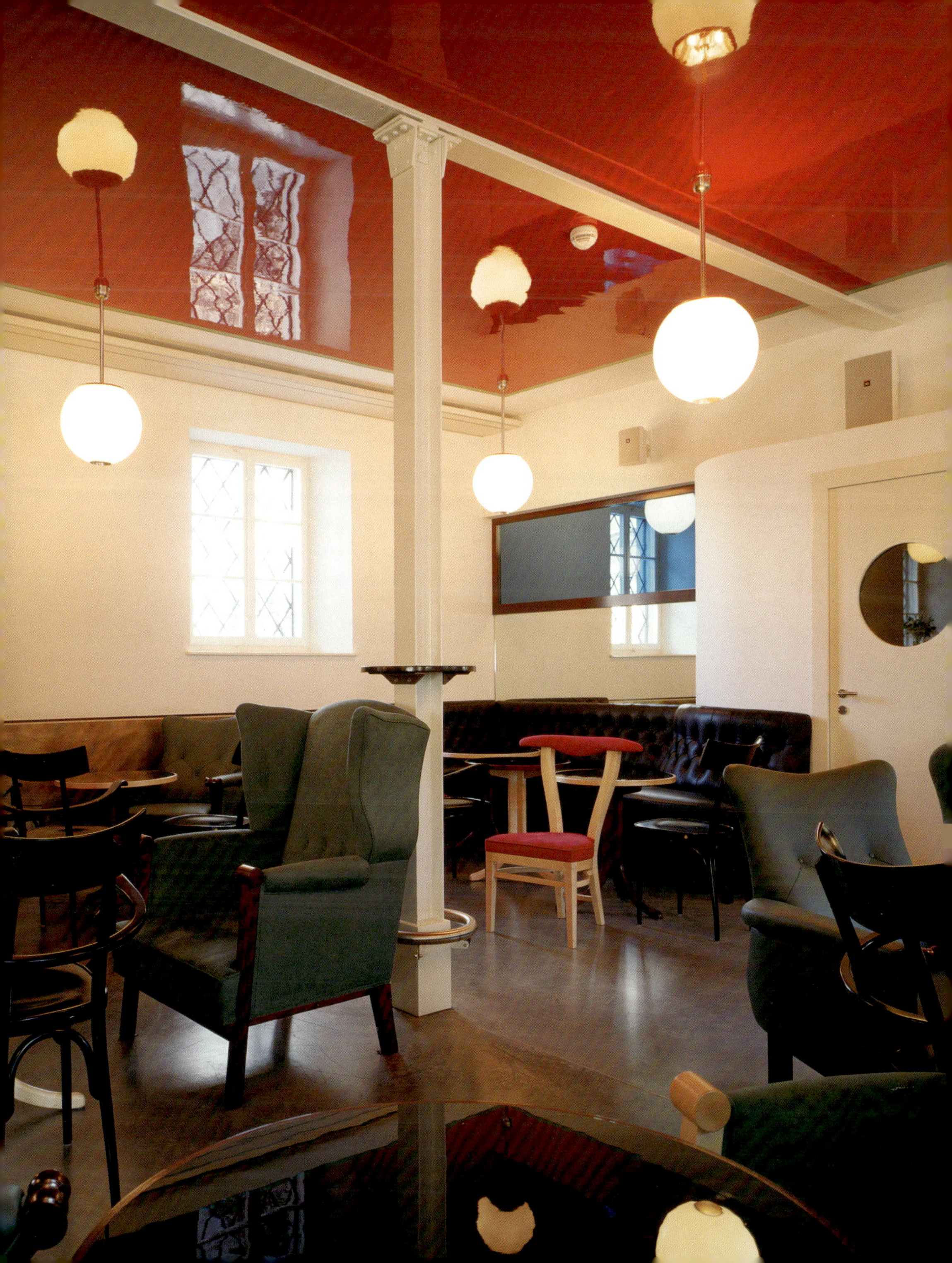

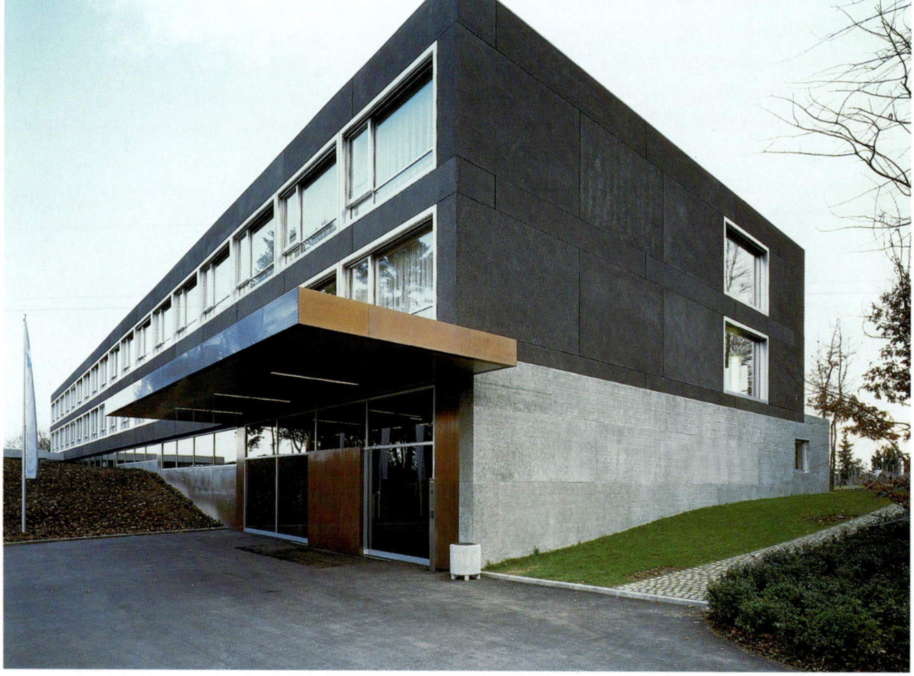

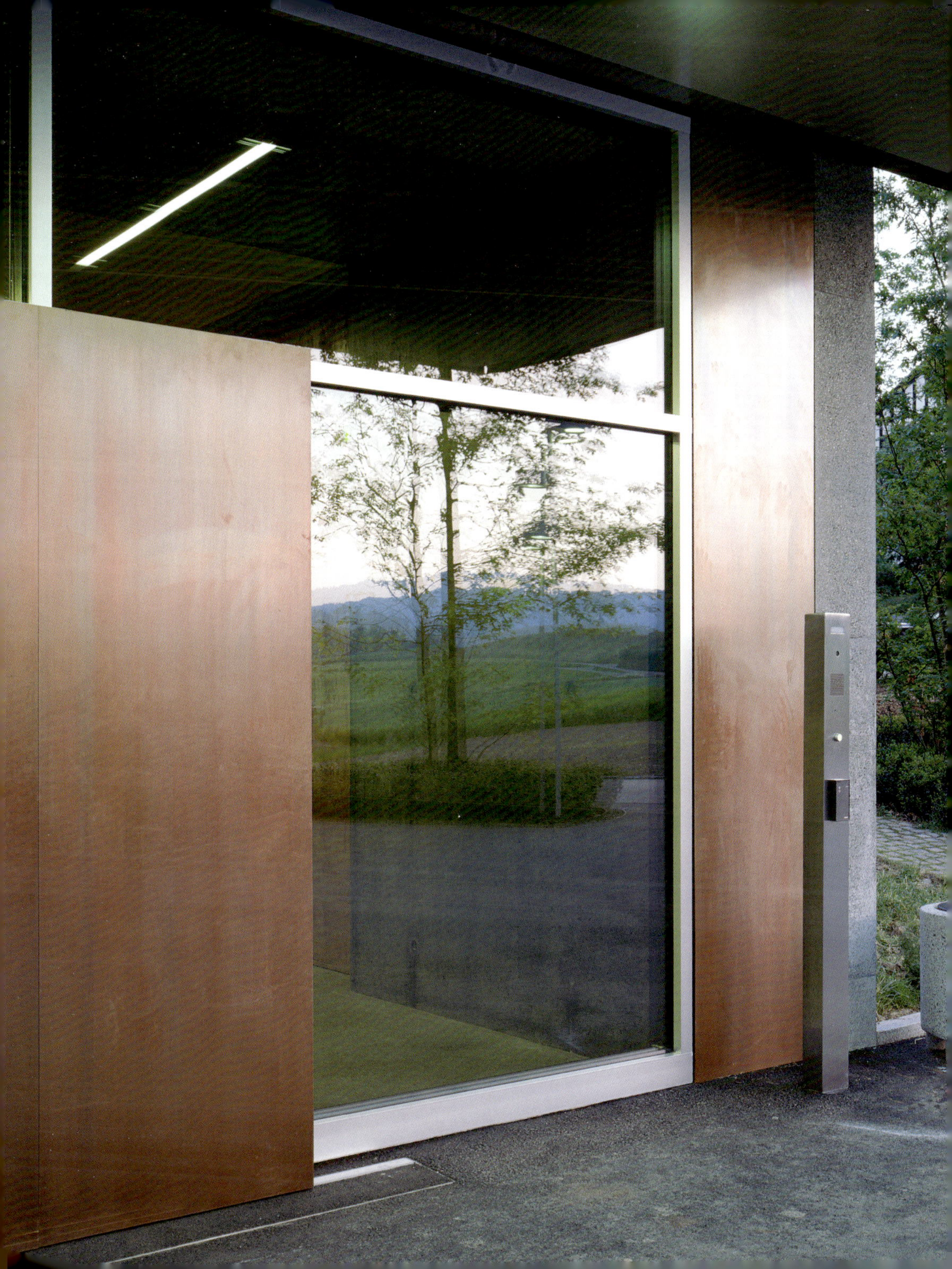

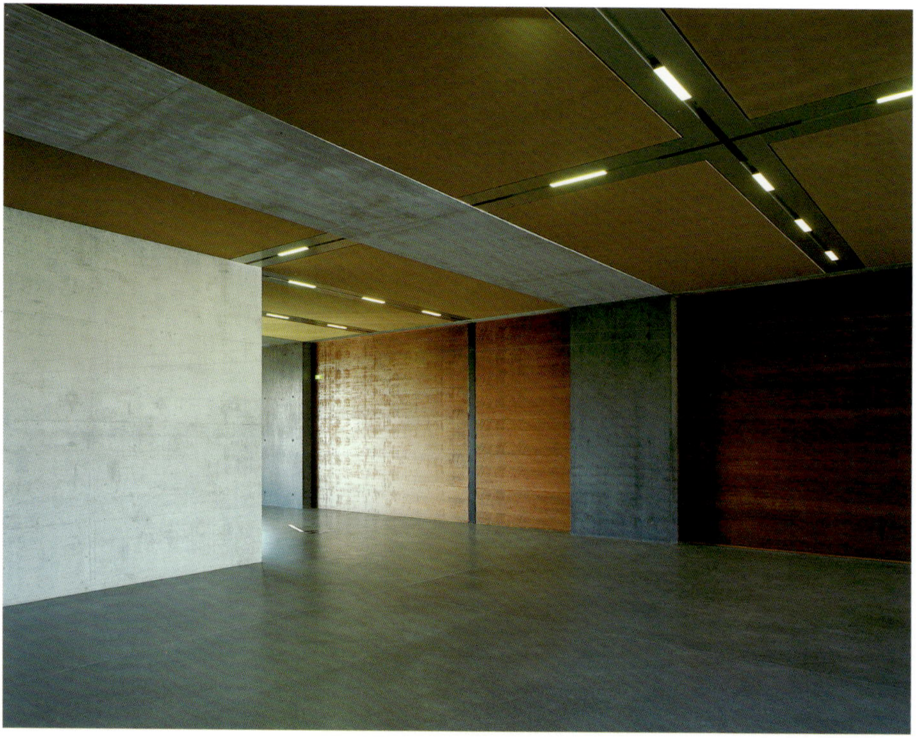

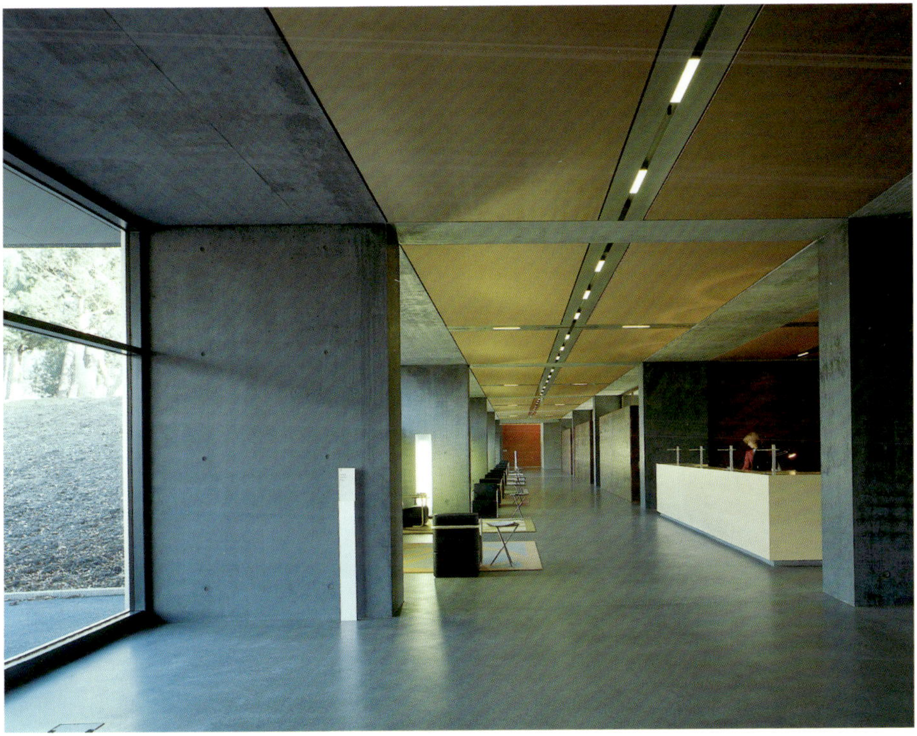

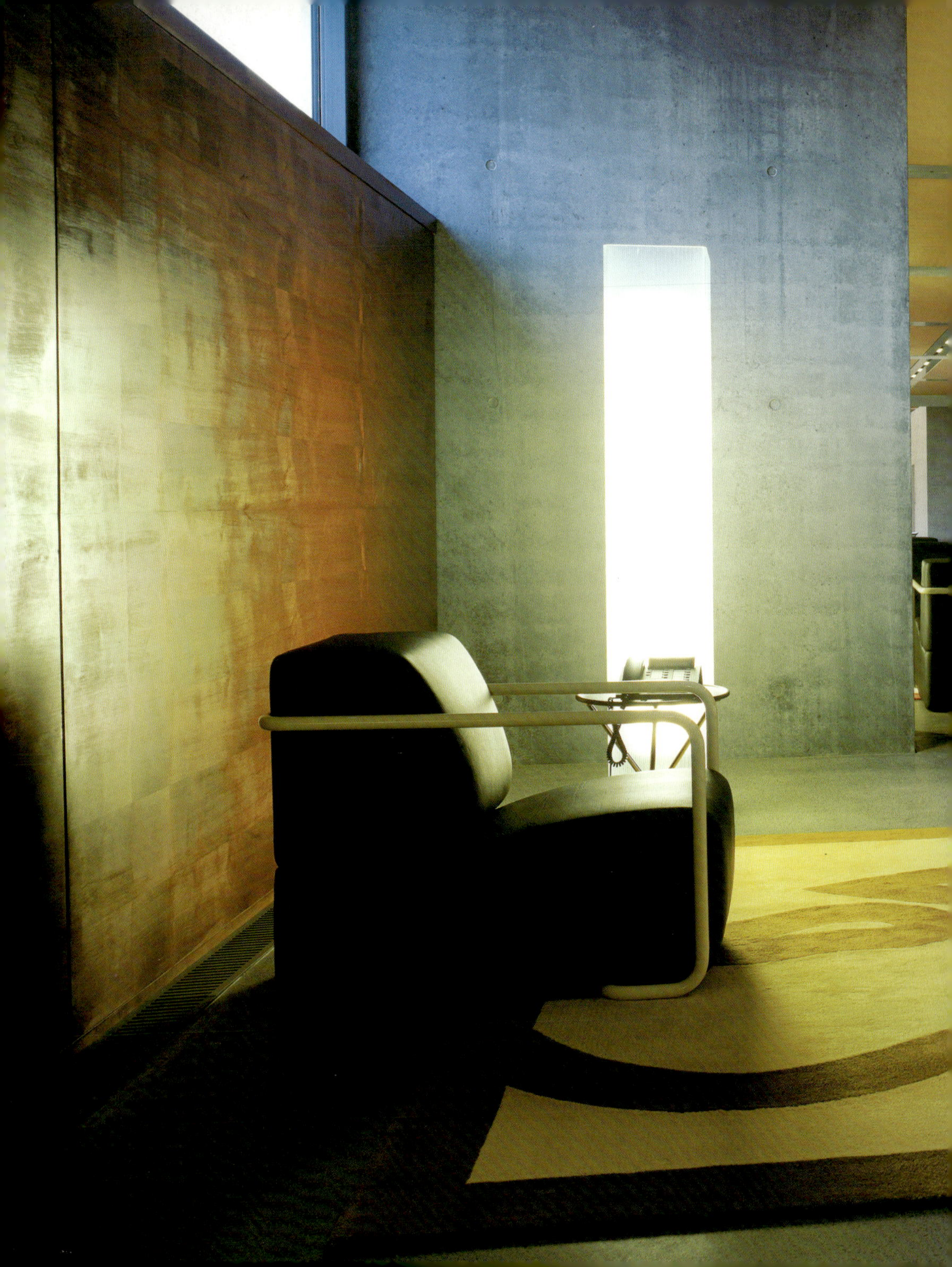

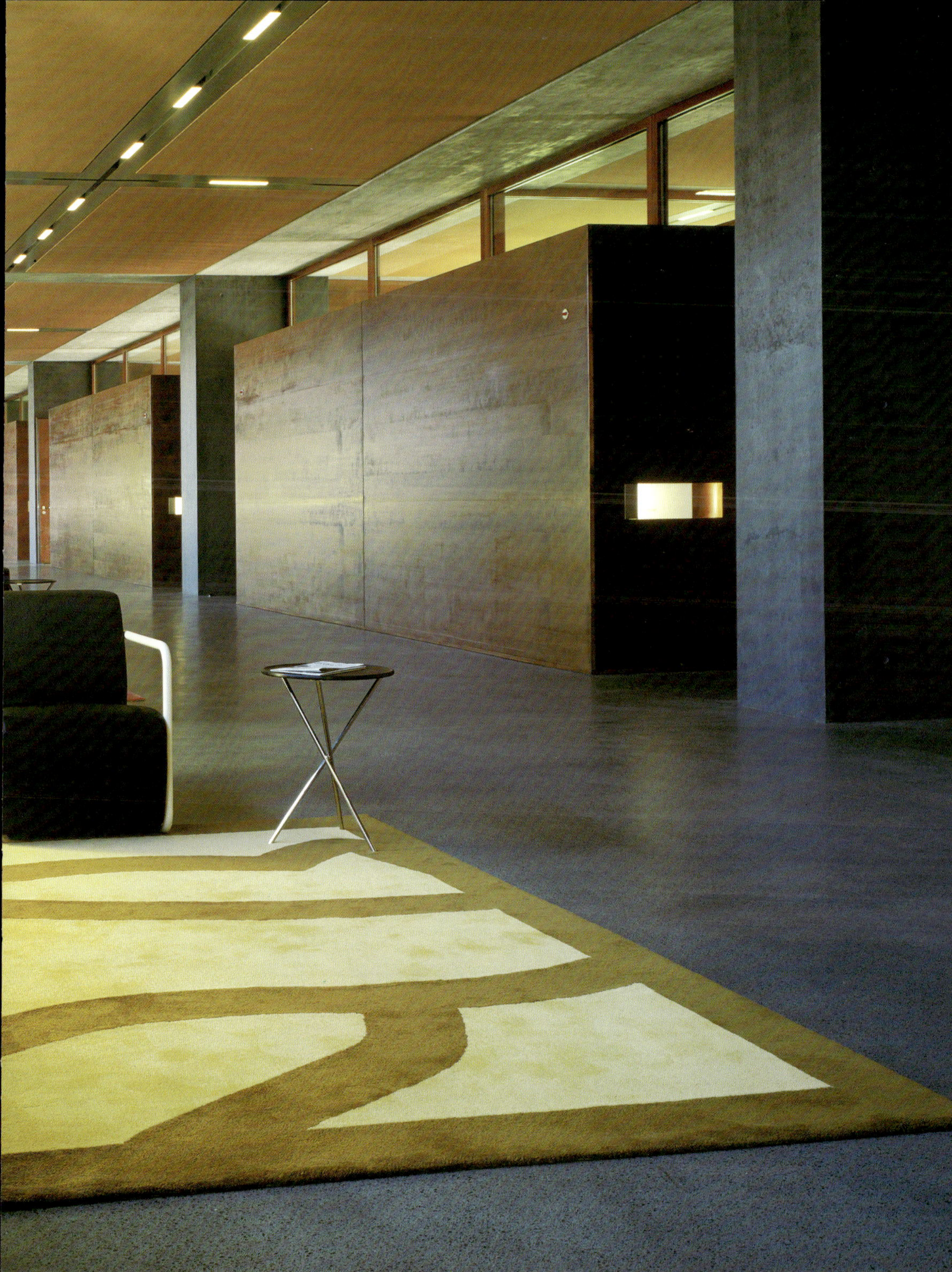

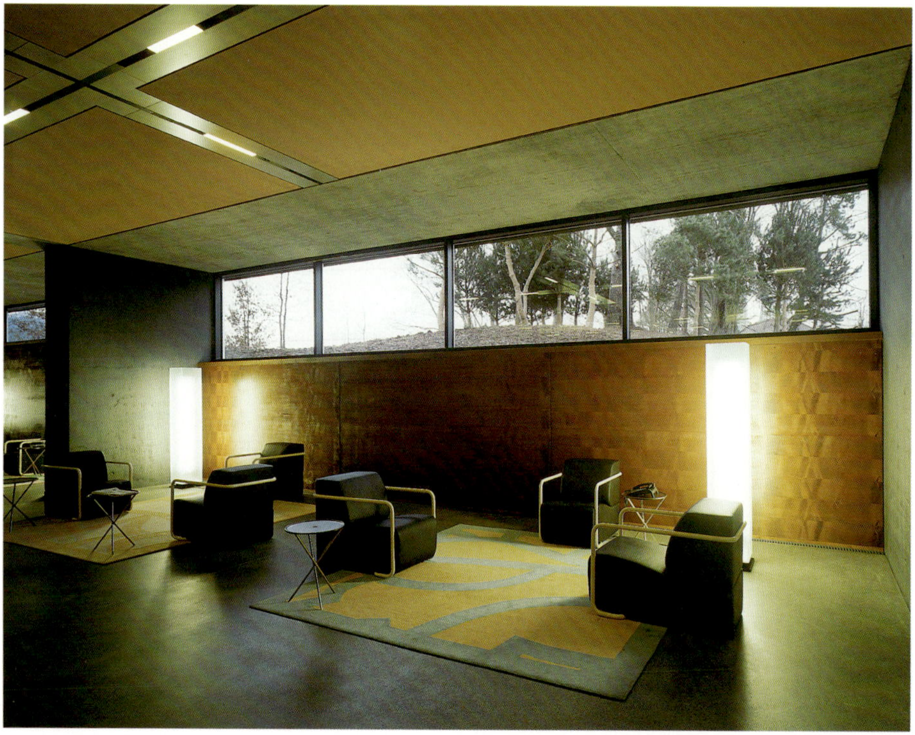

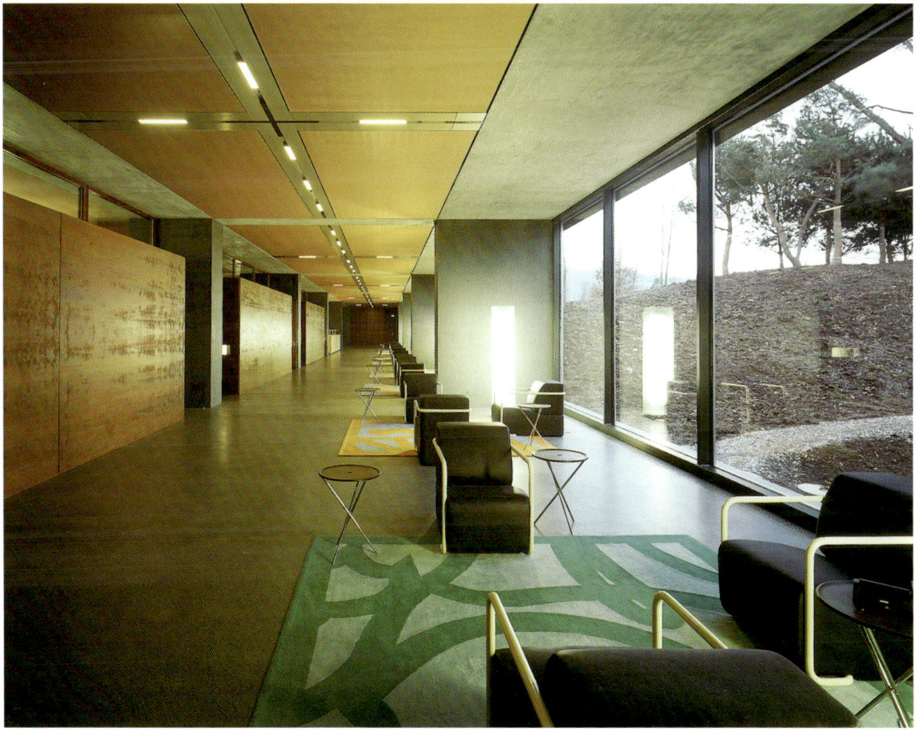

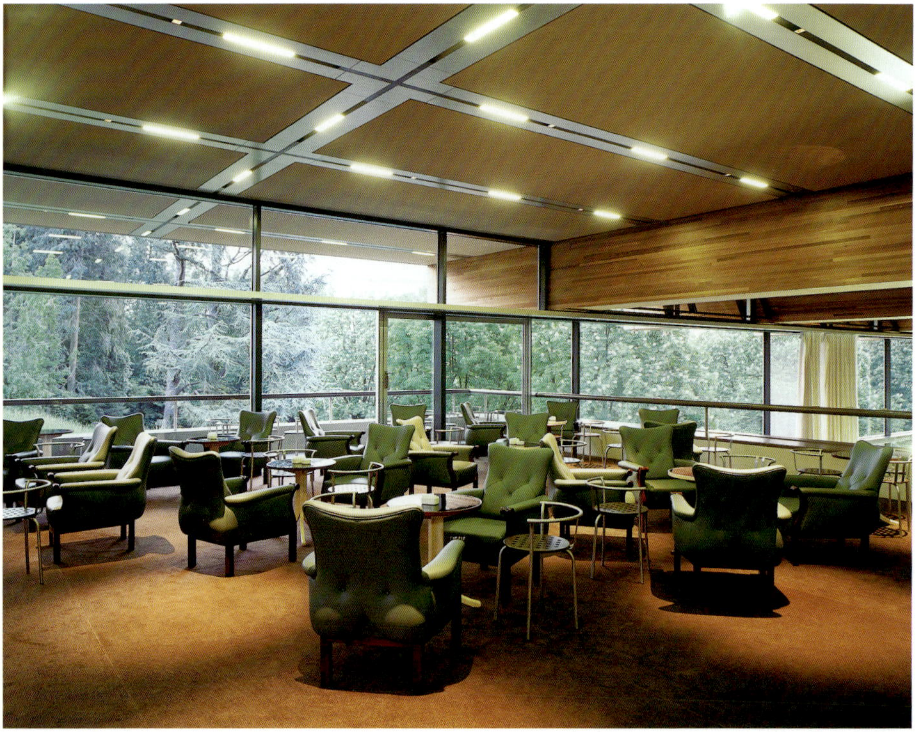

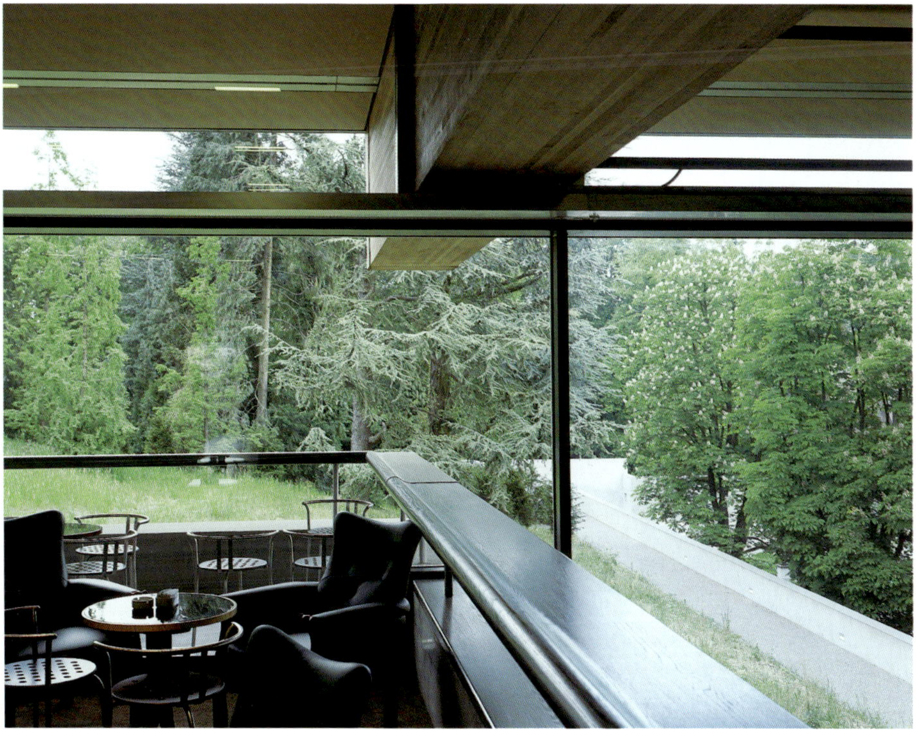

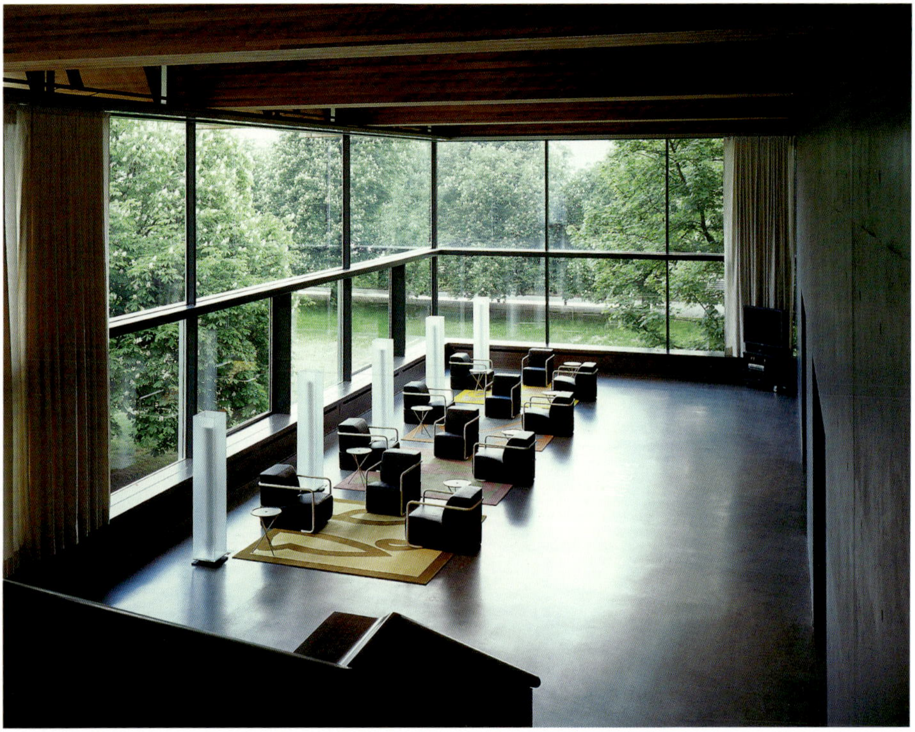

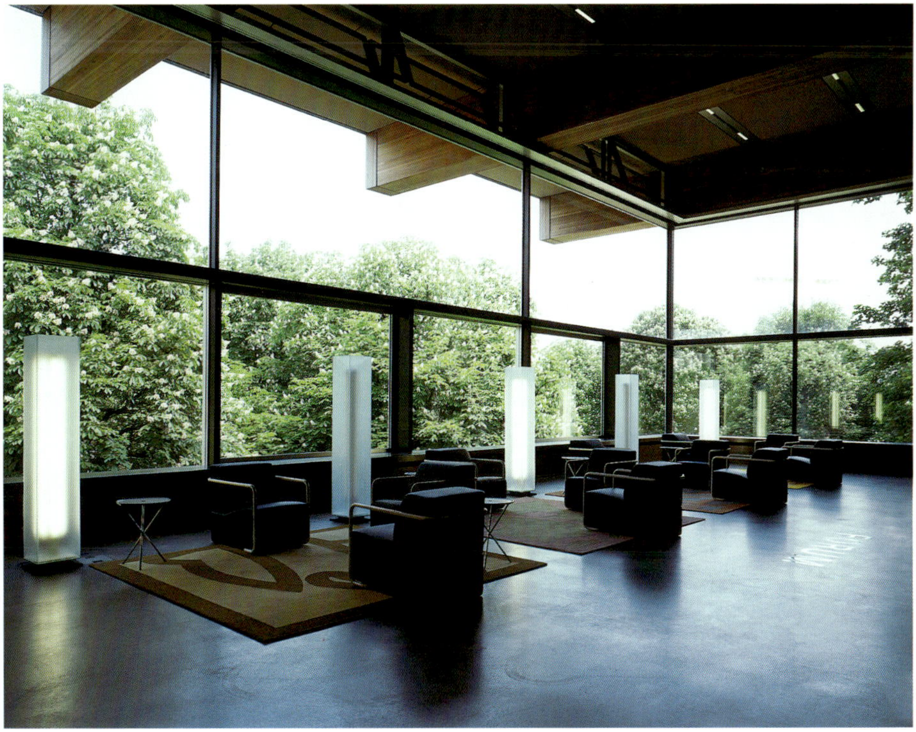

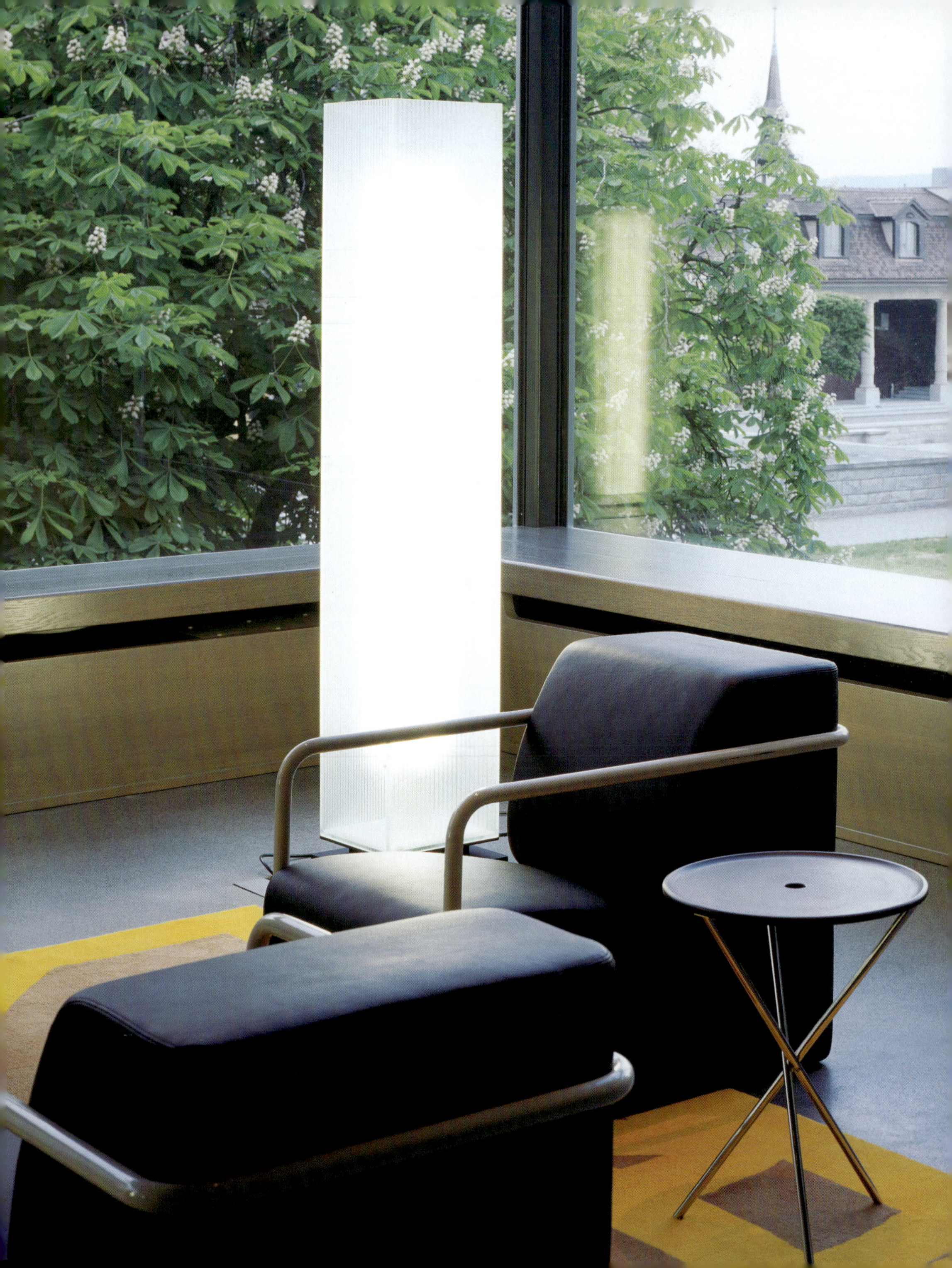

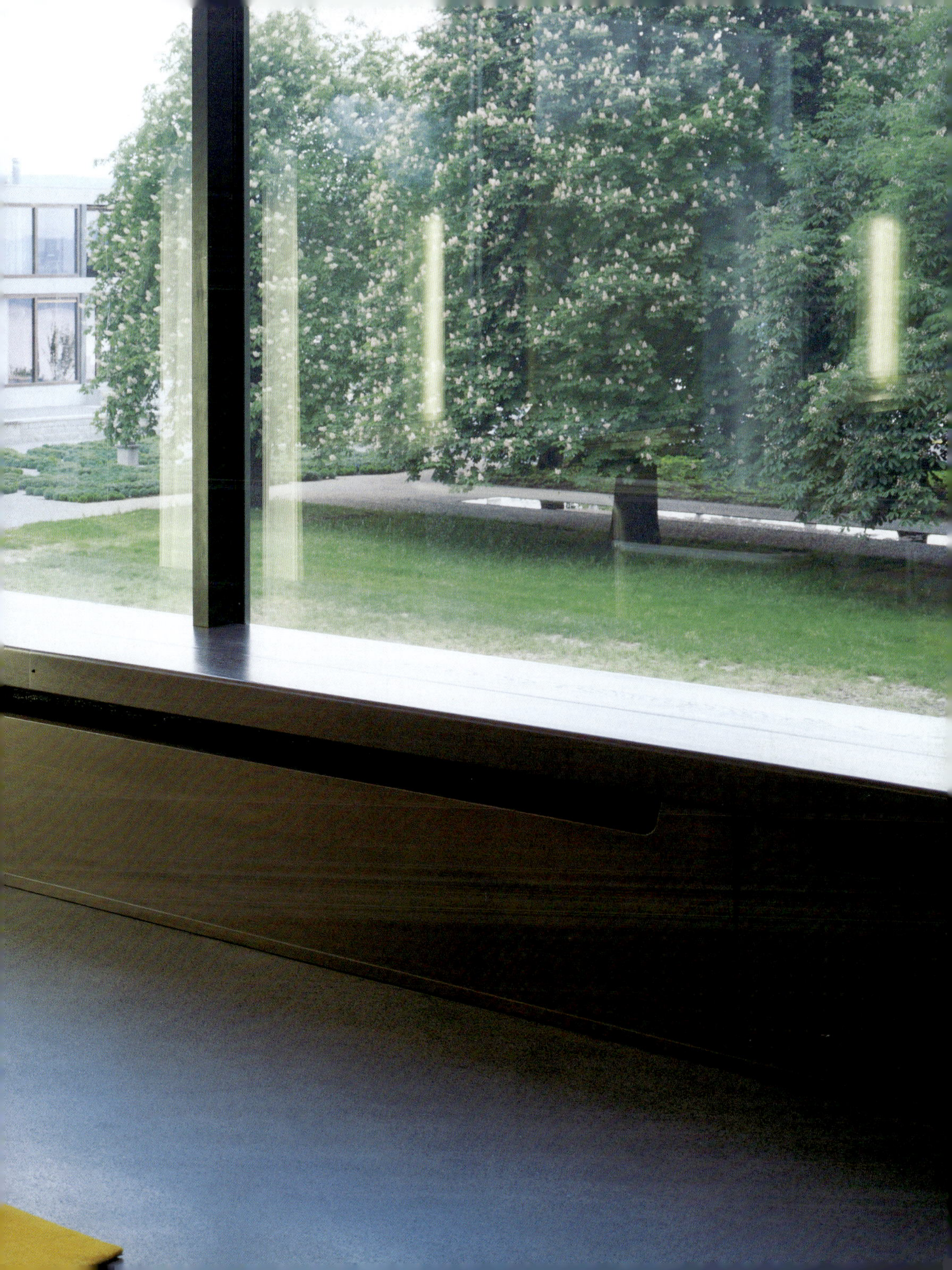

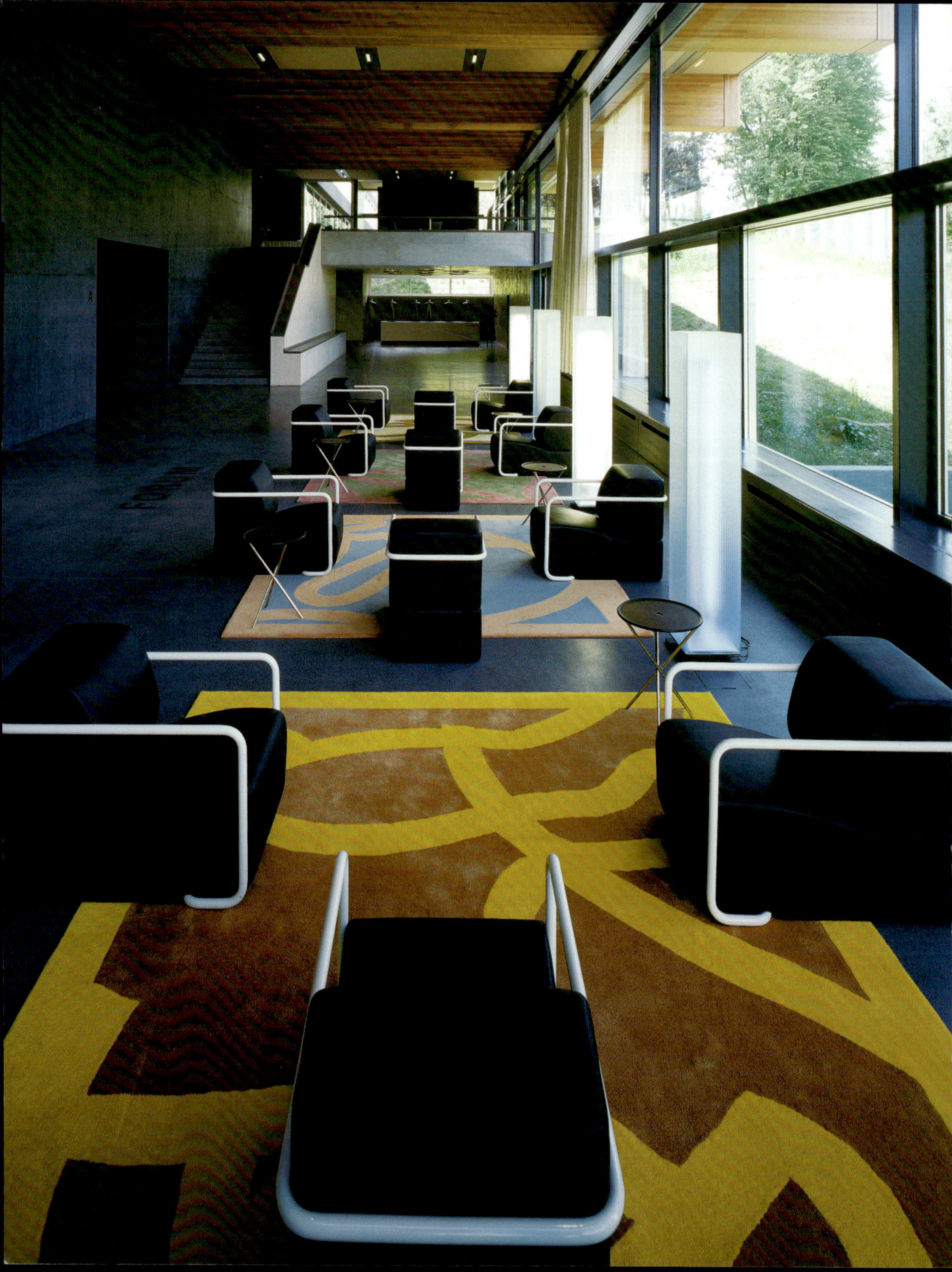

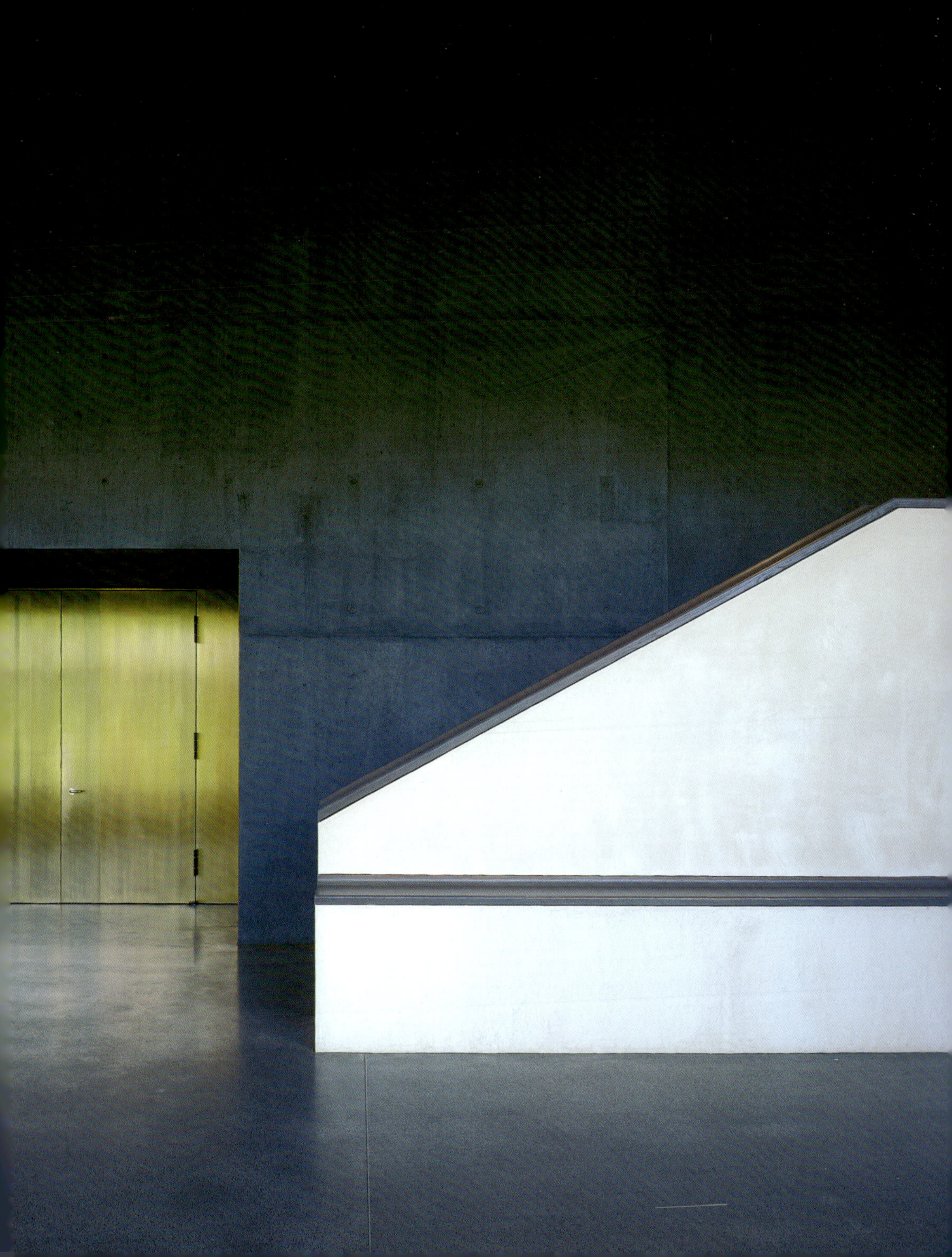

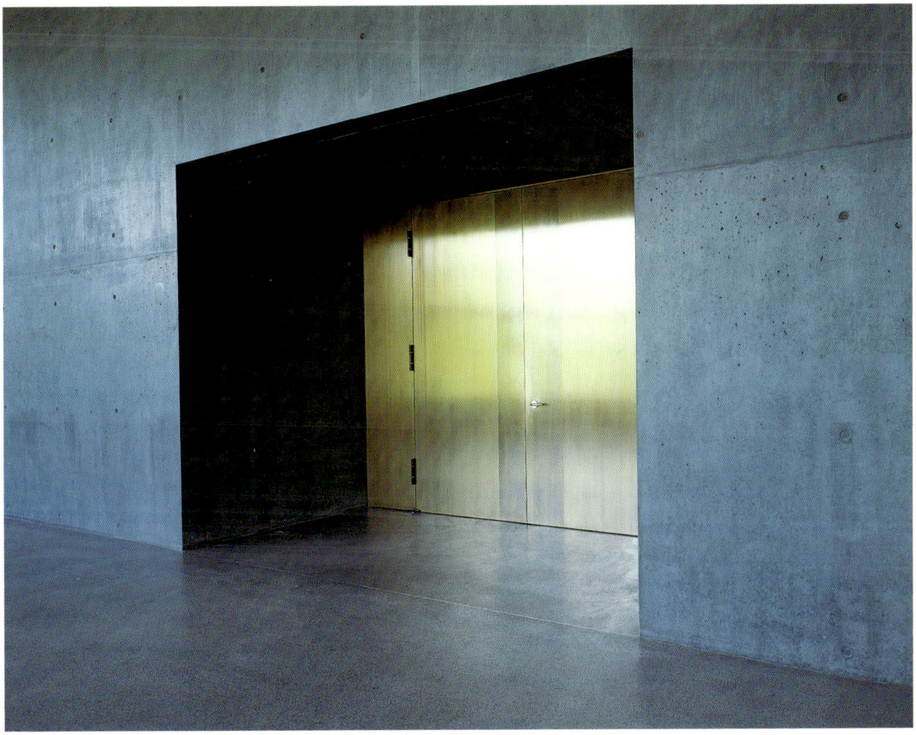

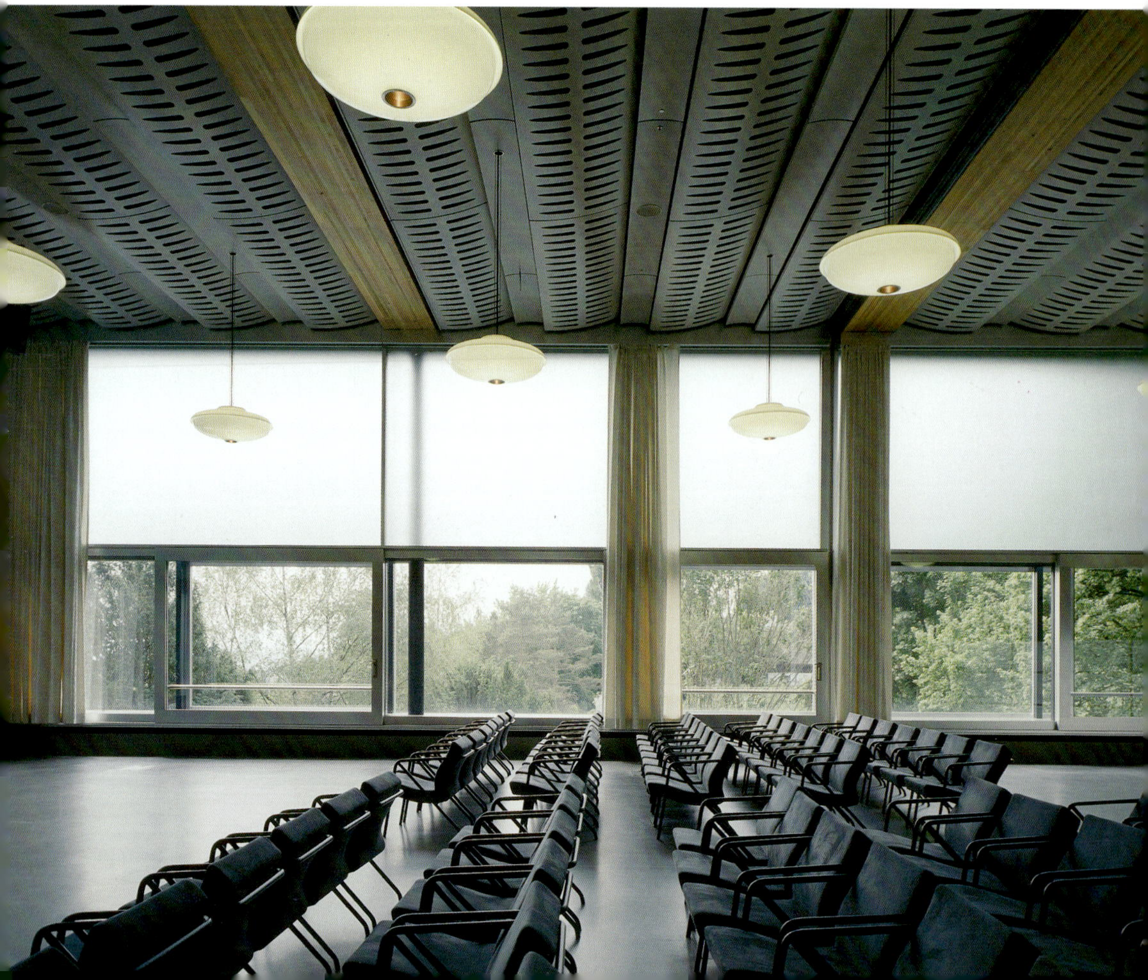

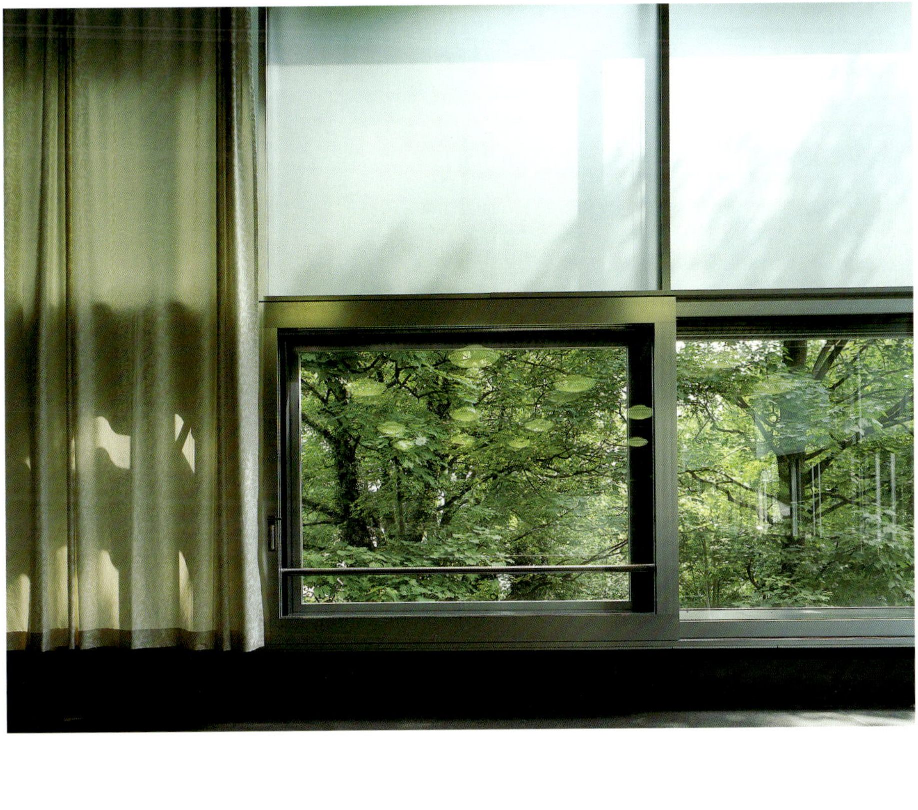

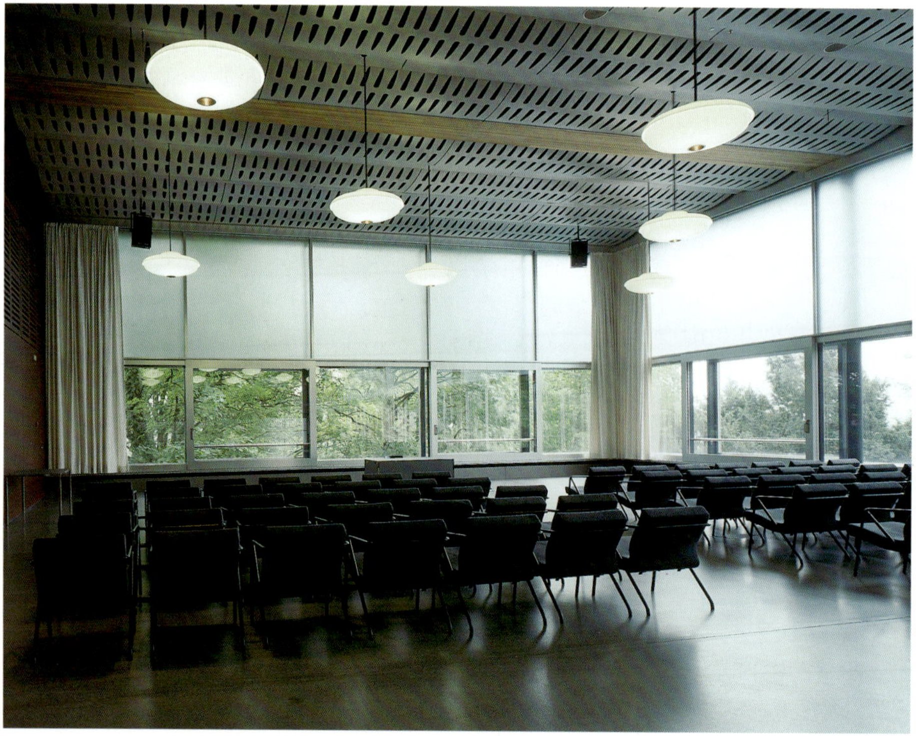

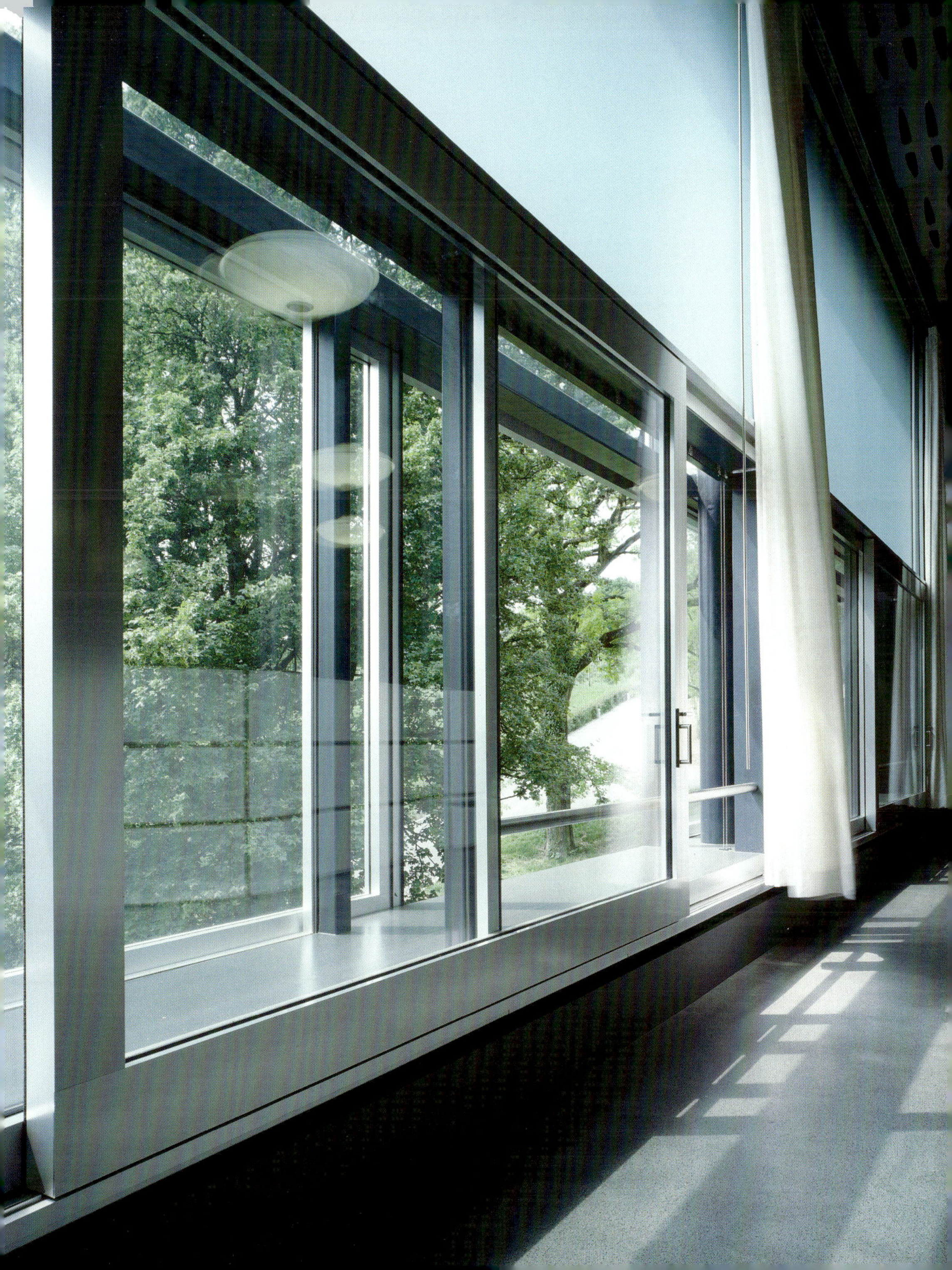

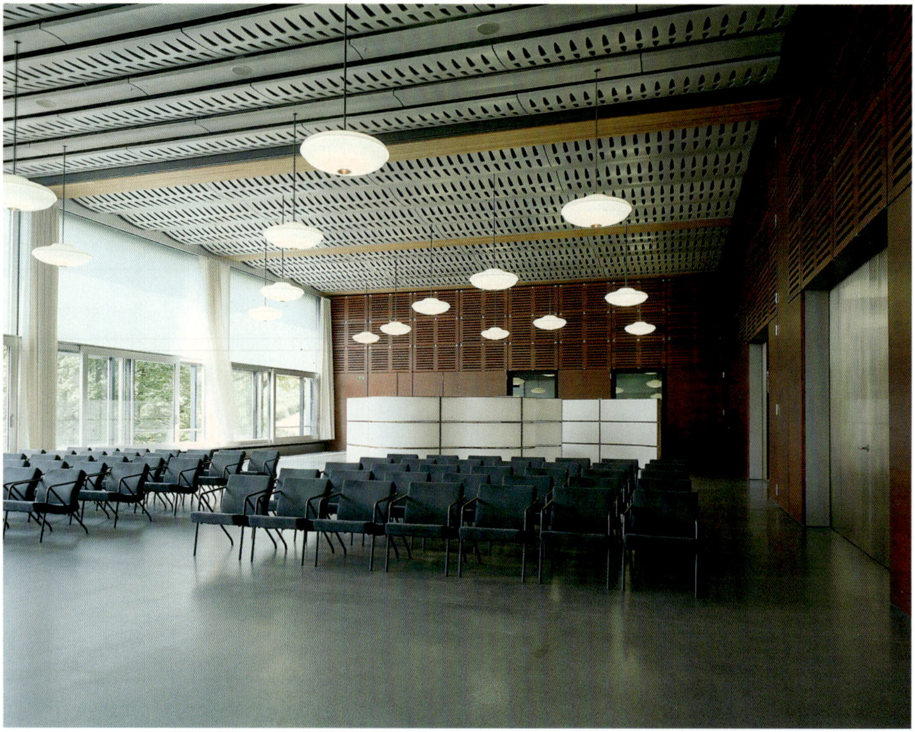

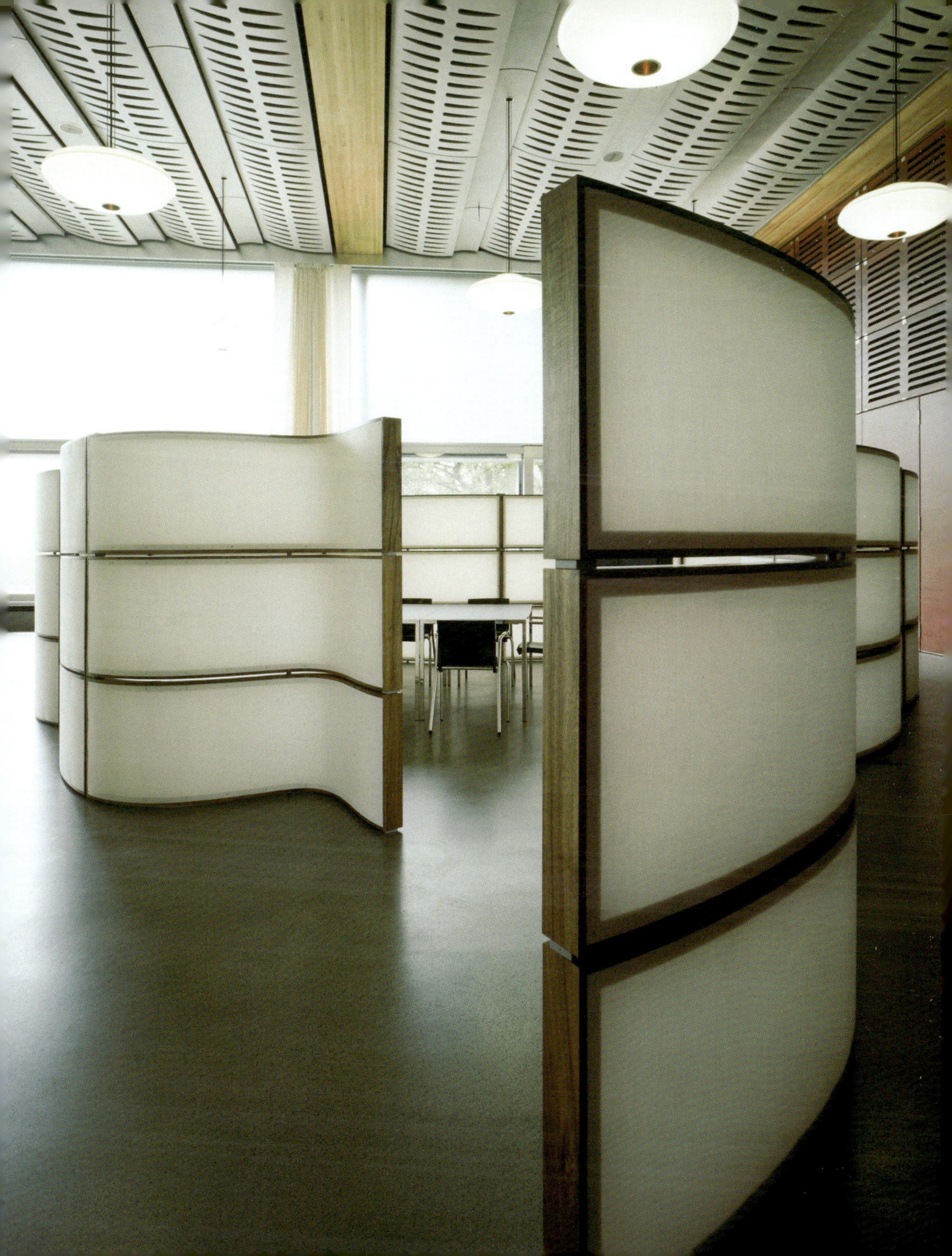

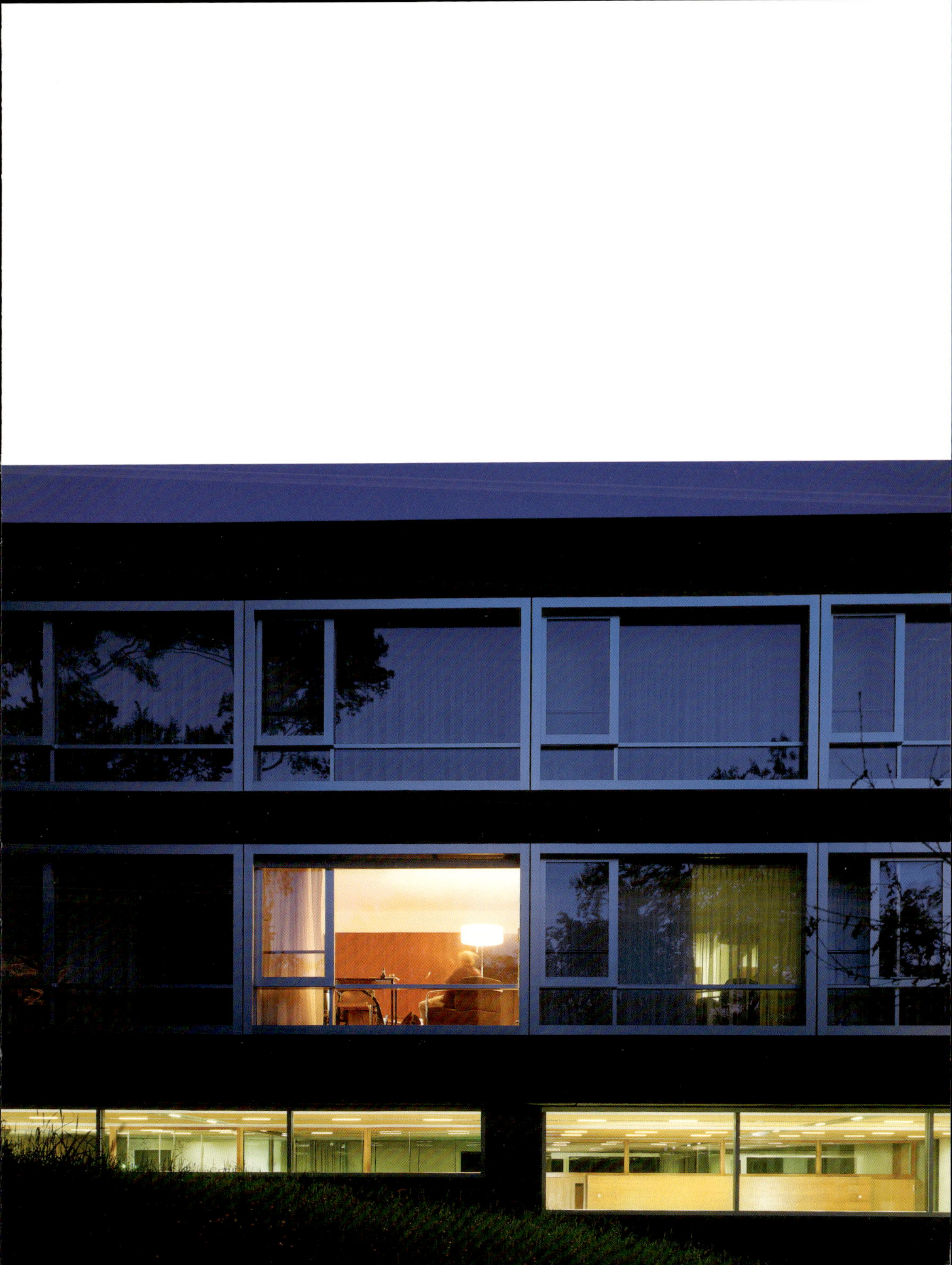

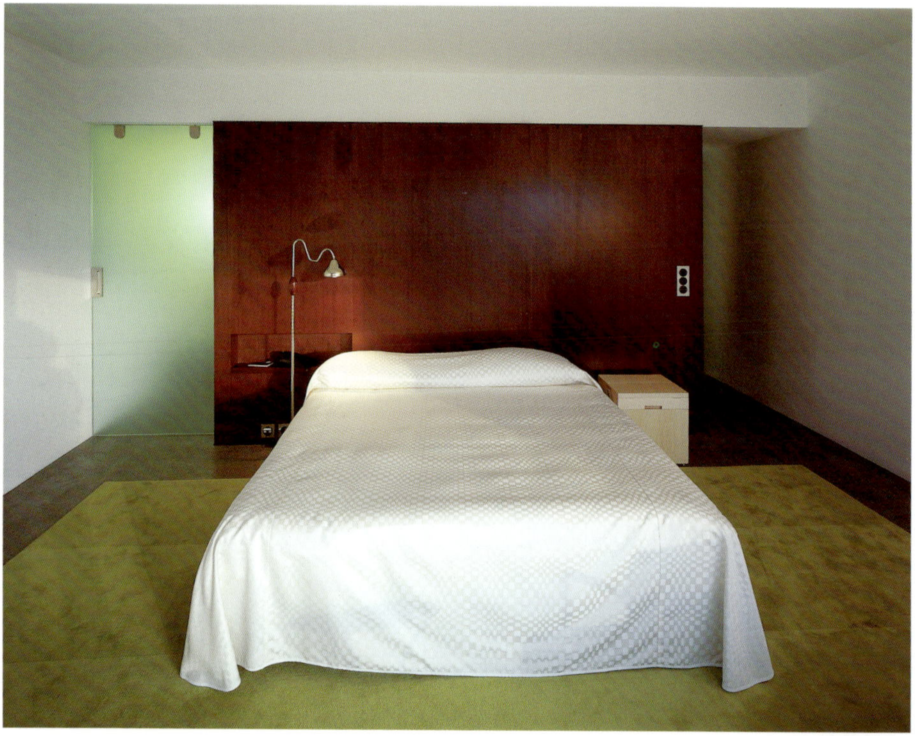

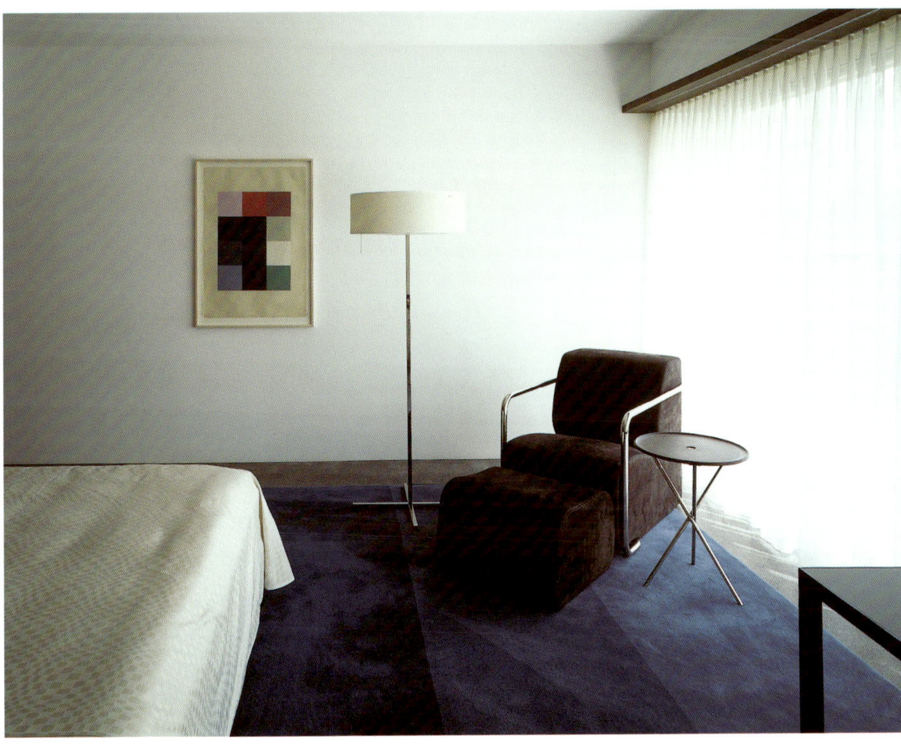

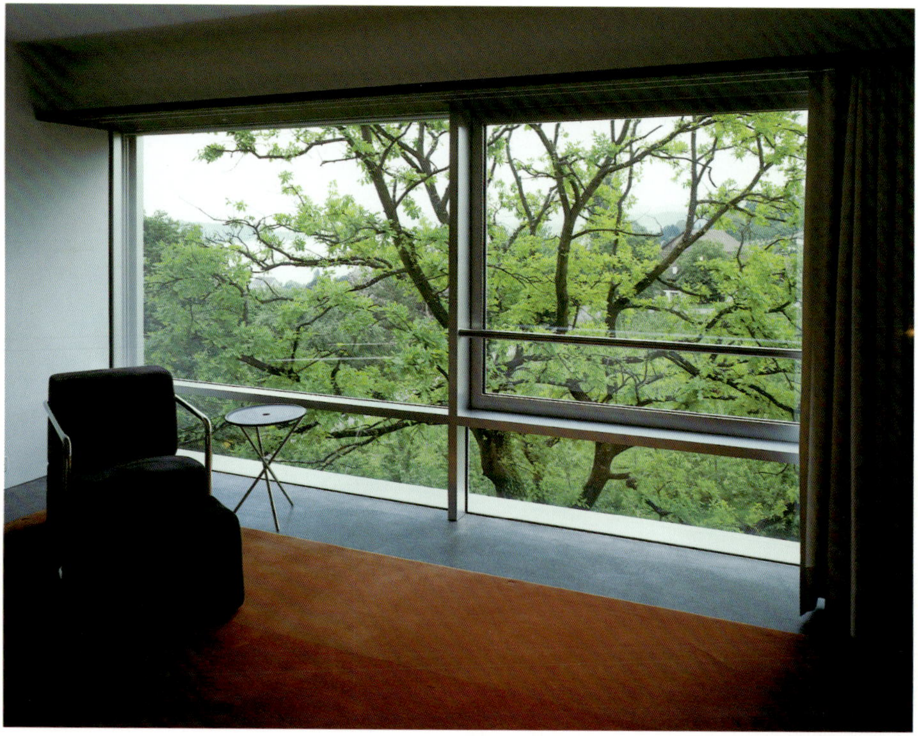

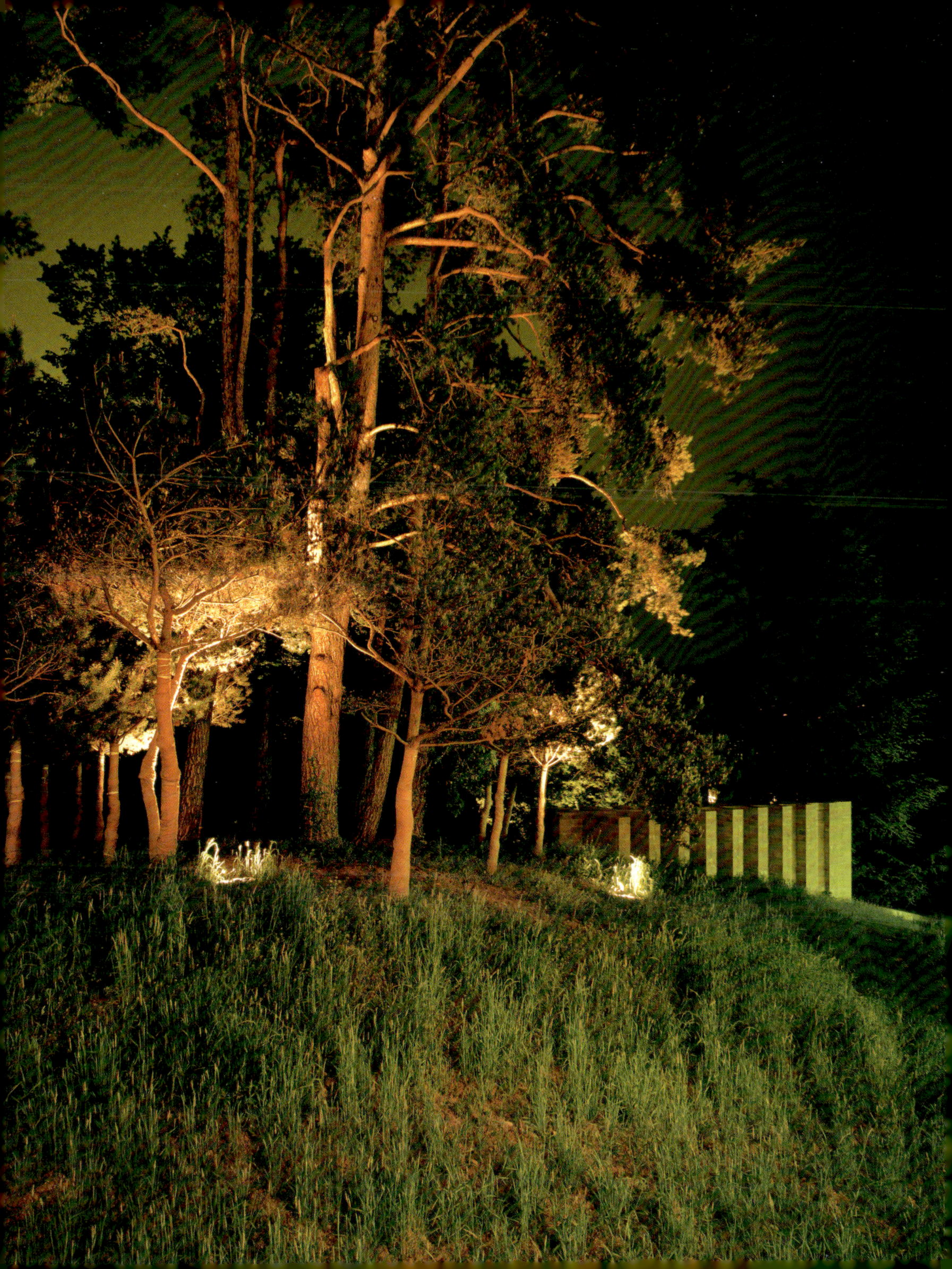

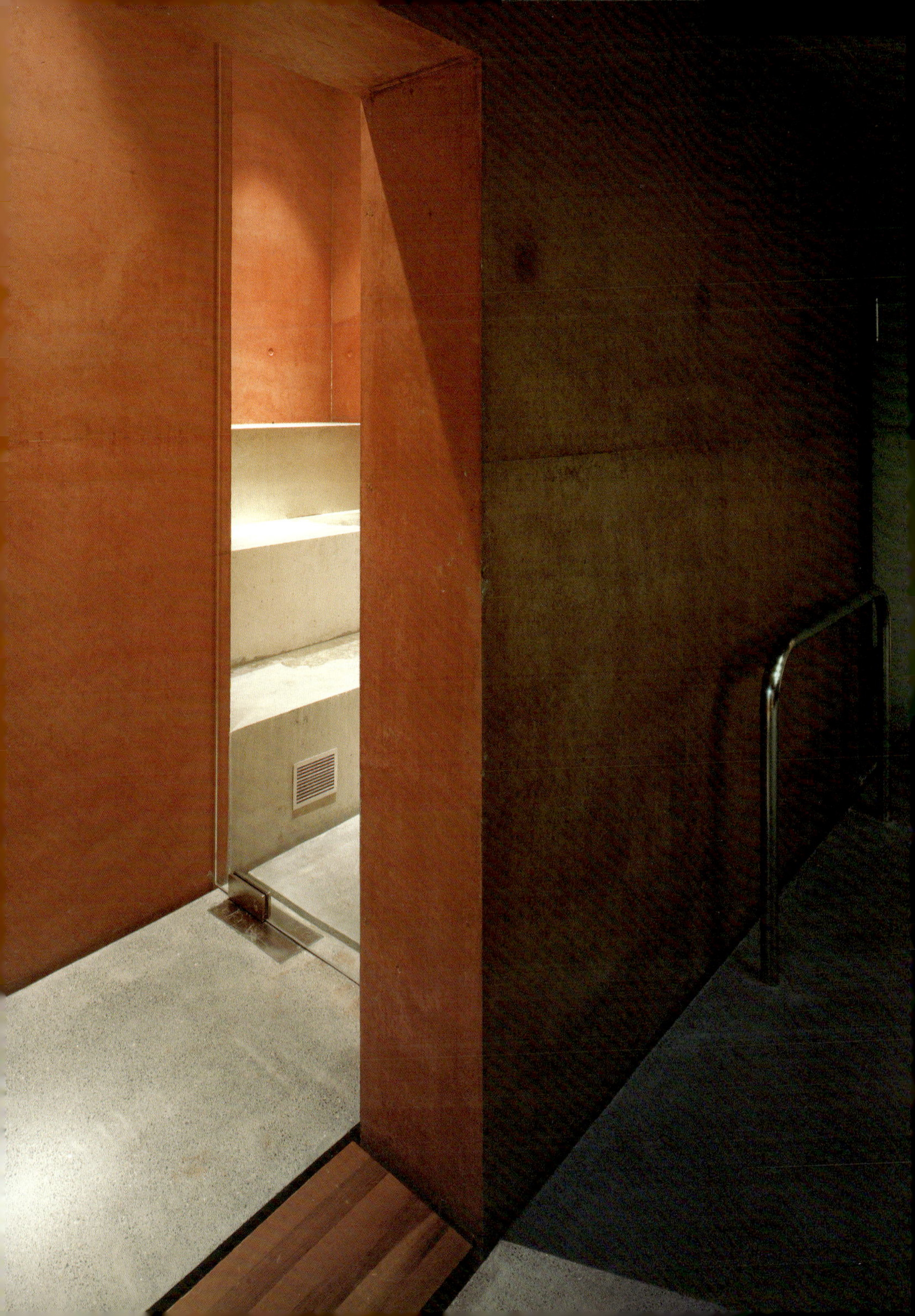

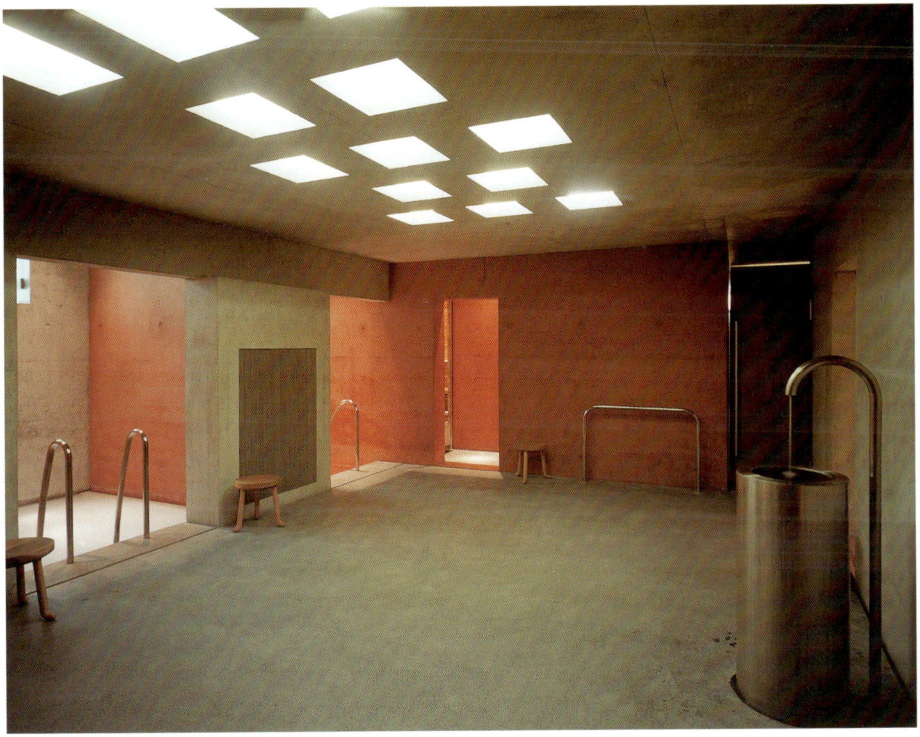

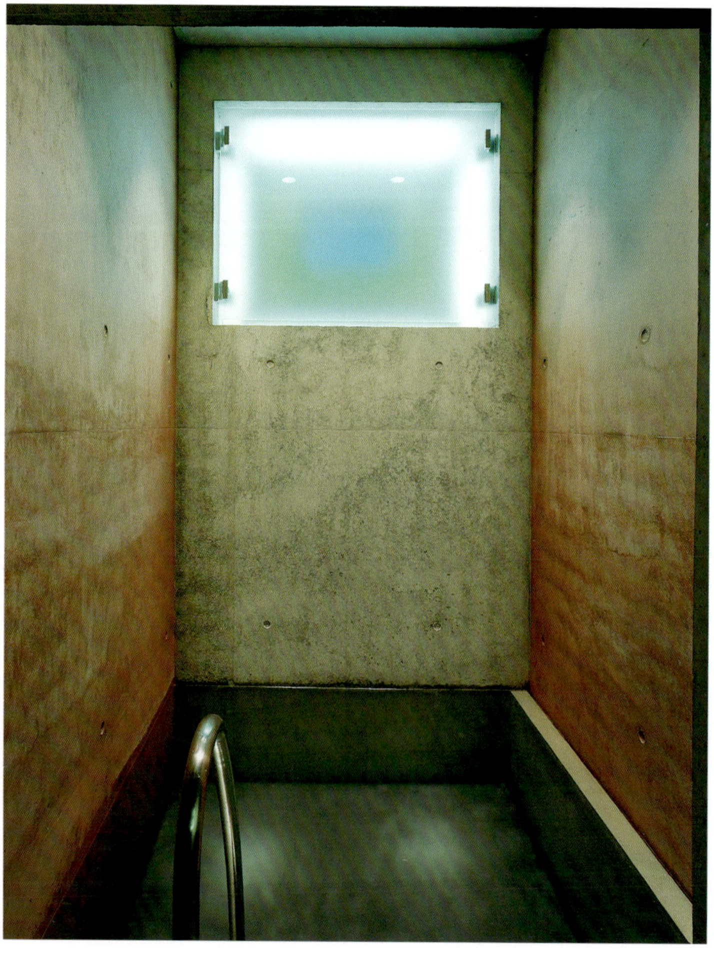

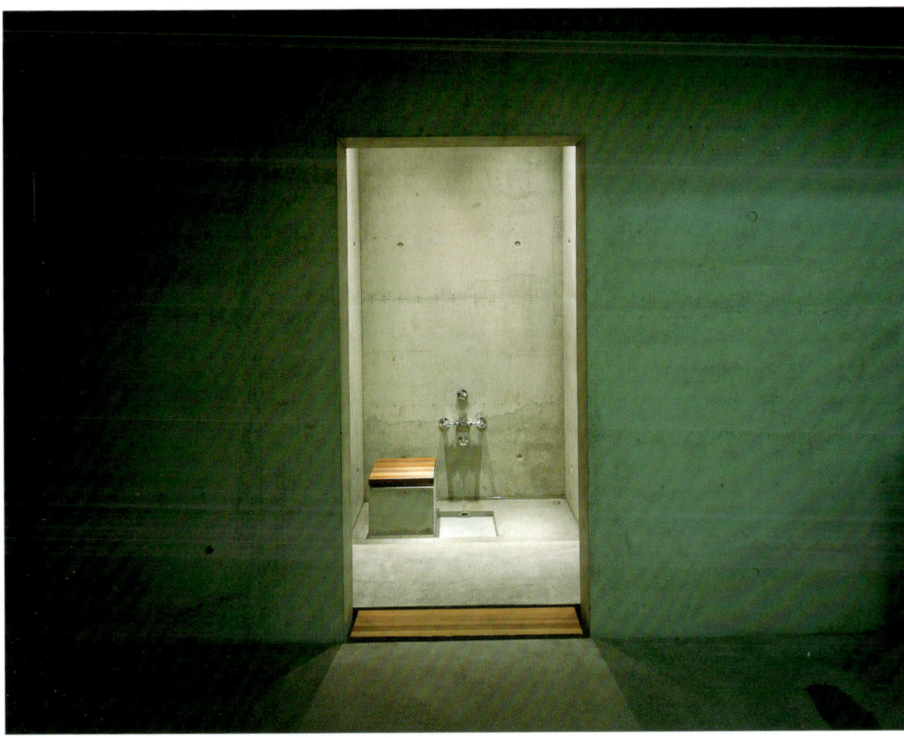

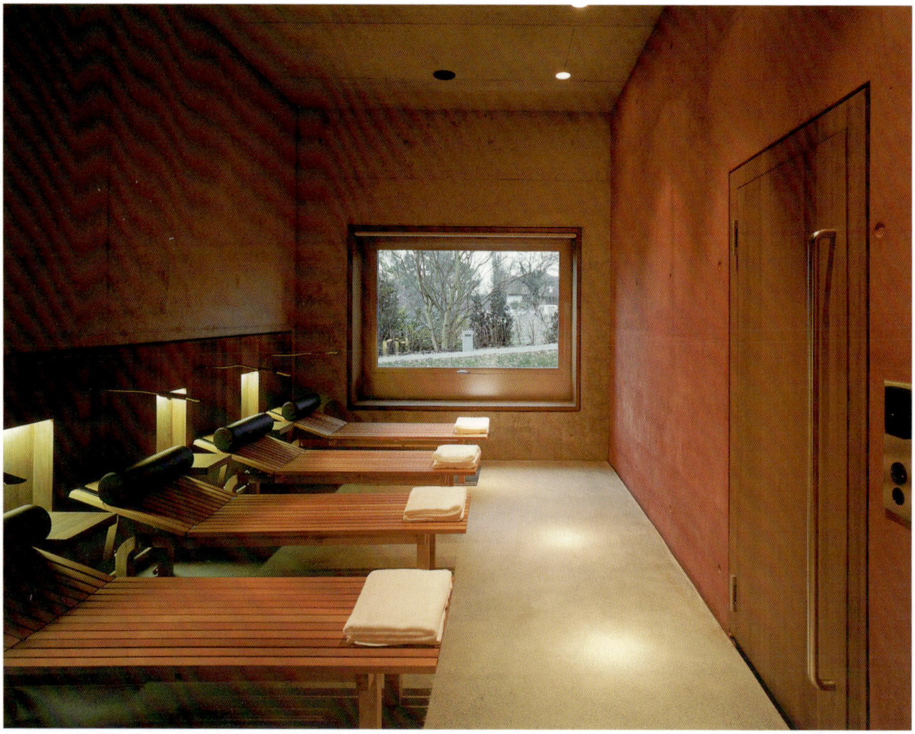

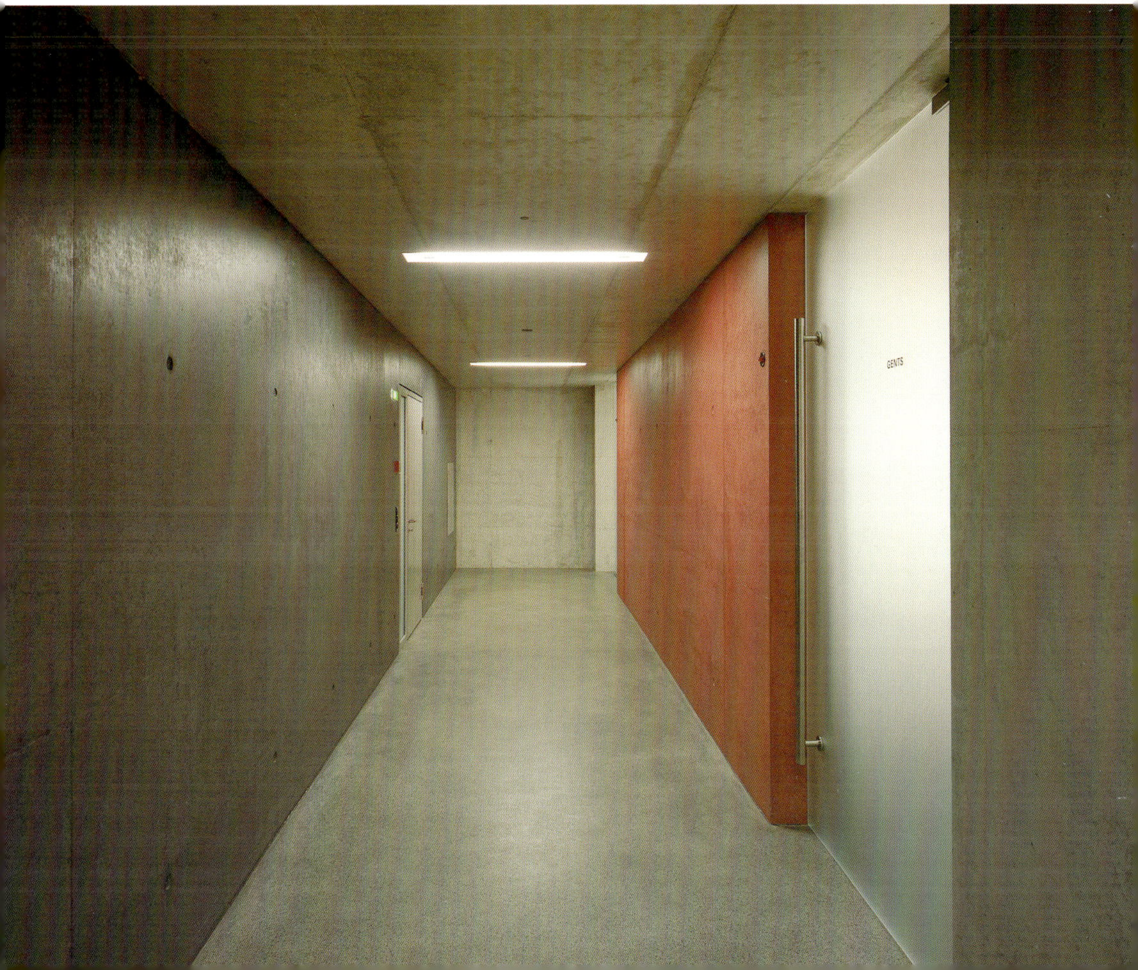
GENTS

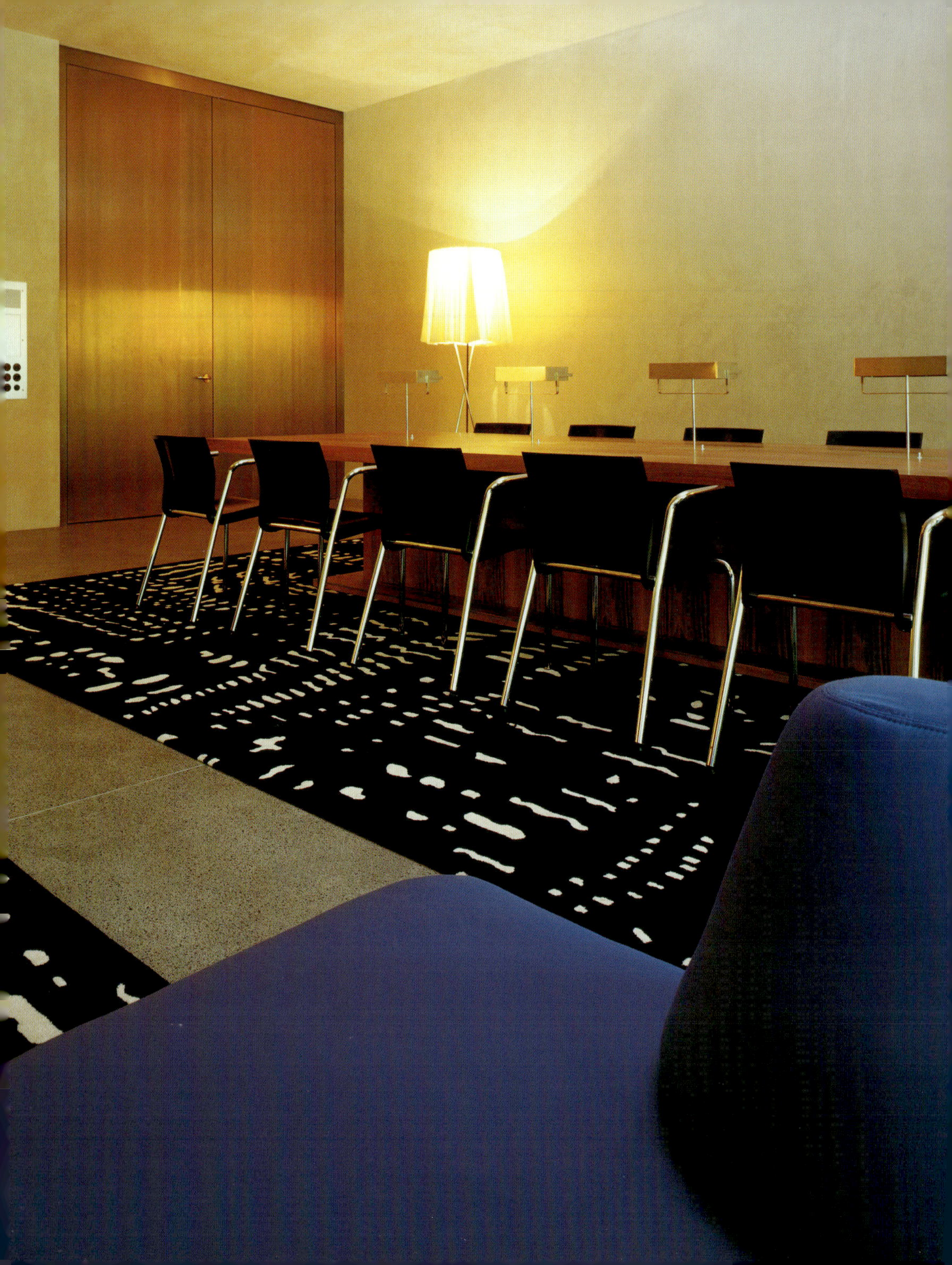

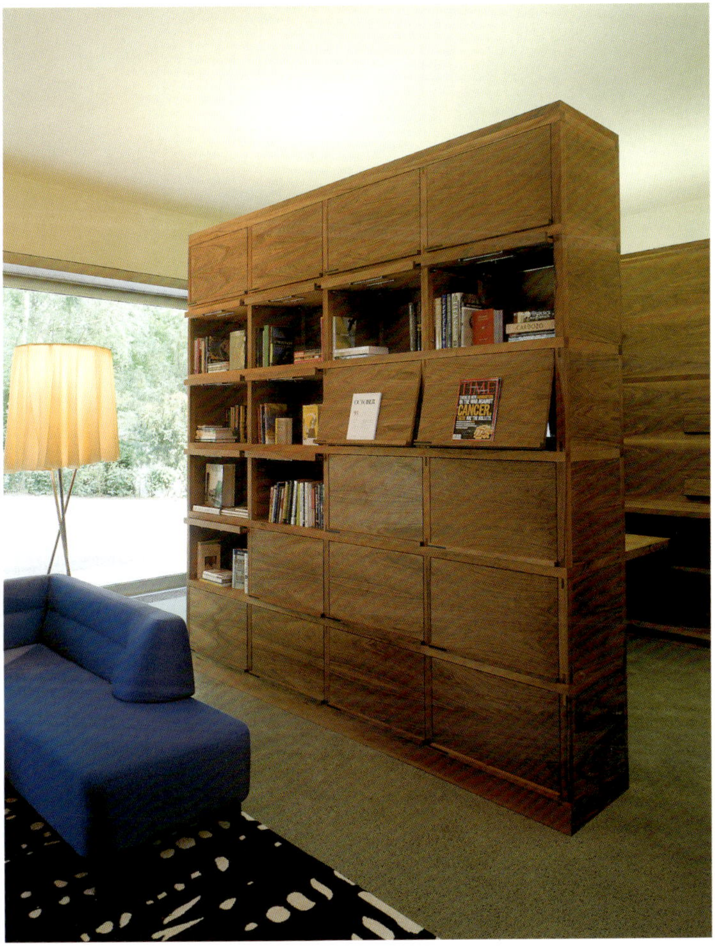

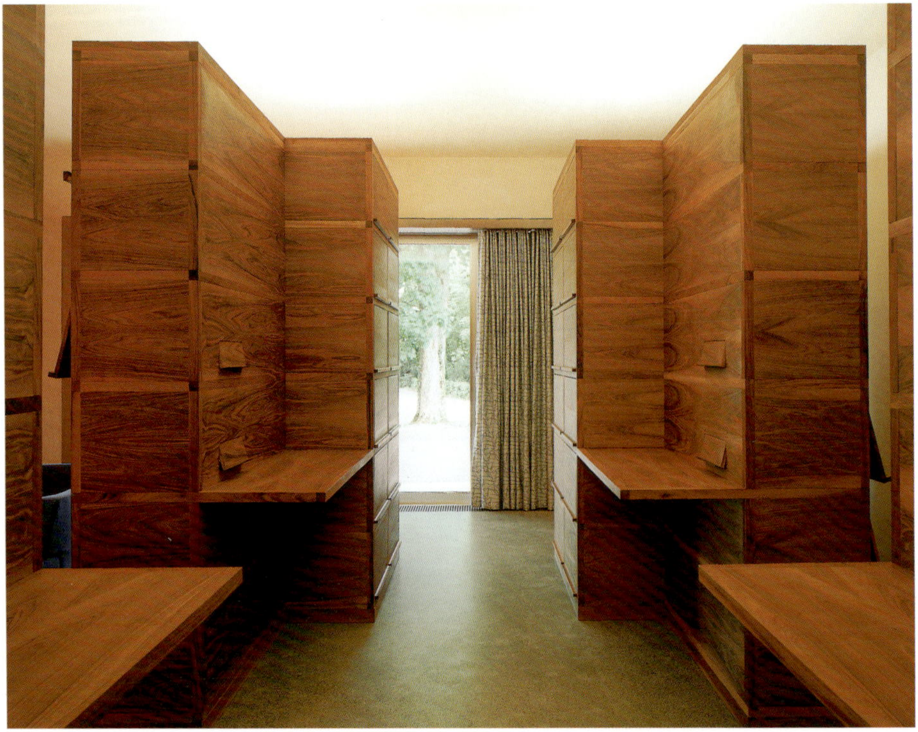

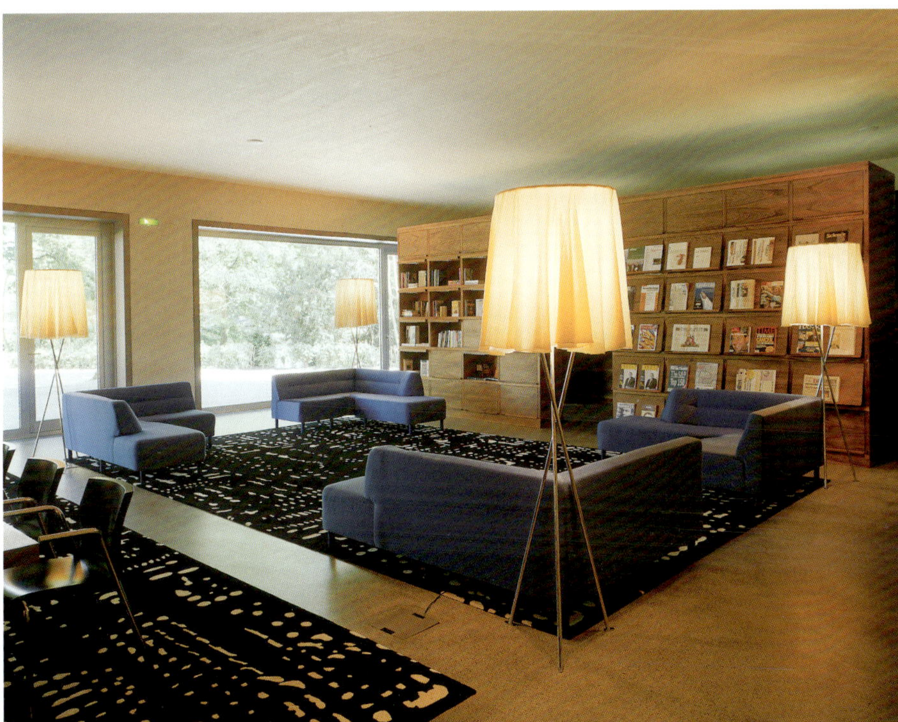

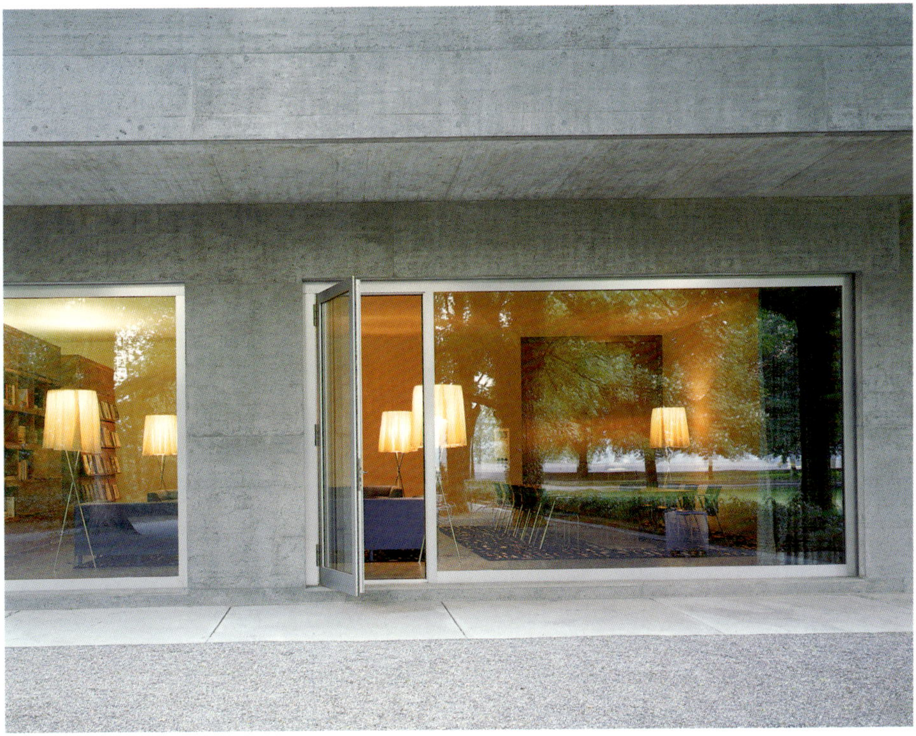

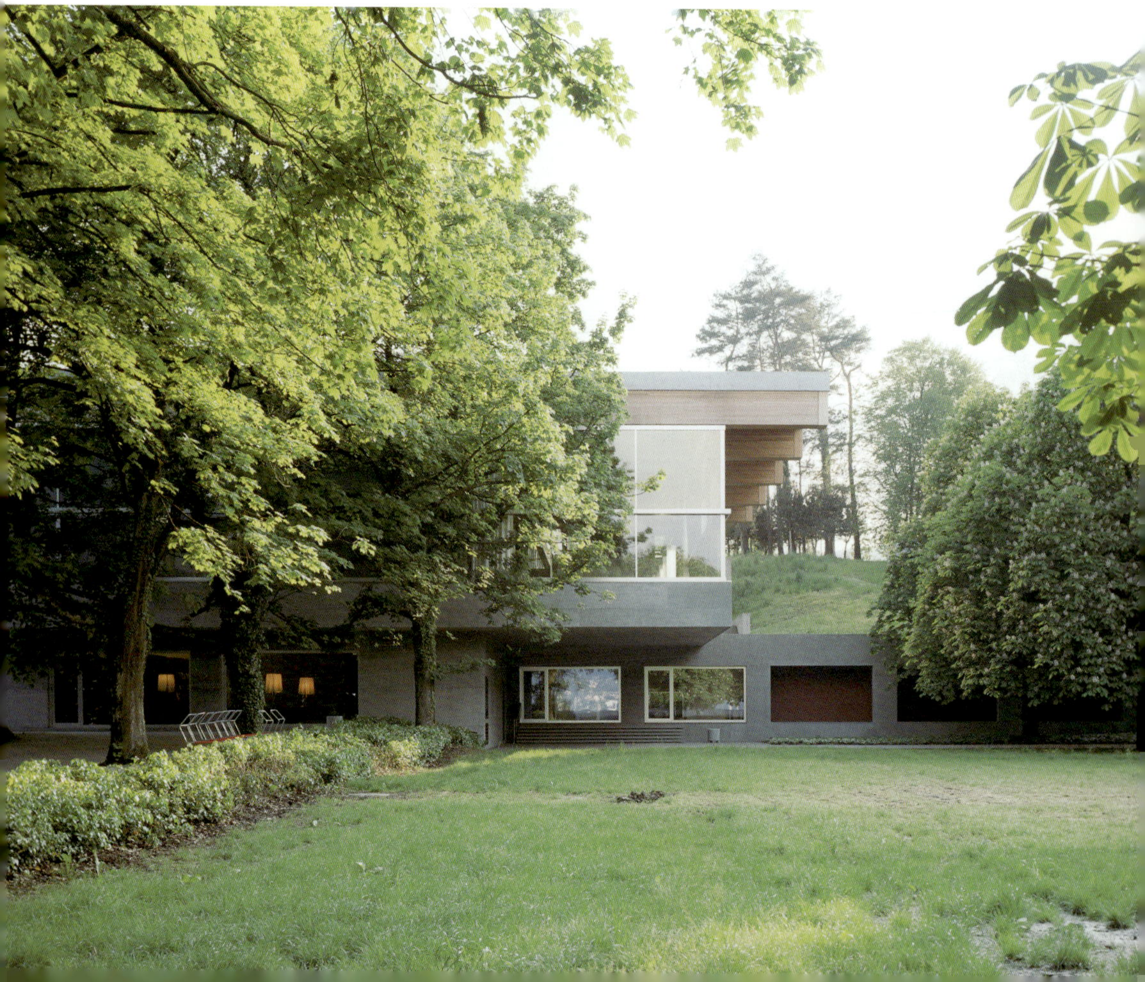

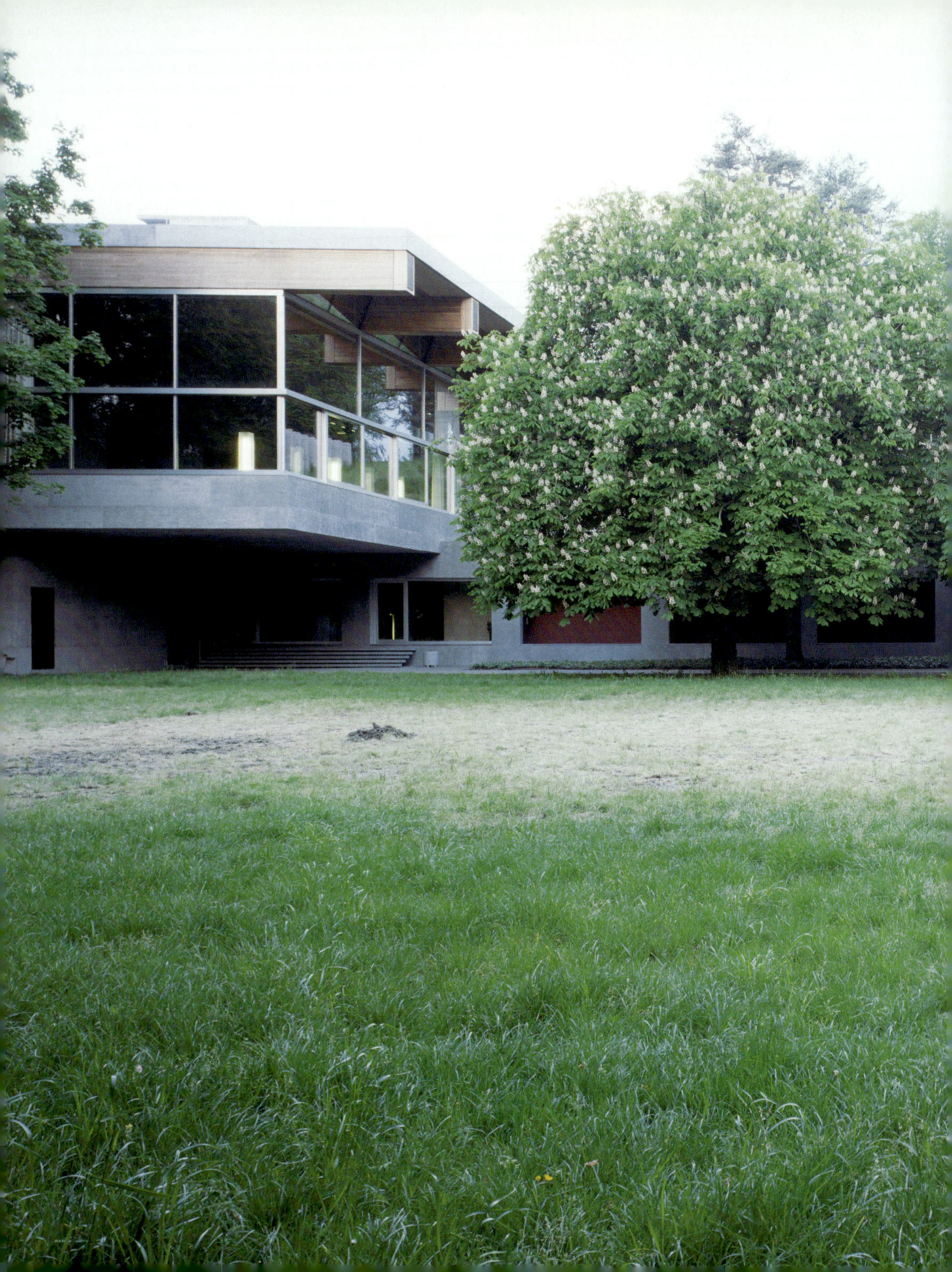

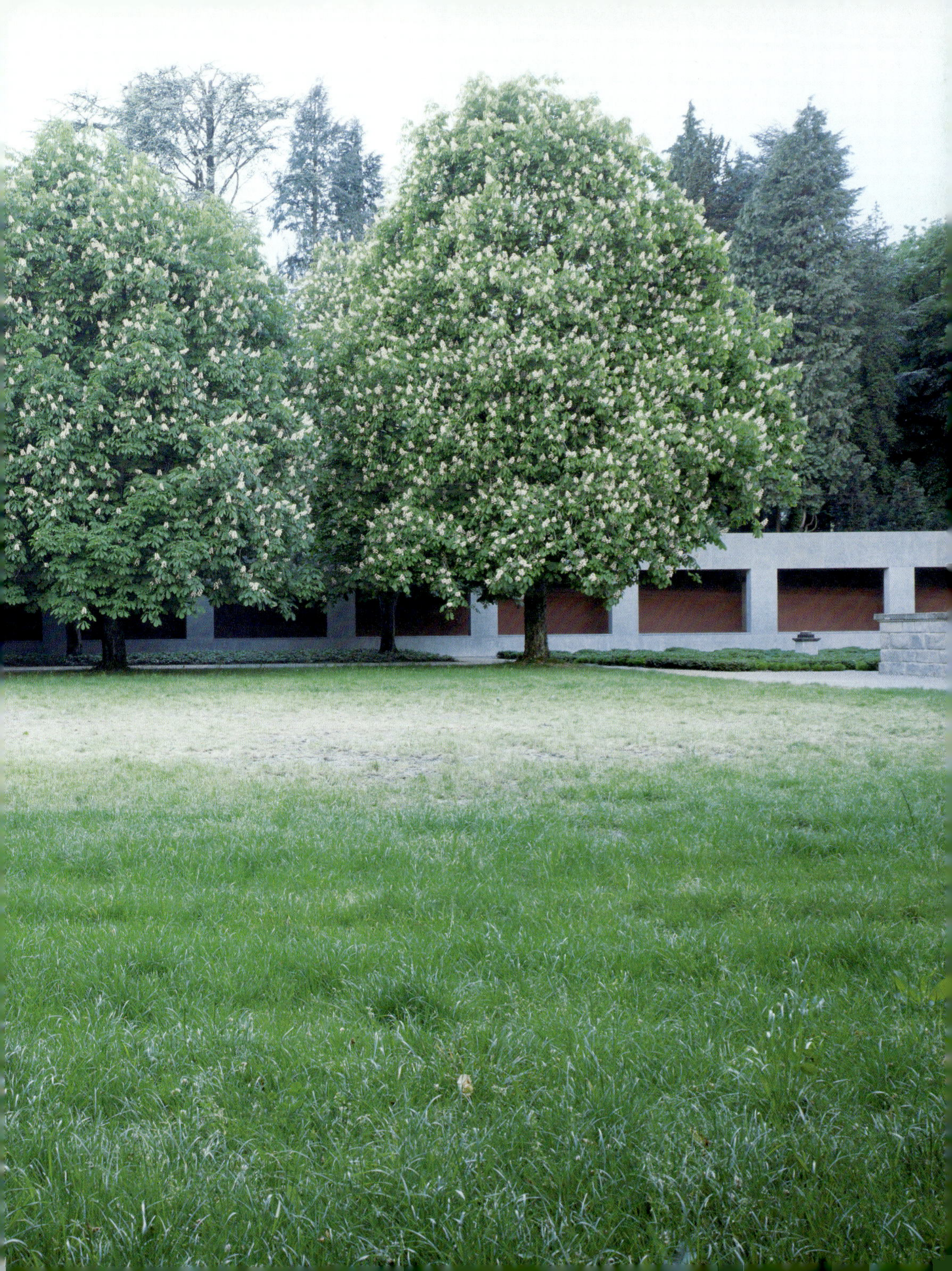

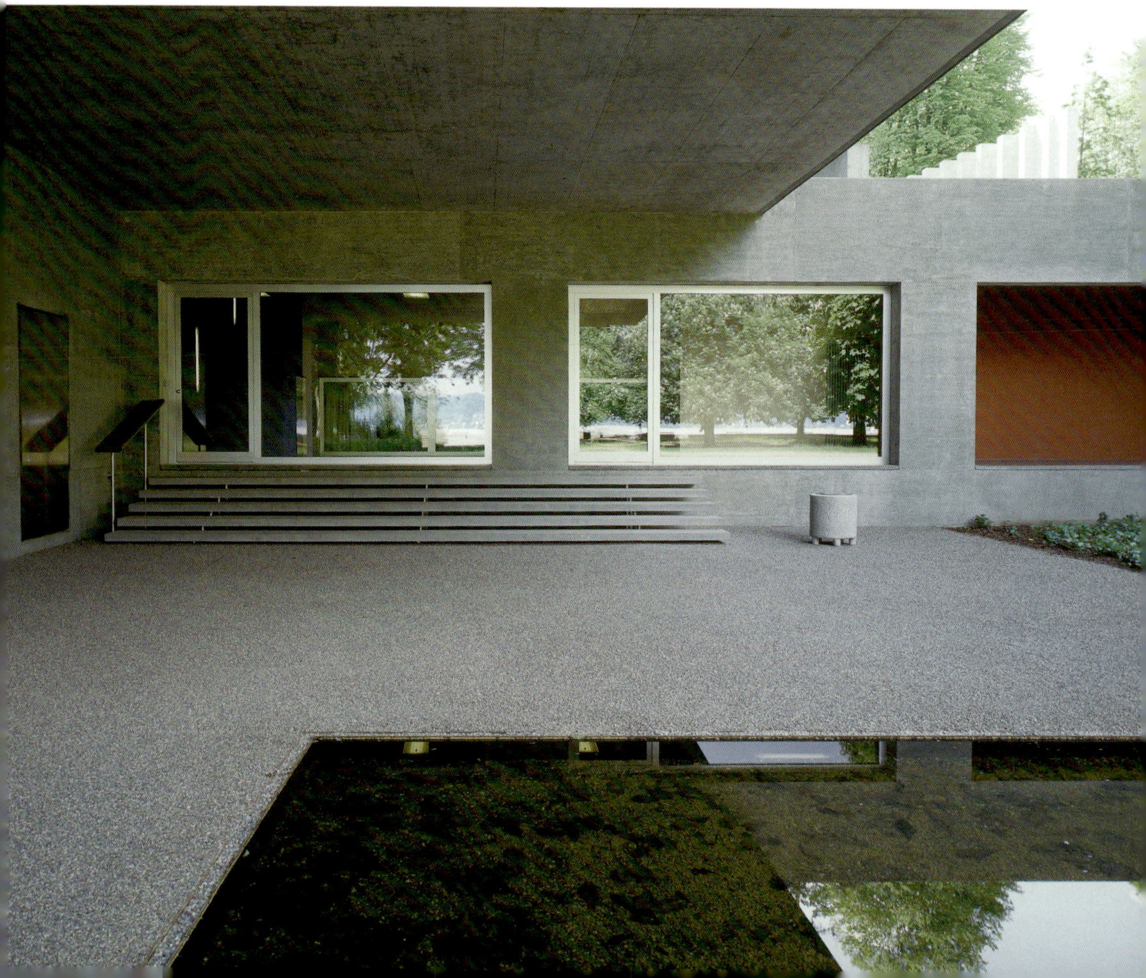

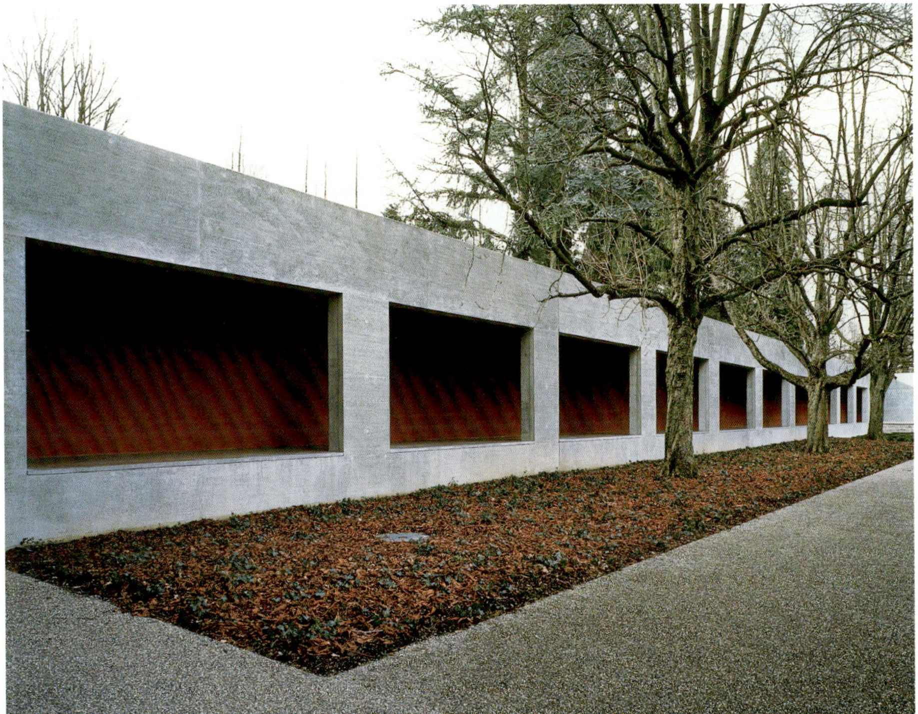

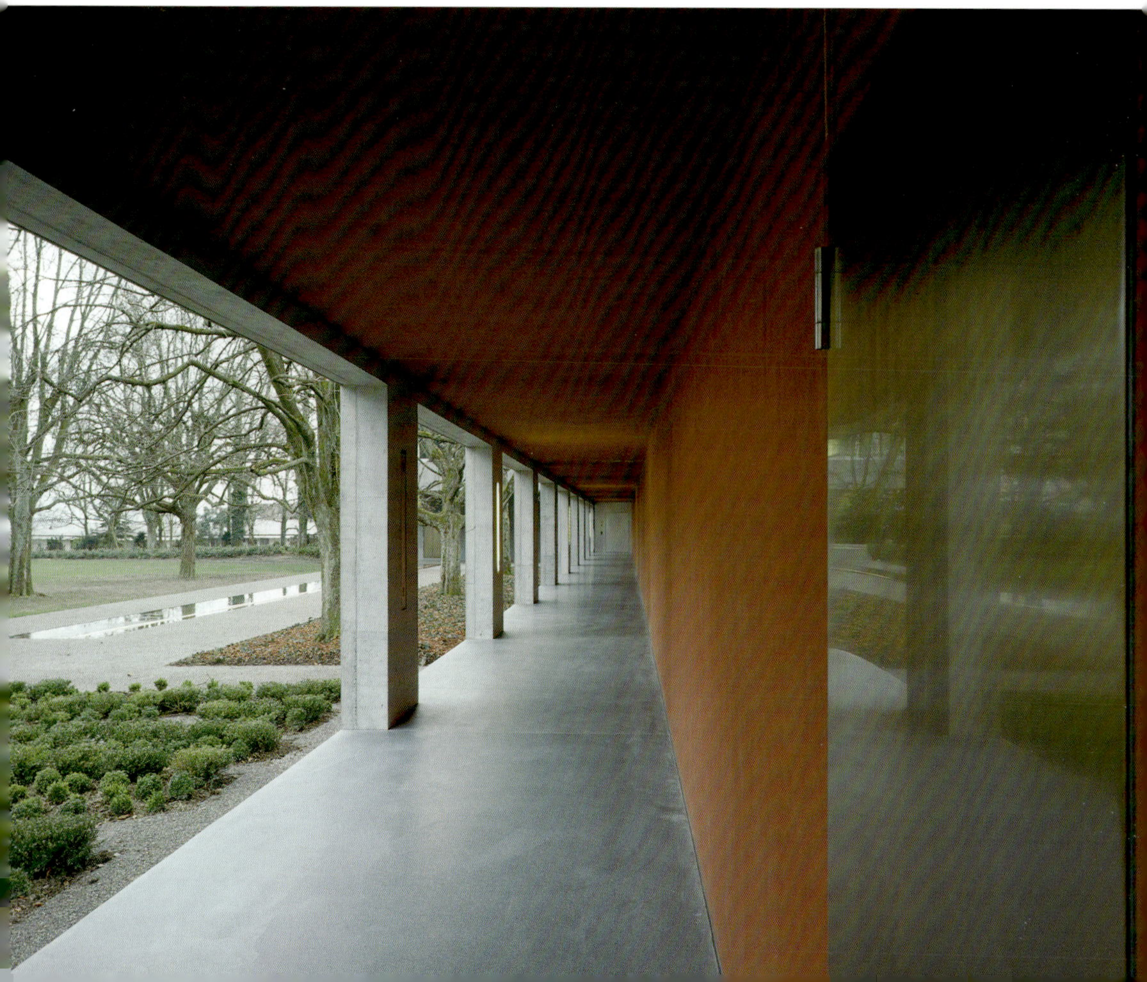

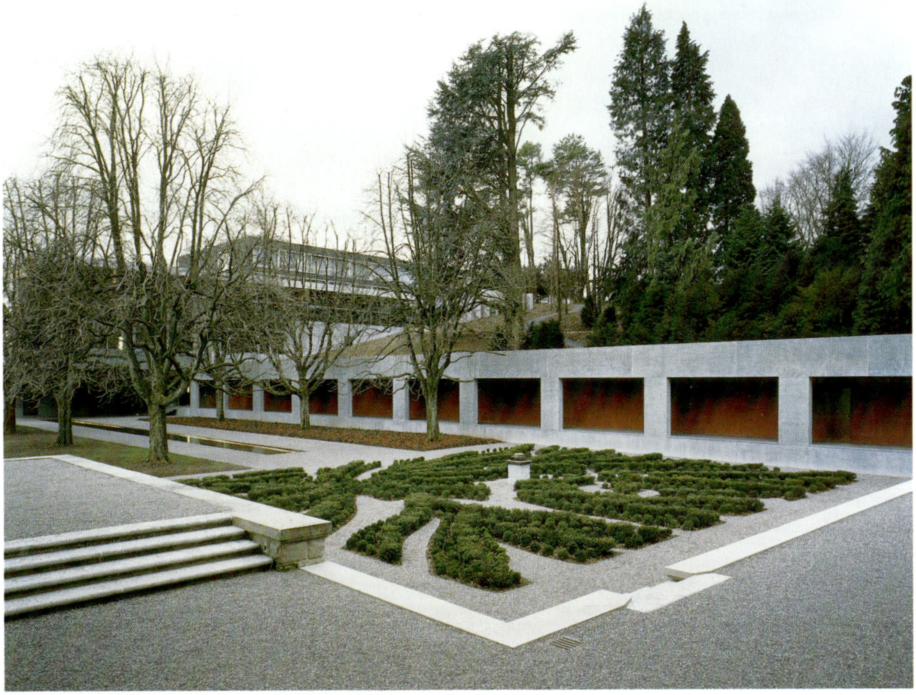

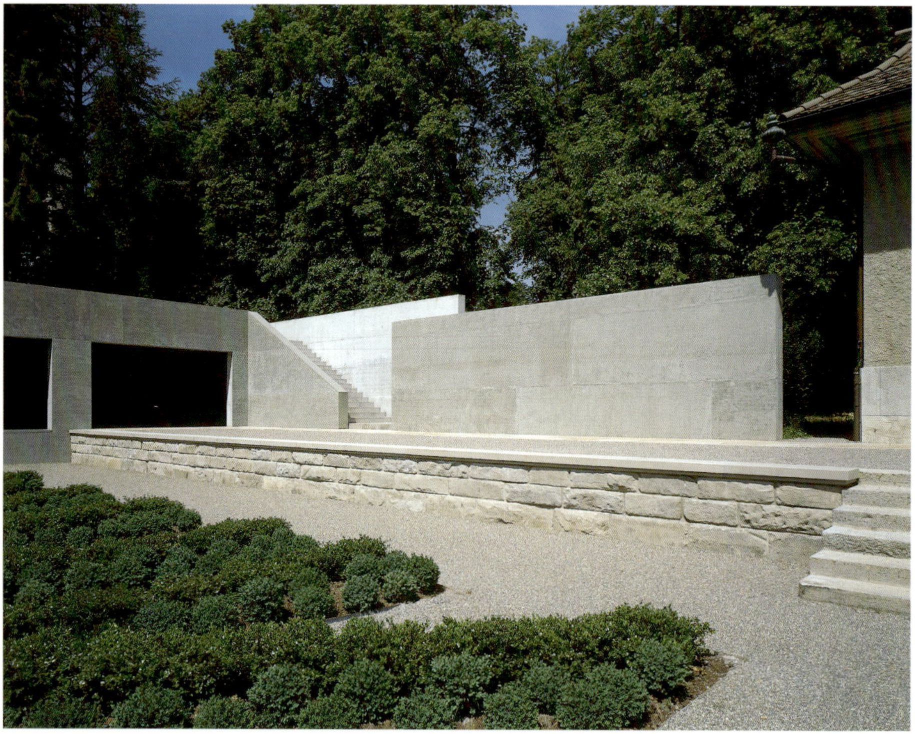

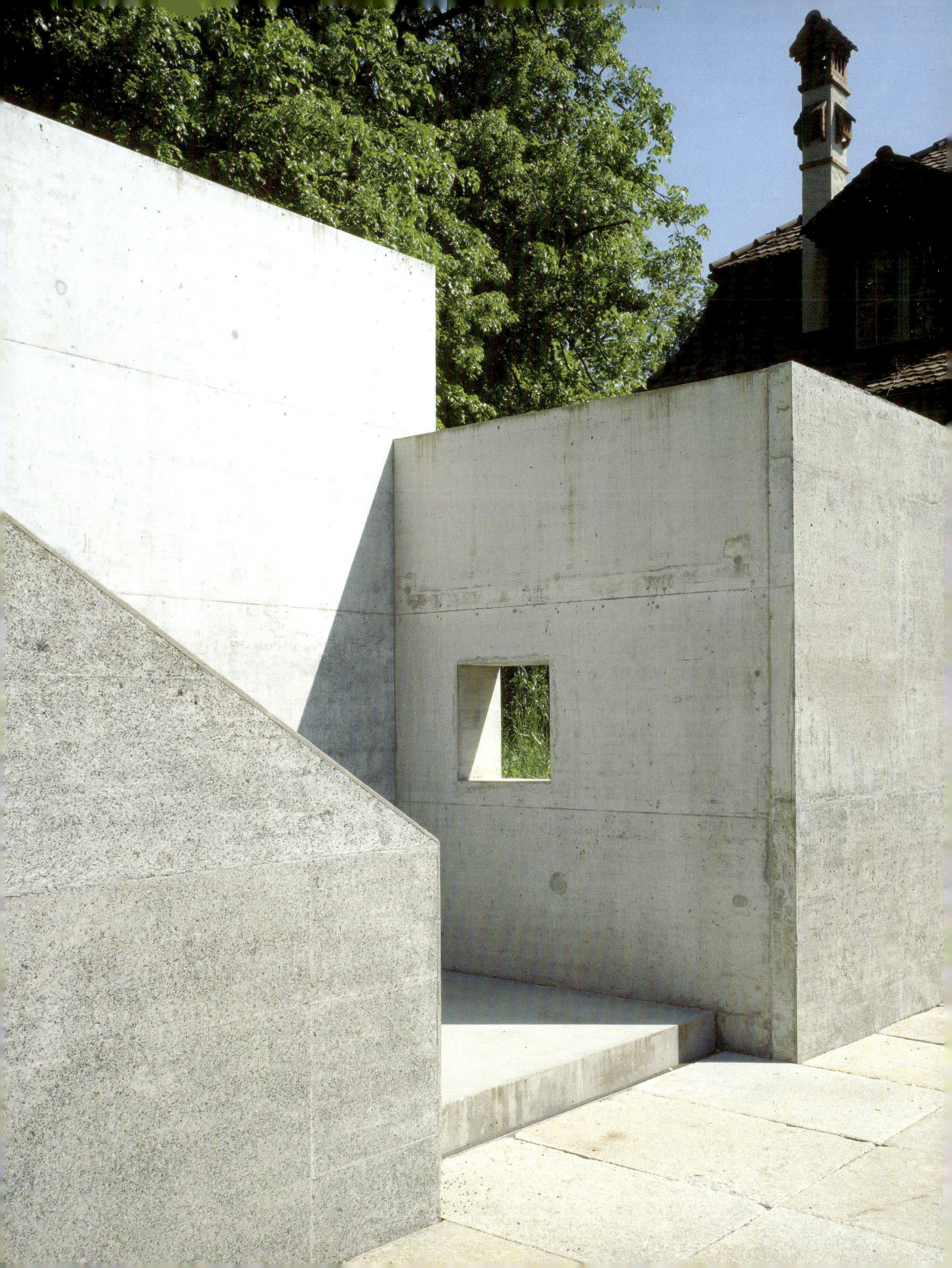

                                Acer palmatum ›Osakazuki‹
                                Acer platanoides
                                Acer platanoides ›Schwedleri‹
                                Acer pseudoplatanus
                                Acer rufinerve
                                Acer trunctatum
                                Acer zoeschense ›Annae‹
                                Achillea decolorans
                                Aesculus hippocastanum
                  Abies alba   Allium schoenoprasum
           Acer buergerianum   Aloysia triphylla
              Acer campestre   Anethum graveolens
              Acer capillipes   Anthriscus cerefolium
     Acer davidii ssp. grosseri   Artemisia dracunculus
   Acer japonicum ›Acontifolium‹   Betula pendula
              Acer palmatum   Betula pubescens

Calendula officinalis
Calocedrus deccurens
Carpinus betulus
Cedrus atlantica
Cercidiphyllum japonicum
Chamaecyparis lawsoniana ›Alumii‹
Chamaecyparis lawsoniana ›Columnaris‹
Chamaecyparis lawsoniana ›Globus‹
Chamaecyparis lawsoniana ›Minima Glauca‹
Betula verrucosa   Chamaecyparis lawsoniana ›Parsons‹
Borago officinalis   Chamaecyparis lawsoniana ›Triomf von Boskoop‹
Buxus sempervirens   Chamaecyparis nootkatensis ›Glauca‹
Buxus sempervirens ›Blauer Heinz‹   Chamaecyparis obtusa ›Draht‹
Buxus sempervirens ›Faulkner‹   Chamaecyparis obtusa ›Graciosa‹
Buxus sempervirens ›Green Velvet‹   Chamaecyparis obtusa ›Hartekamp‹
Buxus sempervirens ›Suffruticosa‹   Chamaecyparis obtusa ›Nana Gracilis‹

	Clematis Hybr. ›John Huxtable‹
	Clematis macropetala ›Blue Bird‹
	Clematis macropetala ›Jan Lindmark‹
	Clematis macropetala ›White Swan‹
	Clematis montana ›Rubens‹
	Clematis viticella ›Etoile‹
	Clematis viticella ›Polish Spirit‹
	Cochlearia officinalis
	Cornus florida
Chamaecyparis pisifera ›Filifera Nana‹	Cornus kousa var chinensis
Chamaecyparis pisifera ›Pendula‹	Cornus nutallii
Citrus sinensis	Crocus ›Flower Record‹
Clematis alpina	Crocus ›Golden Yellow‹
Clematis fargesoides ›Summer Snow‹	Crocus ›Grand Maitre‹
Clematis Hybr. ›Anita‹	Crocus ›Remembrance‹
Clematis Hybr. ›Huldine‹	Crocus ›Vanguard‹

Geranium himalayense ›Irish Blue‹
Geranium macrorrhizum ›Freundorf‹
Geranium macrorrhizum ›Ingwersen‹
Geranium macrorrhizum ›Spessart‹
Geranium macrorrhizum ›Typ Friedrich‹
Geranium magnificum
Geranium magnificum ›Rosemoor‹
Geranium nodosum
Geranium sylvaticum ›Birch Lilac‹
Geranium sylvaticum ›Mayflower‹
Festuca rubra commutata ›Frida‹   Geranium x oxonianum ›Claridge Druce‹
Festuca rubra commutata ›Olivia‹   Geranium x oxonianum ›Rosenlicht‹
Festuca rubra rubra ›Picnic‹   Hedera helix ›Arborescens‹
Geranium endressii   Hedera helix ›Hibernica‹
Geranium endressii ›Wargrave Pink‹   Hydrangea arborescens ›Annabelle‹
Geranium himalayense   Hydrangea macrophylla ›Blaumeise‹

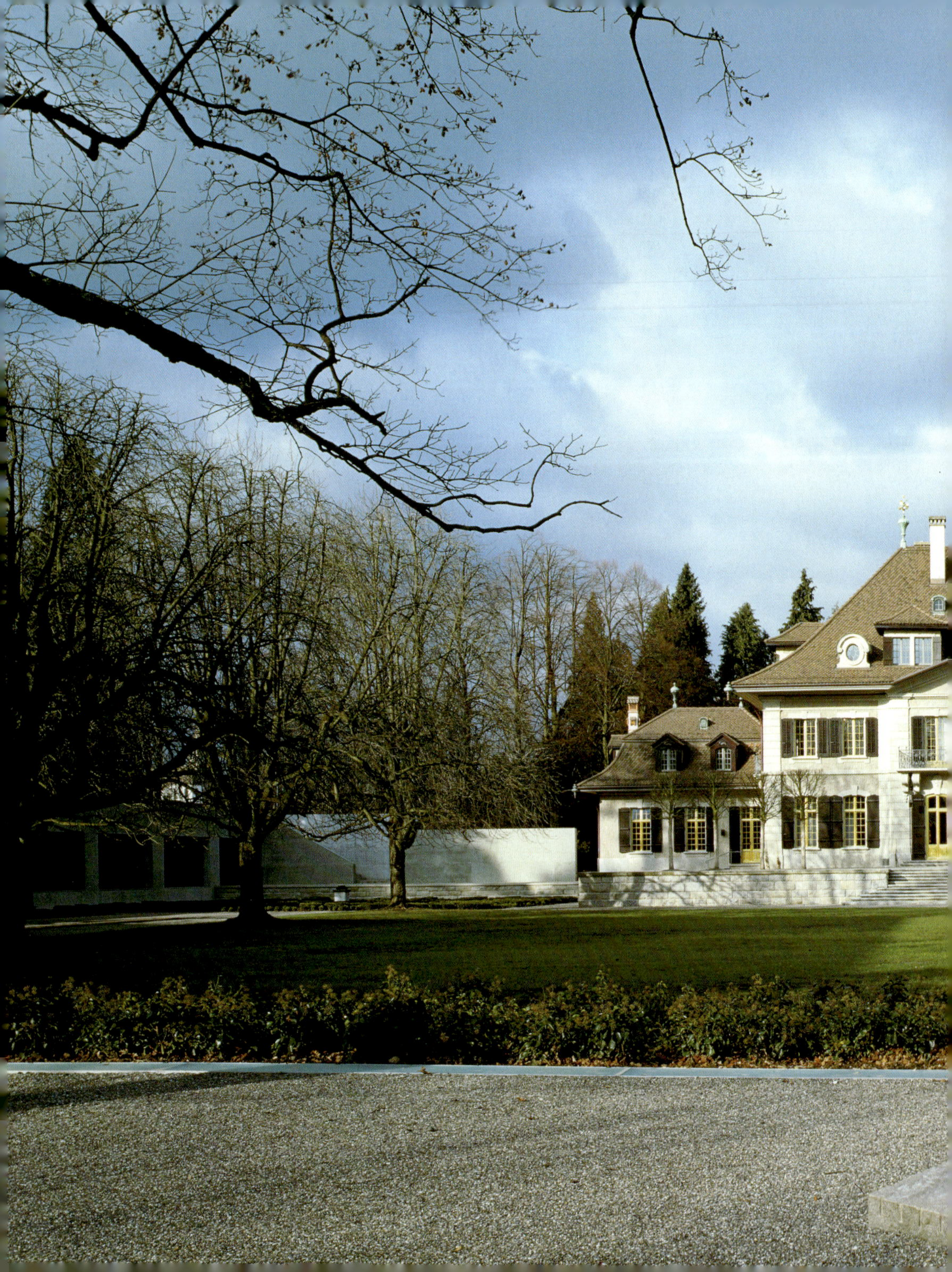

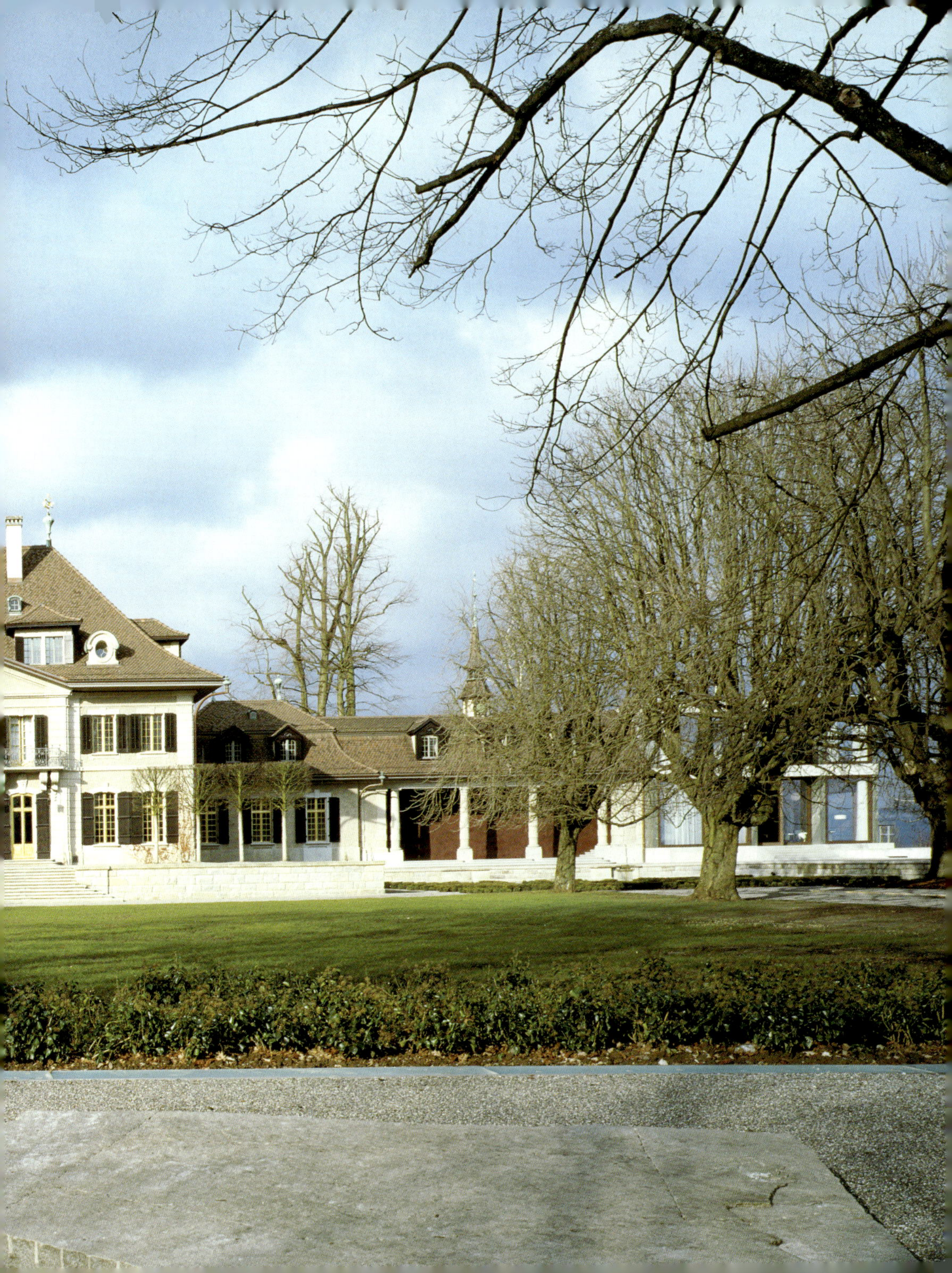

	Hydrangea serrata f. koreana
	Hyssopus officinalis
	Ilex crenata ›Rotundifolia‹
	Ilex meservaea ›Blue Princess‹
	Ilex x meservaea ›Blue Angel‹
	Ilex x meservaea ›Blue Prince‹
	Juniperus chinensis ›Keteleerrii‹
	Laurus nobilis
	Lavandula angustifolia
Hydrangea macrophylla ›Bodensee‹	Levisticum officinale
Hydrangea macrophylla ›Frillibet‹	Ligustrum vulgare ›Atrovirens‹
Hydrangea macrophylla ›Générale Vicomtess de Vibraye‹	Liriodendron tulupifera
Hydrangea paniculata ›Grandiflora‹	Lolium perenne ›Amadeus‹
Hydrangea paniculata ›Kyushu‹	Lolium perenne ›Bellevue‹
Hydrangea quercifolia ›Snow Flake‹	Lolium perenne ›Elegana‹
Hydrangea serrata ›Blue Deckle‹	Magnolia kobus

	Metasequoia glyptostroboides
	Monarda didyma
	Narcissus ›Ice Follies‹
	Narcissus ›Mount Hood‹
	Ocimum basilicum ›Dark Opal‹
	Ocimum basilicum var minimum
	Ocimum citriodorum
	Origanum majorana
	Origanum vulgare
Magnolia stellata ›Dr. Mervel‹	Parrotia persica
Magnolia x loebneri ›Leonard Messel‹	Petroselinum crispum
Melissa officinalis	Picea abies
Mentha crispa	Picea orientalis
Mentha rotundifolia ›Apfelminze‹	Picea speziosa
Mentha spicata ›Spalinger‹	Pinus nigra
Mentha x gentilis ›Variegata‹	Pinus sylvestris

	Prunus subhirtella ›Autumnalis‹
	Prunus x hillieri ›Spire‹
	Quercus cerris
	Quercus coccinea
	Quercus palustris
	Quercus petraea
	Rosa ›Cedric Morris‹
	Rosa ›Multiflora carnea‹
	Rosa ›Multiflora cathayensis‹
Poa pratensis ›Broadway‹	Rosa ›Multiflora platyphylla‹
Poa pratensis ›Cocktail‹	Rosa ›Paul's Himalayan Musk‹
Poa pratensis ›Limousine‹	Rosa ›Rambling Rector‹
Populus nigra ›Italica‹	Rosmarinus officinalis
Prunus ›Accolade‹ Prunus incisa	Ruta graveolens
Prunus laurocerasus	Salix caprea
Prunus mume	Salvia officinalis

	Thuja occidentalis ›Columbia‹
	Thuja occidentalis ›Columna‹
	Thuja occidentalis ›Smaragd‹
	Thuja plicata ›Atrovirens‹
	Thujopsis dolabrata
	Thymus citriodorus
	Thymus vulgaris
	Tilia platyphyllos
	Tilia x euchlora
Sanguisorba minor	Tilia oliveri
Satureja montana	Tropaeolum majus
Sedum reflexum	Viburnum carlesii
Sequoiadendron giganteum	Viburnum farreri
Taxodium distichum	Viburnum plicatum ›Mariesii‹
Taxus baccata	Viburnum x burkwoodii
Thuja occidentalis ›Brabant‹	Viburnum x carlcephalum

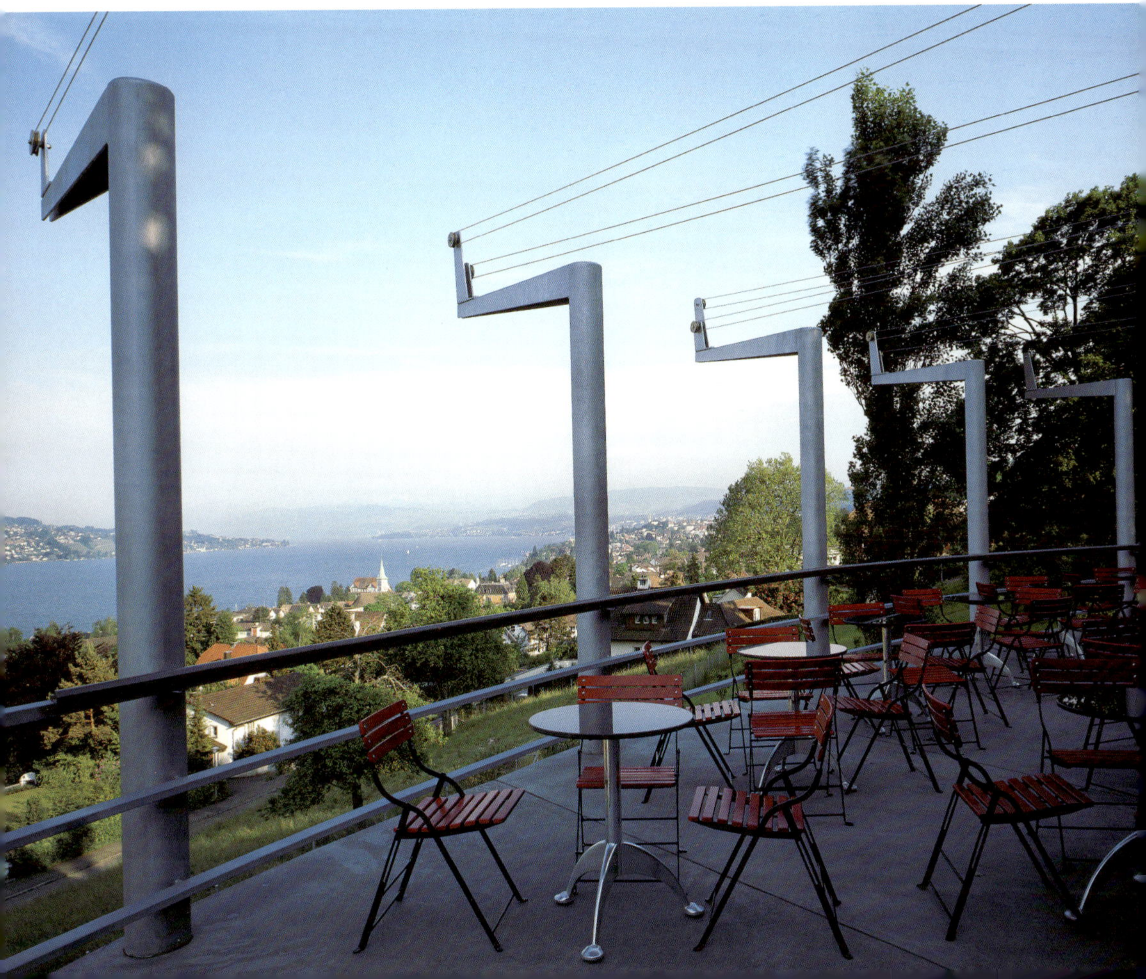

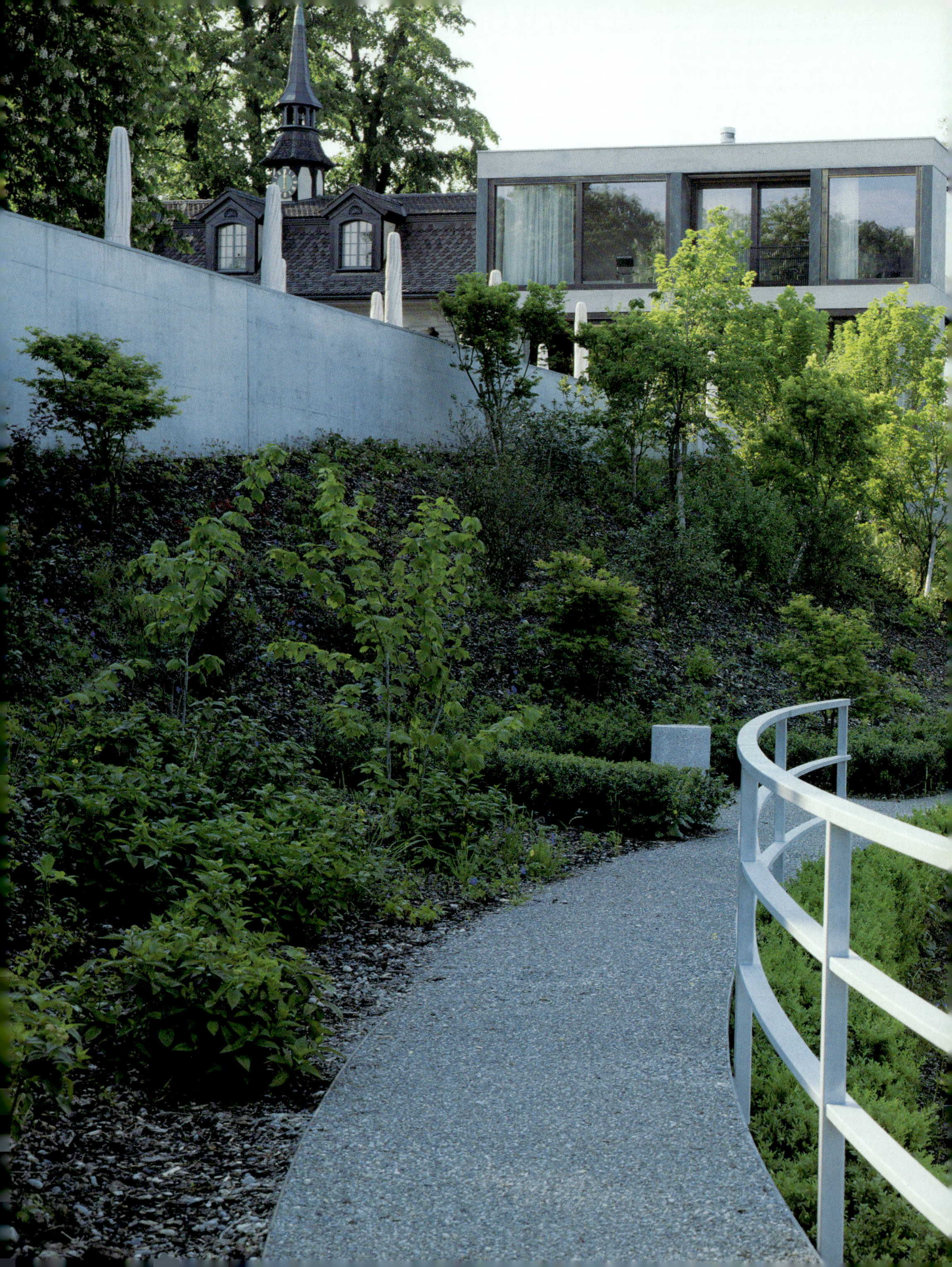

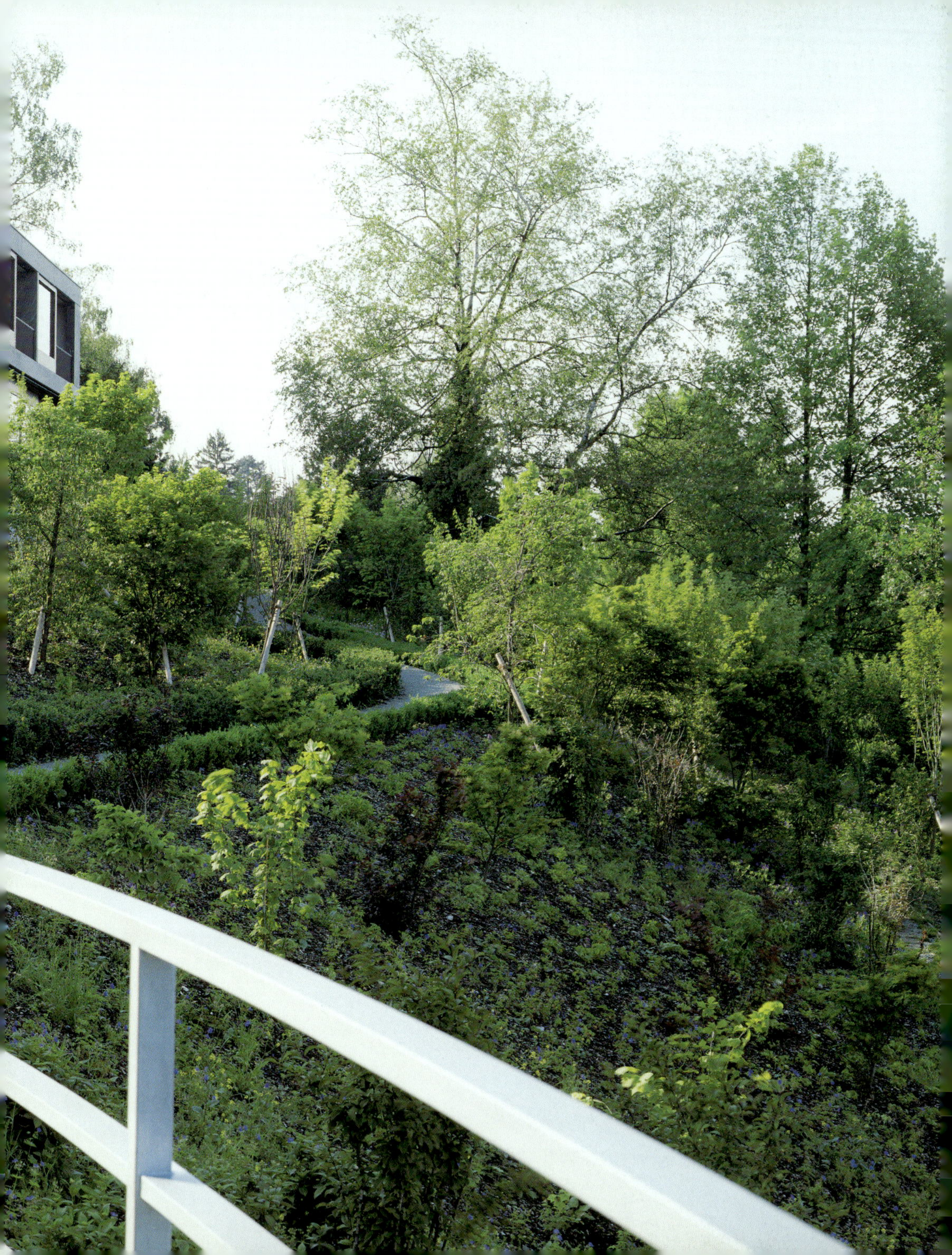

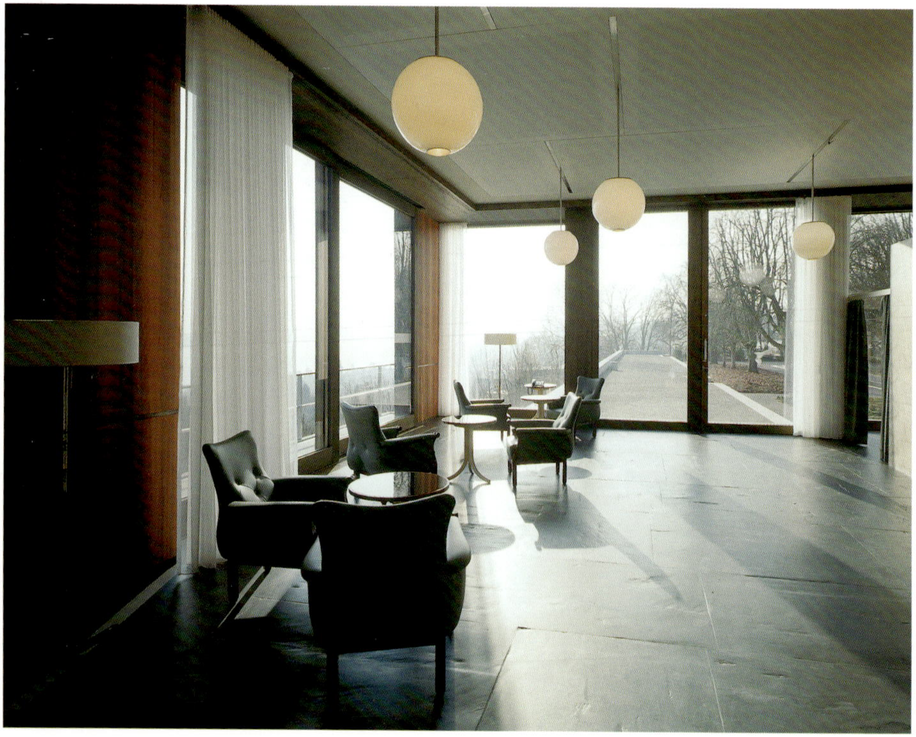

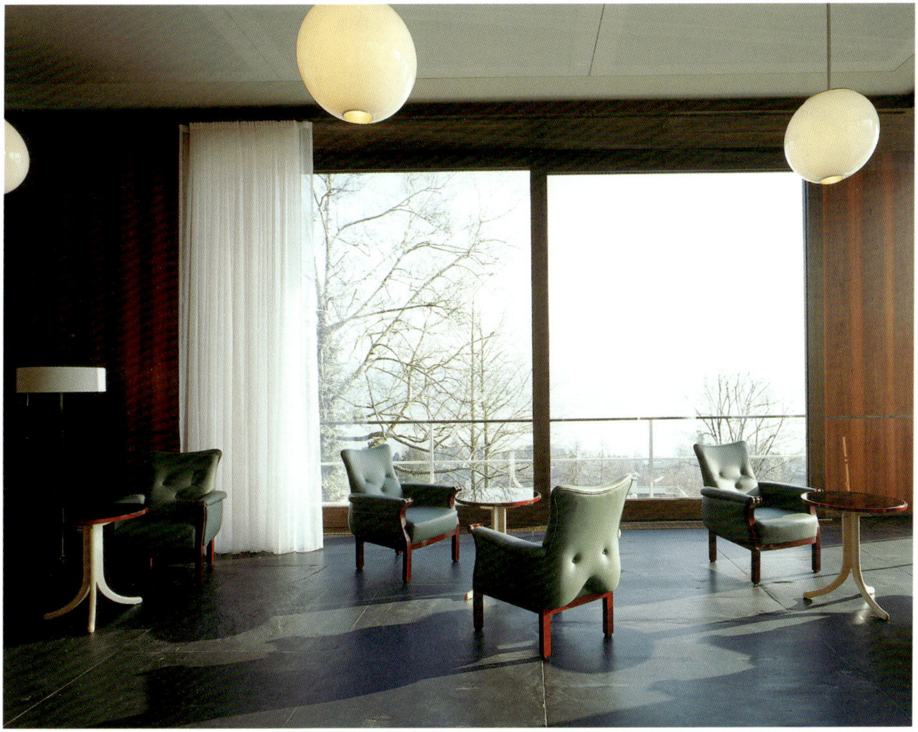

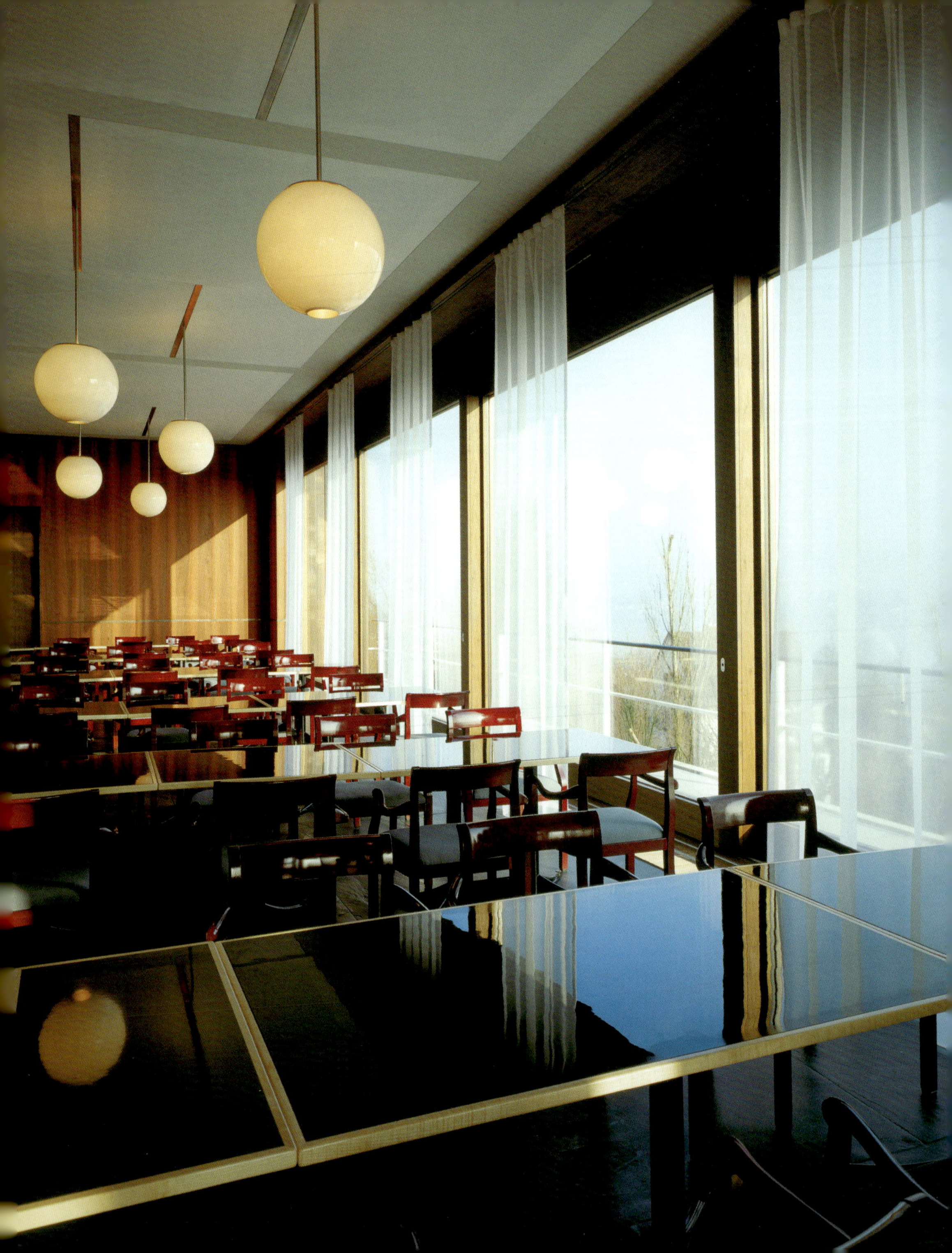

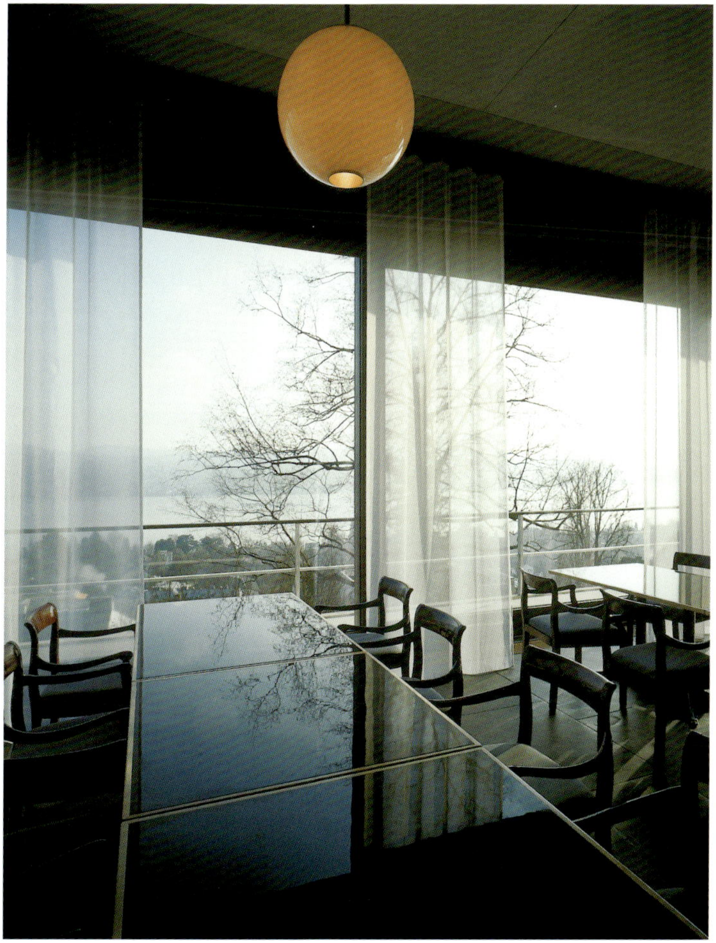

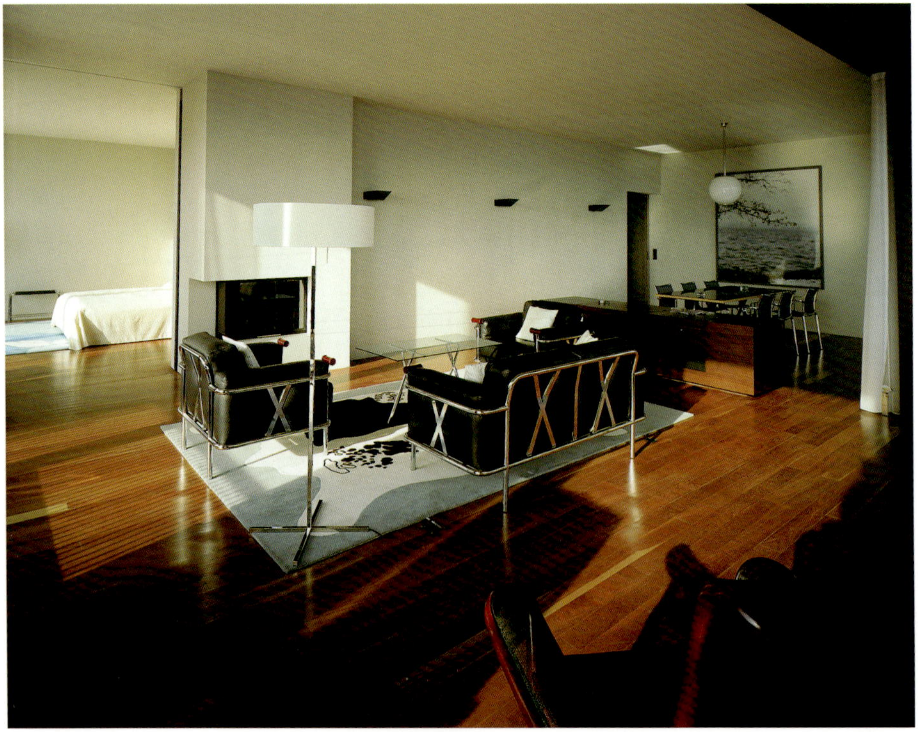

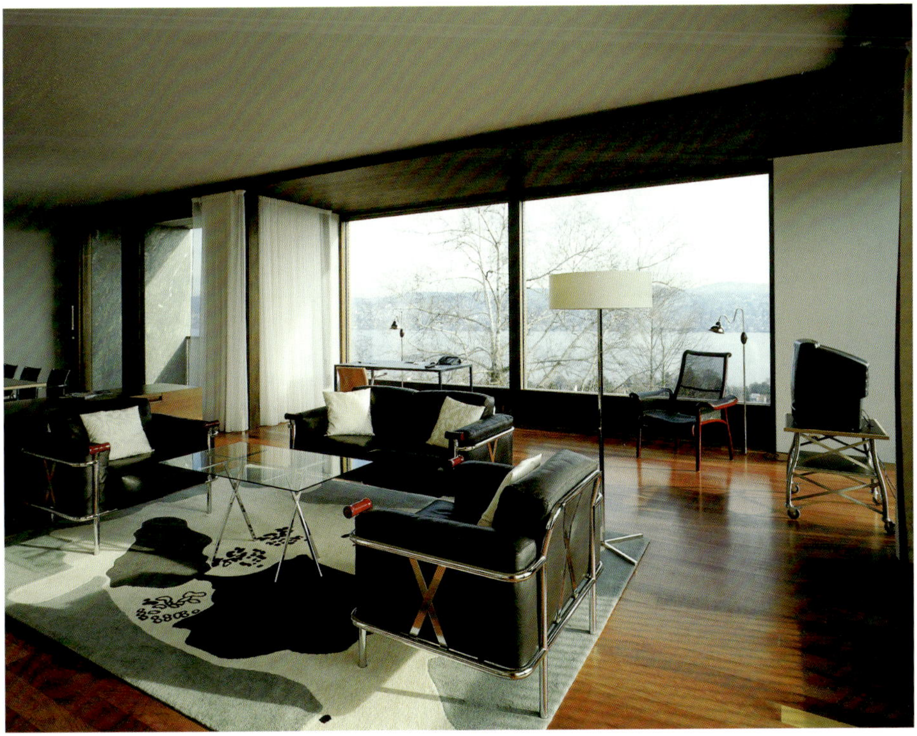

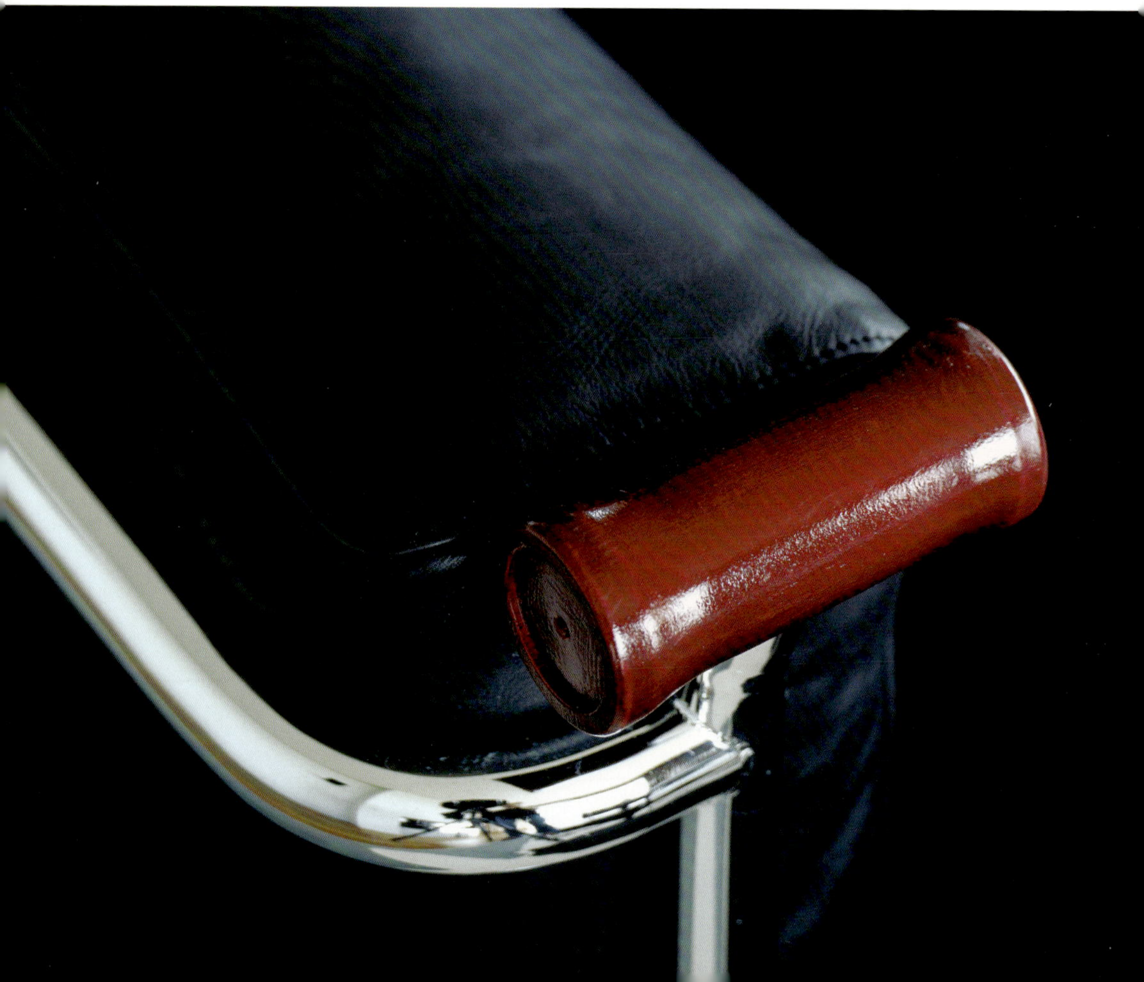

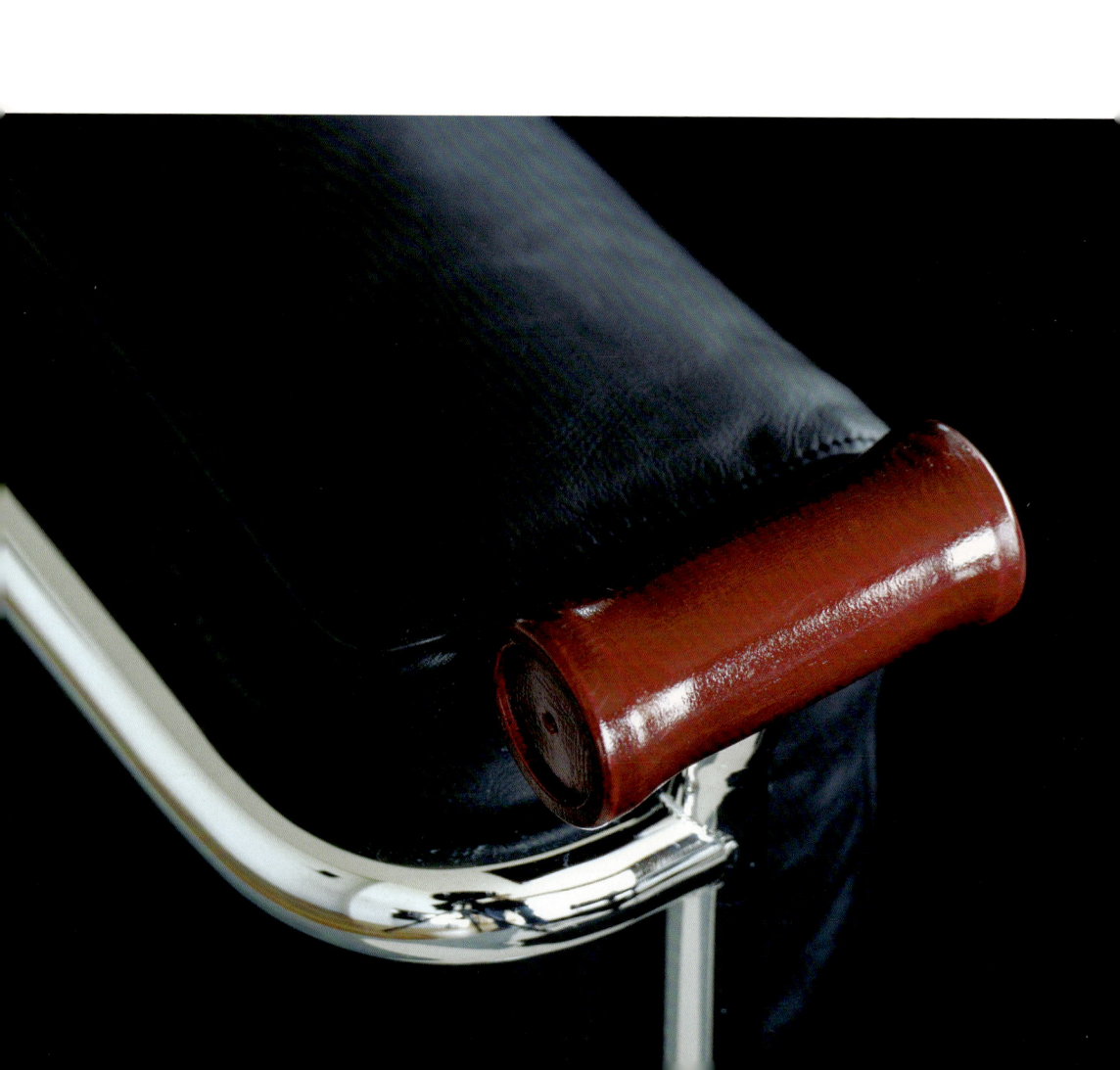

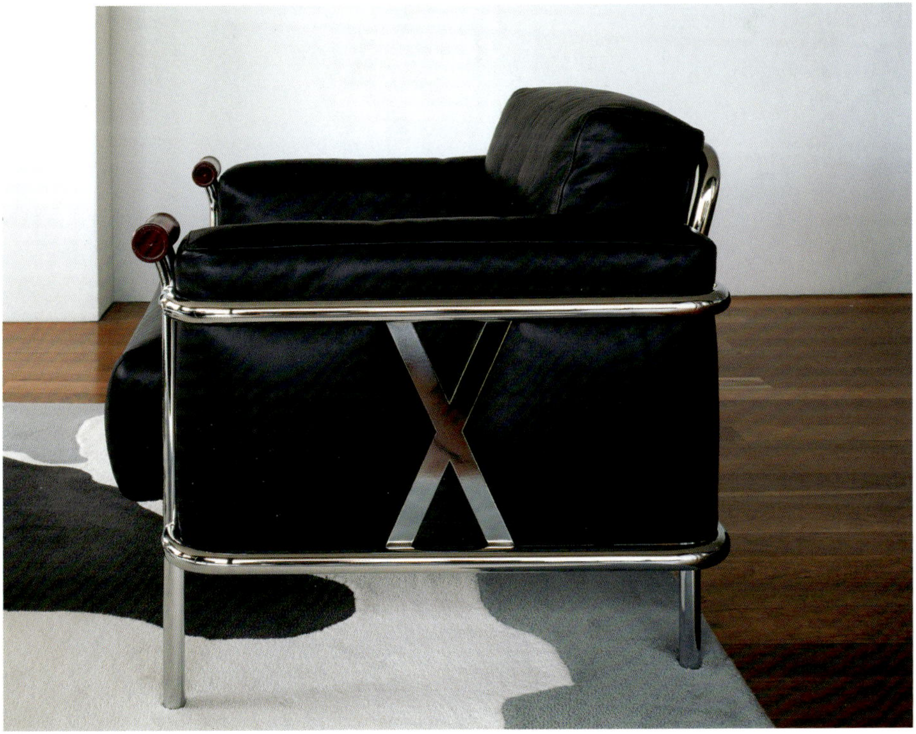

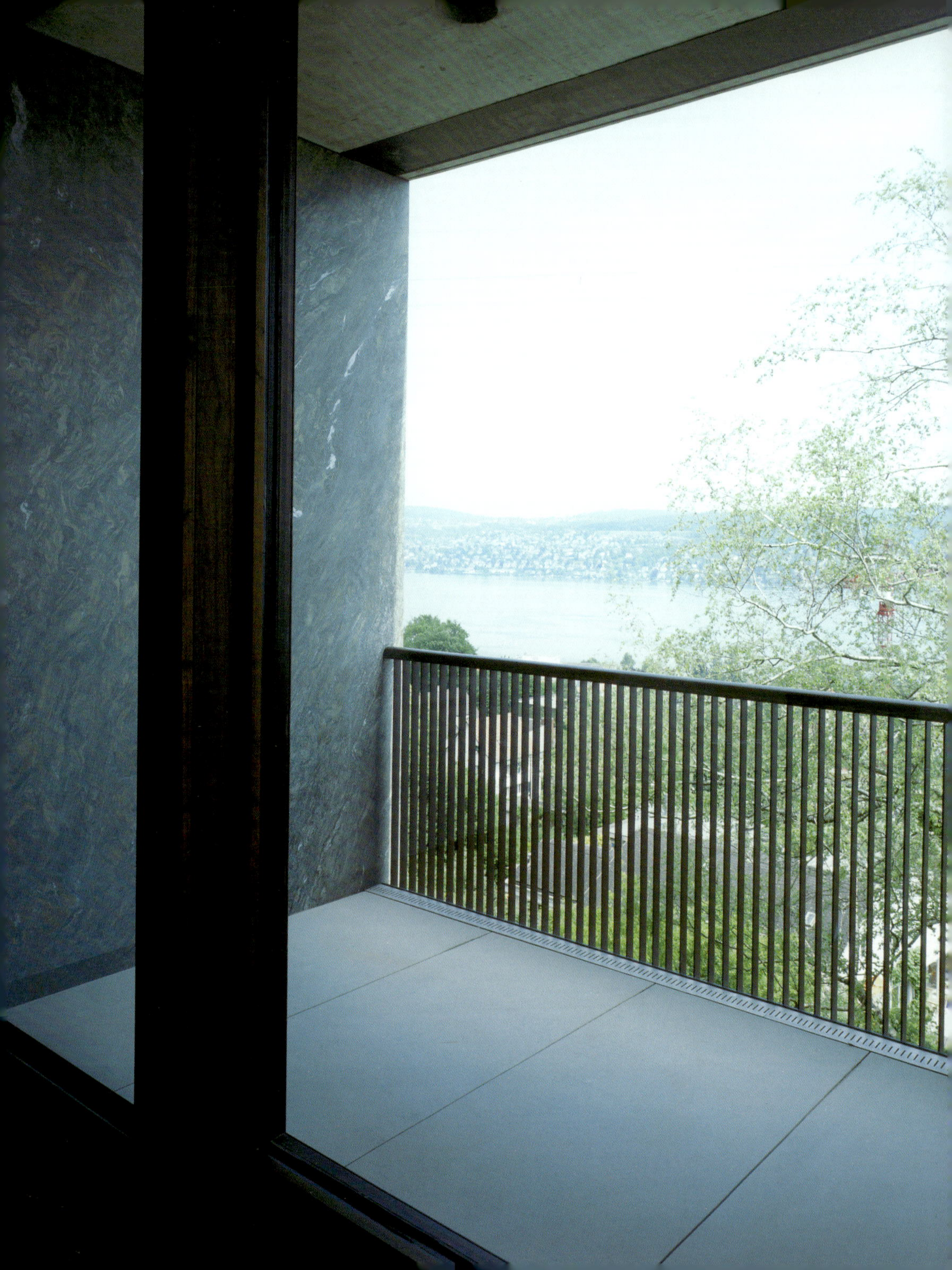

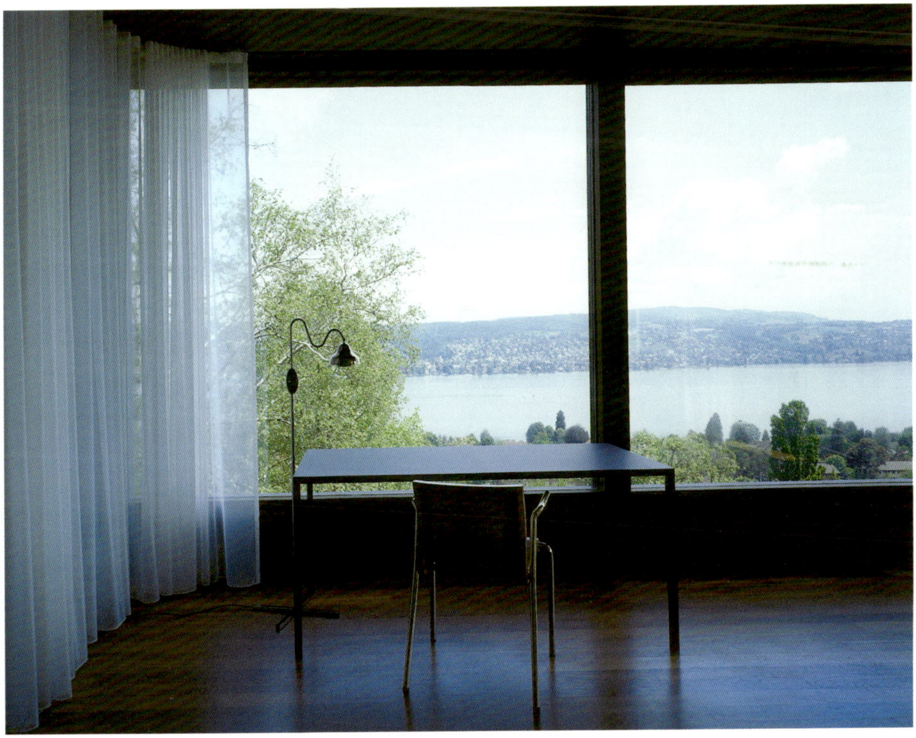

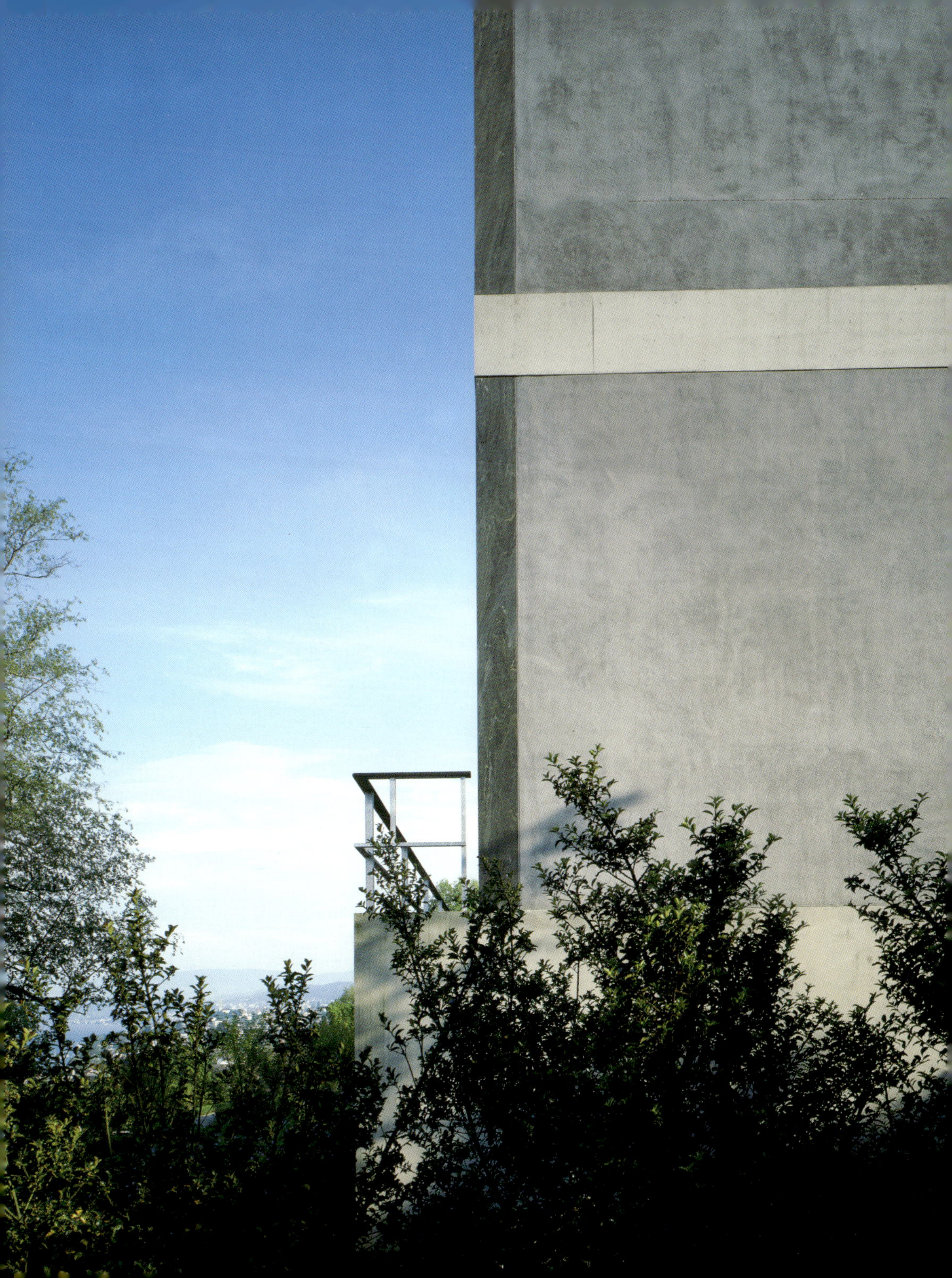

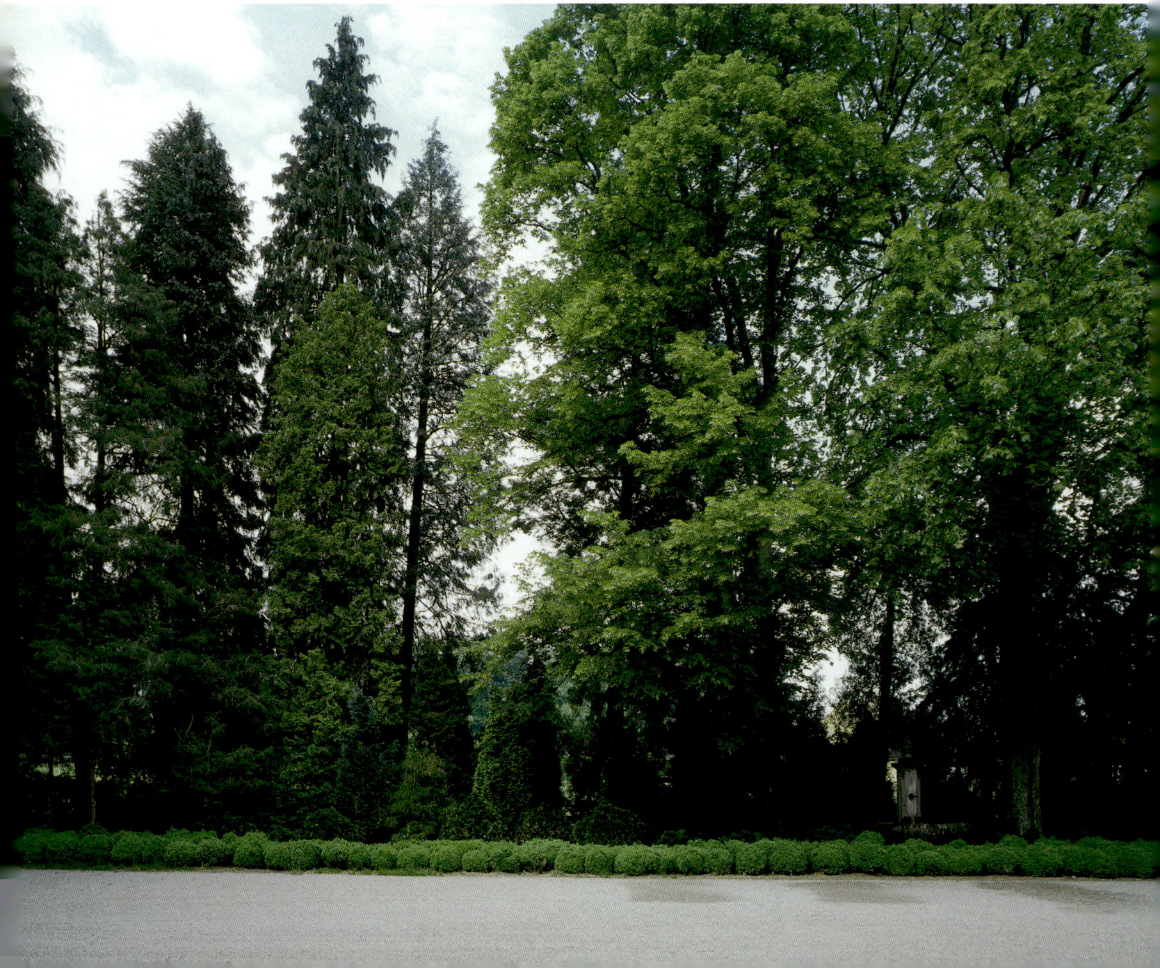

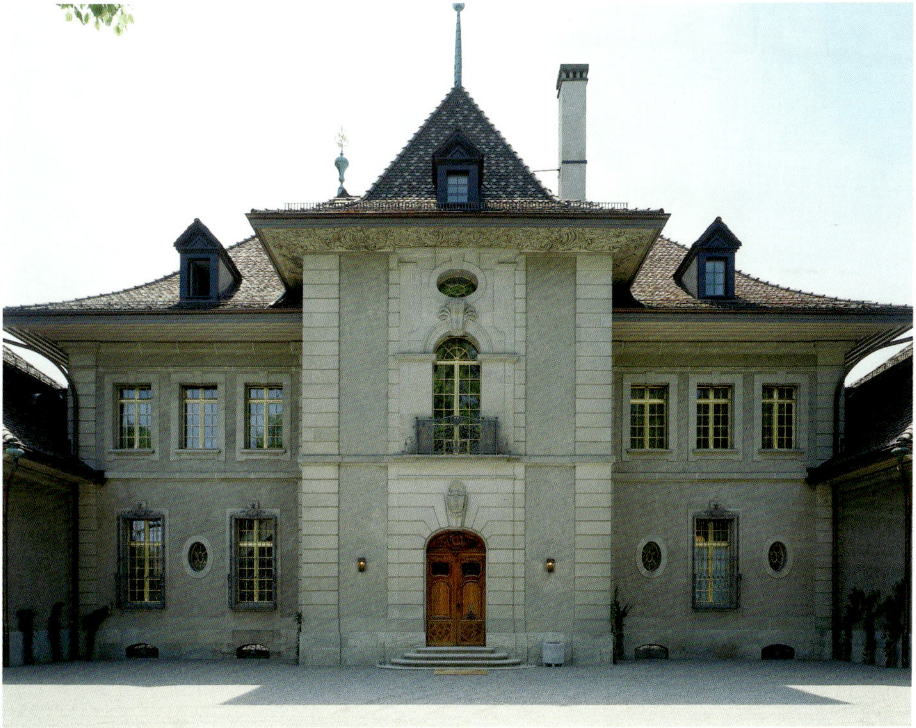

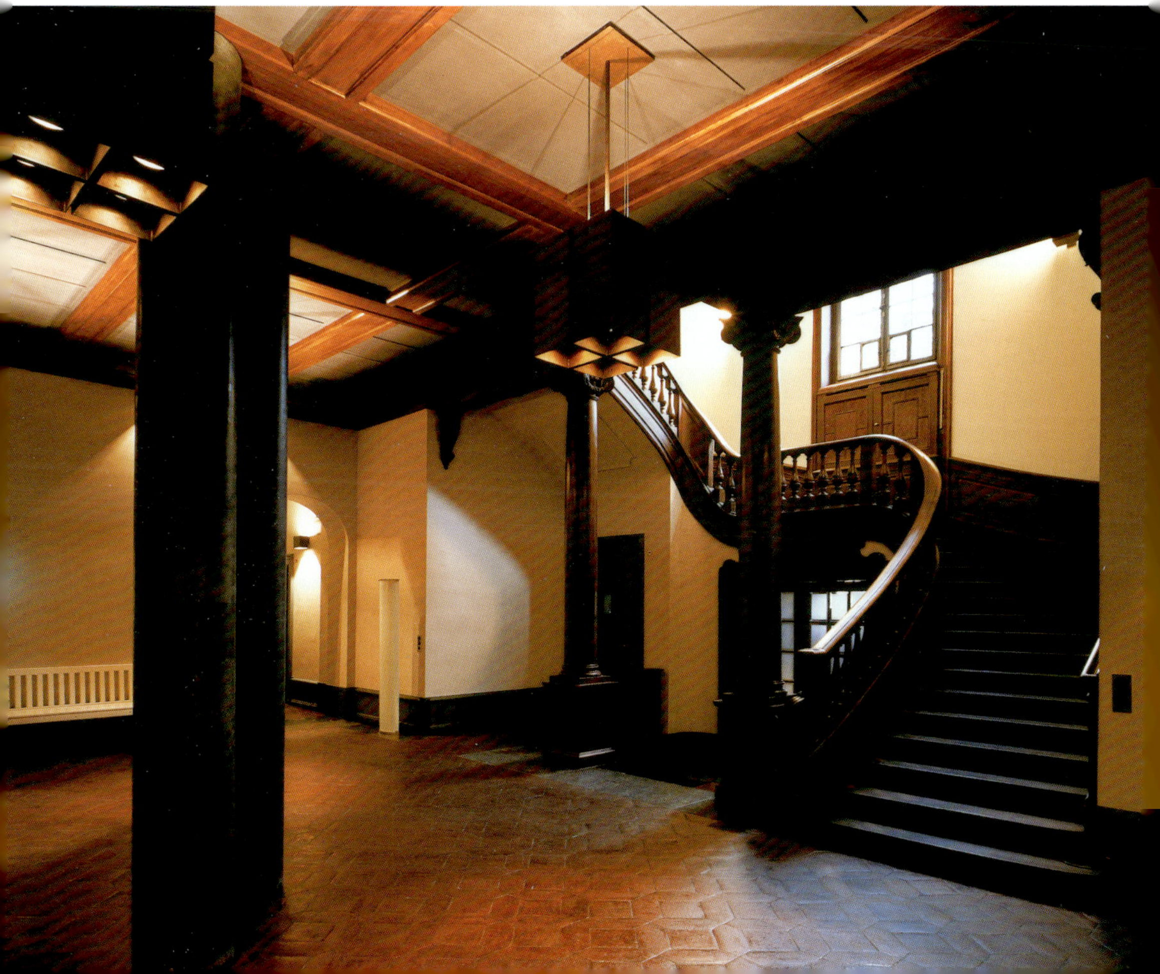

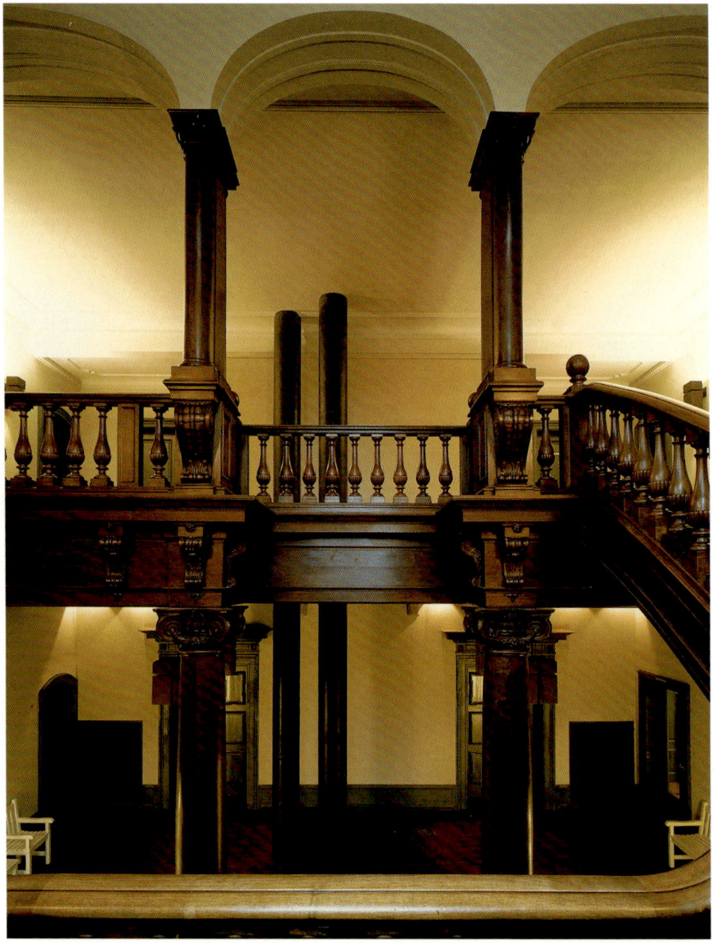

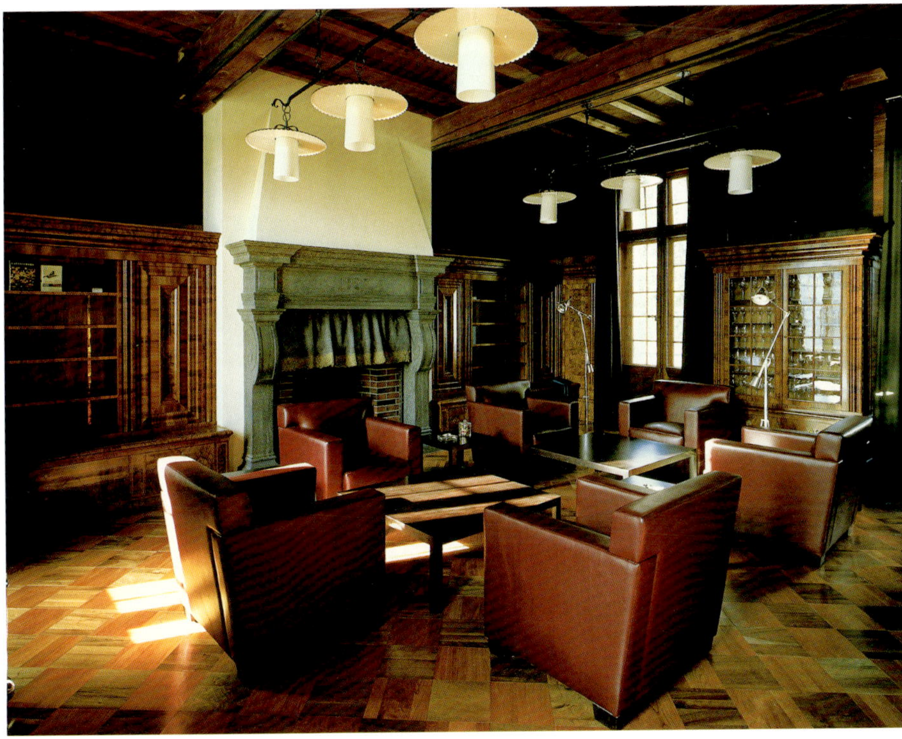

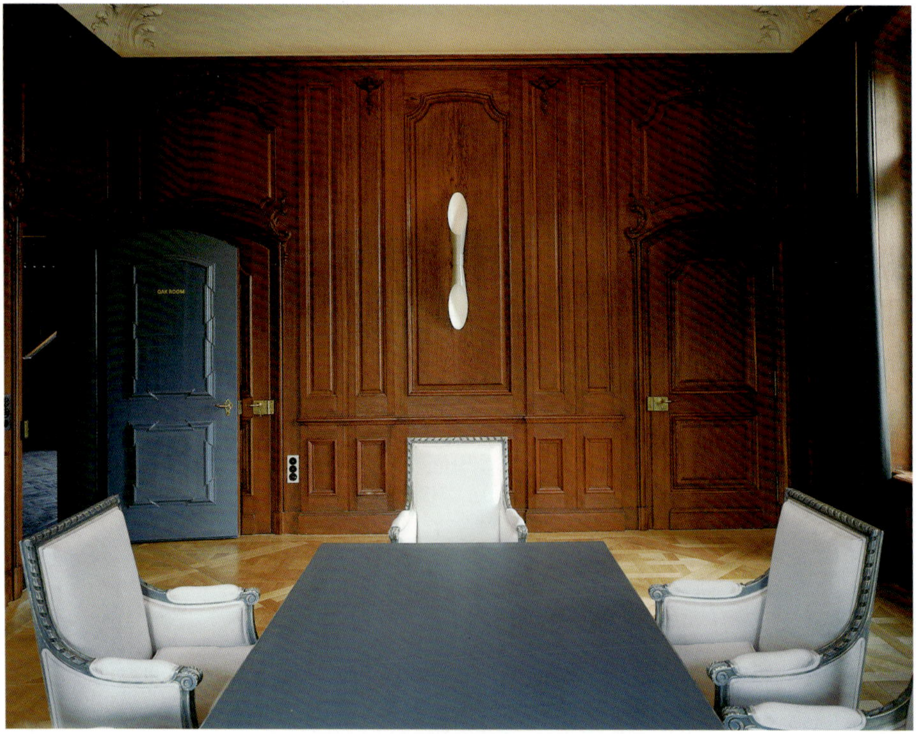
OAK ROOM

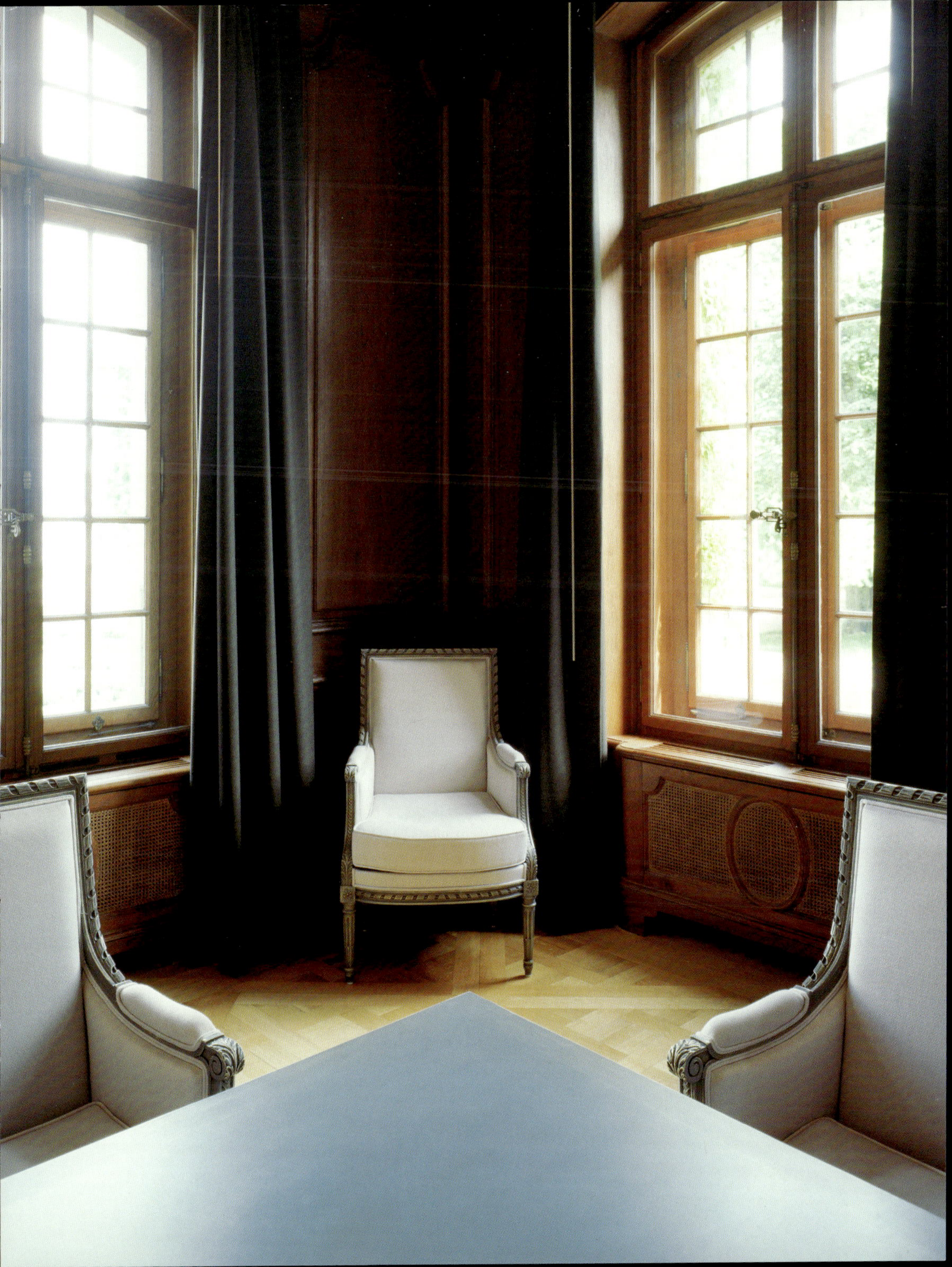

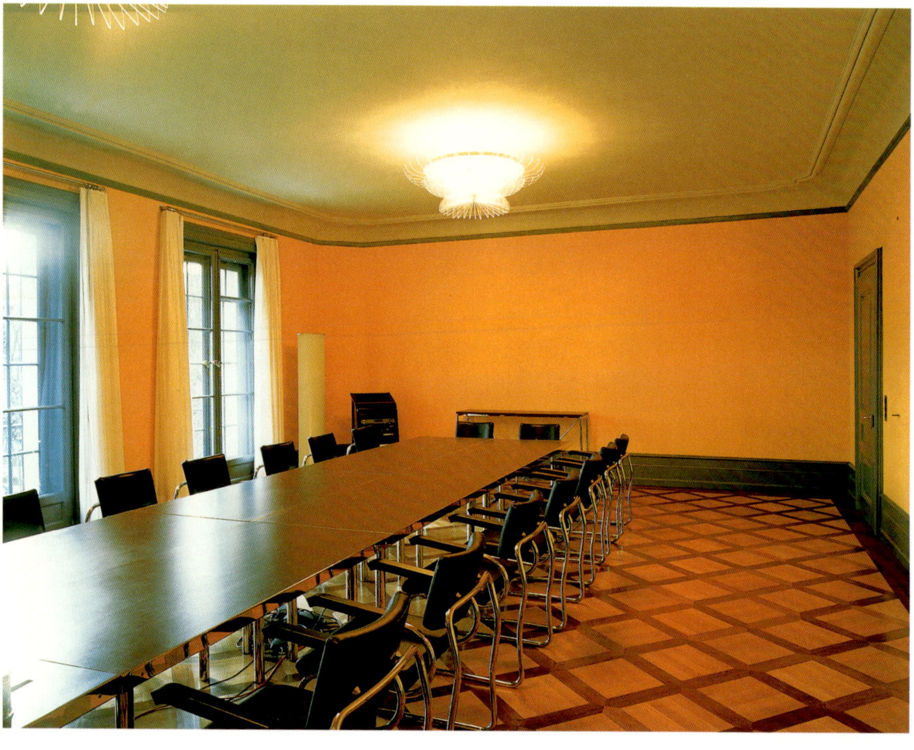

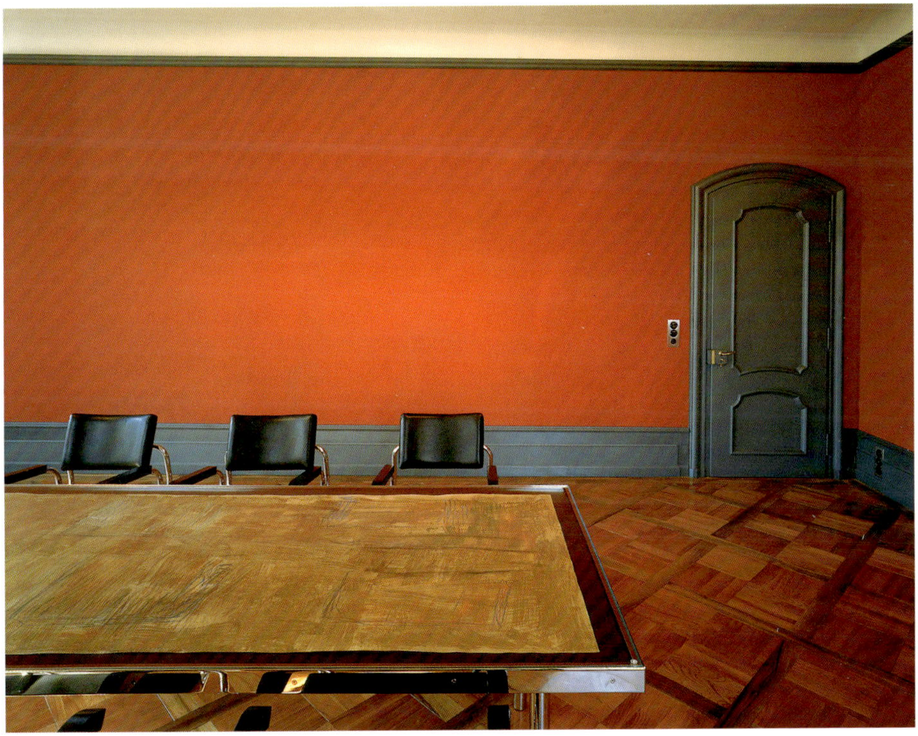

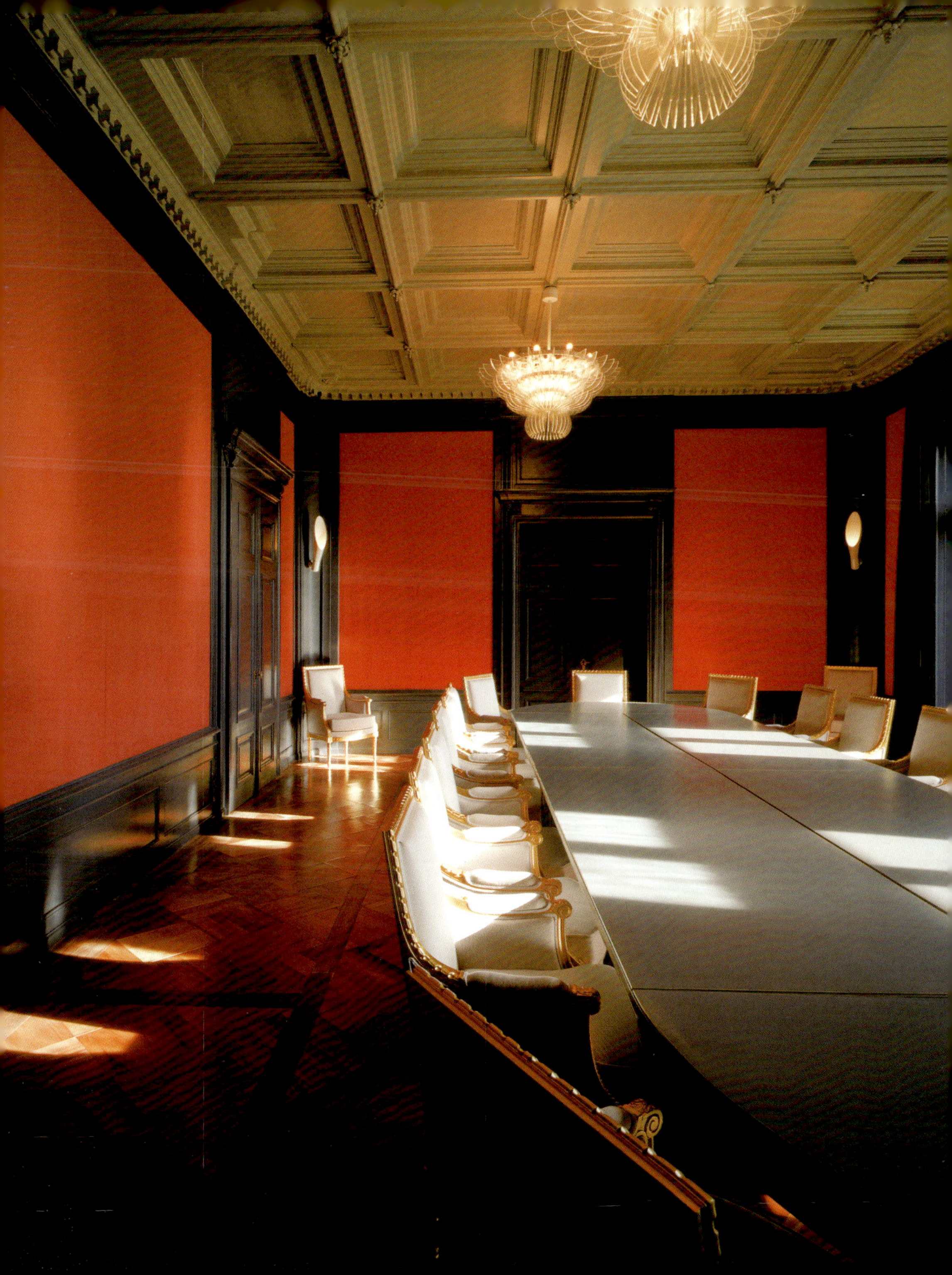

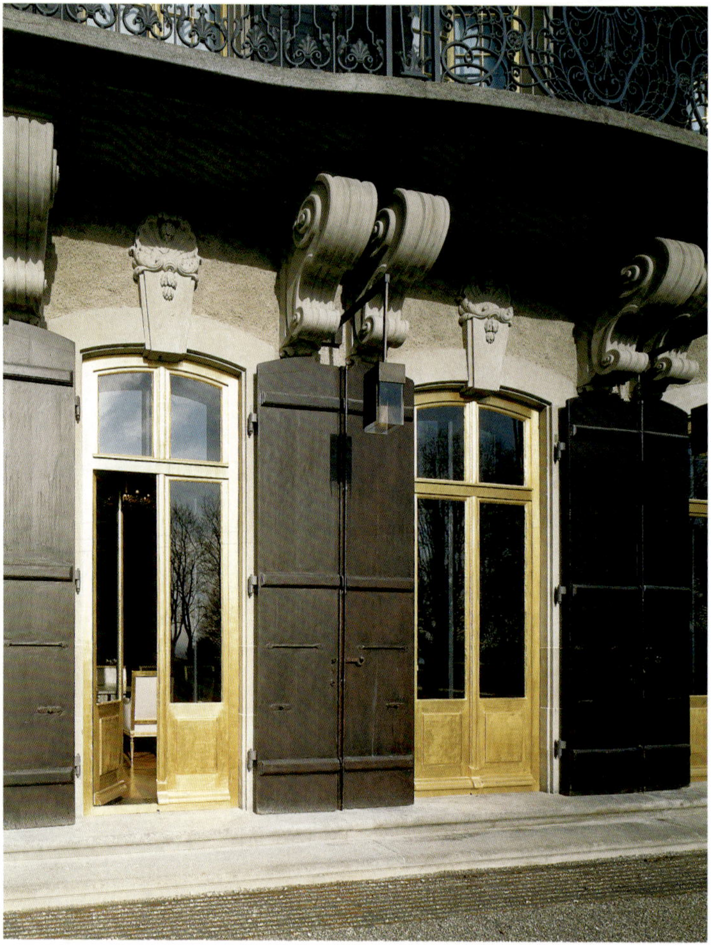

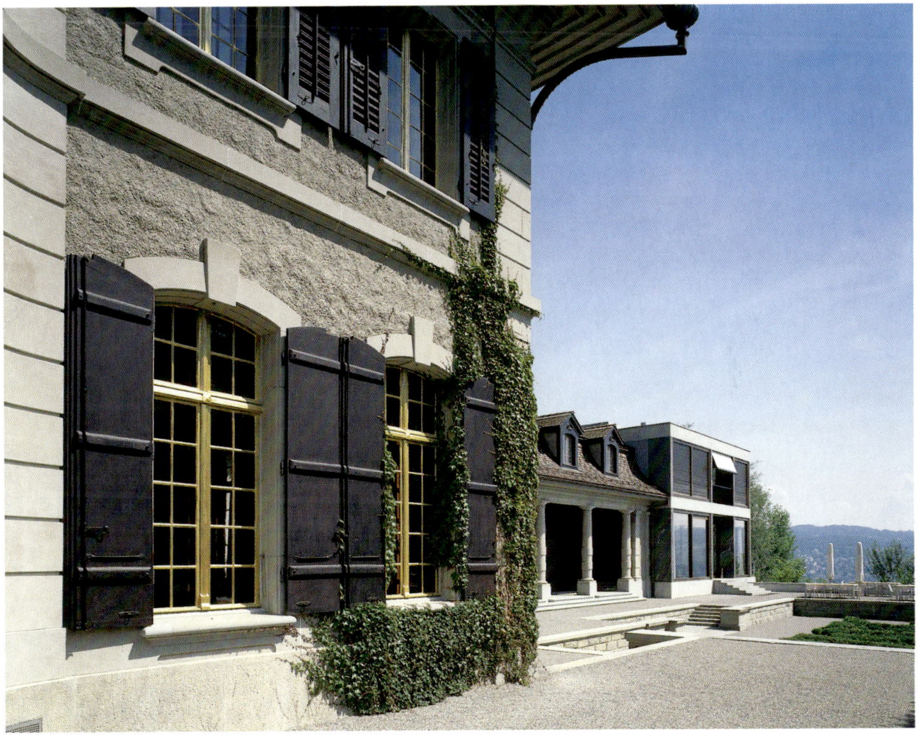

Biografische Daten

Biographical Data

Gilbert Bretterbauer

Geboren 1957 in Wien ıMatura an der HTL für Textilindustrie, Wien, Bundesheer ıStudium an der Universität für angewandte Kunst, Wien ı Zusammenarbeit mit der Galerie Peter Pakesch ı Zweijähriger Aufenthalt in Japan (Mombusho Stipendium) ıLehrtätigkeit an der Universität für angewandte Kunst, Wien ıeinjähriger Aufenthalt in Los Angeles ıMAK-Schindlerstipendium Los Angeles ıLectures am Art Center Pasadena ı lebt und arbeitet in Wien und Los Angeles

Hermann Czech

Geboren in Wien ıStudent bei Konrad Wachsmann und Ernst A. Plischke ı1985 Preis der Stadt Wien für Architektur ı1985–86 Gastprofessor an der Hochschule für angewandte Kunst, Wien ı 1988–89 und 1993–94 Gastprofessor an der Harvard University, Cambridge, Mass.

Werke ıAuswahl

1967	U-Bahn-Netzentwurf für Wien (mit F. Kurrent, J. Spalt, H. Potyka, O. Steinmann)
1974	Wettbewerbsprojekt, Donauinsel
1980	Teilnahme an der Architektur-Biennale, Venedig
1984	Umbau Palais Schwarzenberg, Wien
1984	von hier aus, Ausstellungsgestaltung, Düsseldorf
1989	Wohnbau Petrusgasse, Wien
1989	Wunderblock, Ausstellungsgestaltung, Wien
1991	Teilnahme an der Architektur-Biennale, Venedig
1994	Wohnbebauung Perchtoldsdorf bei Wien
1994	Rosa Jochmann-Schule, Wien-Simmering
1995	Winterverglasung der Loggia der Wiener Staatsoper
1996	XIX. Triennale di Milano, Ausstellungsgestaltung
1997	Einzelausstellung, Architekturmuseum Basel
1997	Einzelausstellung, Architekturforum Tirol, Innsbruck
1997	Umbau Hauptgebäude Bank Austria
2000	Teilnahme an der Architektur-Biennale, Venedig

Zahlreiche kritische und theoretische Publikationen zur Architektur

Günther Förg

1952 geboren in Füssen, Deutschland | lebt in Areuse bei Neuchâtel, Schweiz | 1992–98 Professur an der Staatlichen Hochschule für Gestaltung in Karslruhe | seit 1999 Professur an der Akademie der Bildenden Künste in München | 1996 Wolfgang-Hahn-Preis, Köln

Einzelausstellungen | Auswahl

1985	Stedelijk Museum Amsterdam (mit Jeff Wall)
1986	Kunsthalle Bern
1987	Museum Haus Lange, Krefeld
1988	Haags Gemeentemuseum, Den Haag
1989	San Francisco Museum of Modern Art
	Milwaukee Art Museum
	Castello di Rivoli – Museo d'arte contemporanea Rivoli (bei Turin)
1989–90	Museum Boymans-van Beuningen, Rotterdam
1990	The Renaissance Society at the University of Chicago
	Museum van Hedendaagse Kunst, Gent
1990–91	Museum Fridericianum Kassel
	Wiener Secession
1991	Tokyo Museum of Contemporary Art, Tokio
	Musée d'art moderne de la Ville de Paris
1992	Dallas Museum of Art
1994	Kunstmuseum Bonn
	Kunsthalle Winterthur
1995	Stedelijk Museum Amsterdam
1995–96	Kunstverein Hannover
1996–97	Museum Ludwig Köln
1997	Haus für konkrete und konstruktive Kunst, Zürich
2000	Kunsthaus Bregenz, Österreich

Otto Kapfinger

1949 geboren | freischaffender Architekturwissenschafter und Publizist | 1970–78 Mitglied der Experimentalgruppe Missing Link | 1981–90 Architekturkritiker der Tageszeitung »Die Presse« | 1979–90 Redakteur der Zeitschrift »UmBau« | 1997–98 Gastprofessor an der Hochschule für Gestaltung in Linz | Kurator zahlreicher Ausstellungen und Publikationen zur Architektur des 20. Jahrhunderts in Österreich

Dieter Kienast

Geboren 1945 in Zürich, Schweiz | Schulen und Gärtnerlehre in Zürich | Studium der Landschaftsplanung an der Gesamthochschule Kassel, Deutschland

- **1978** Promotion mit einer pflanzensoziologischen Doktorarbeit | Mitinhaber von Stöckli, Kienast & Koeppel, Landschaftsarchitekten
- **1980–91** Professor für Gartenarchitektur am Interkantonalen Technikum Rapperswil
- **1992–97** Professor für Landschaftsarchitektur an der Universität Karlsruhe
- **ab 1997** Professor an der ETH Zürich, Abteilung Architektur
- **ab 1995** Mitinhaber von Kienast Vogt Partner, Landschaftsarchitekten
- **1998** verstorben

Adolf Krischanitz

Geboren 1946 in Schwarzach im Pongau, Österreich | 1955–72 Architekturstudium Wien | seit 1979 freischaffender Architekt in Wien | 1991 Preis der Stadt Wien für Architektur | 1991–93 Präsident der Wiener Secession | seit 1992 Professor für Entwerfen und Stadterneuerung, Hochschule der Künste, Berlin

Werke | Auswahl

- **1987–89** Haus in Salmannsdorf, Wien
- **1987–89** Siedlung Pilotengasse, Wien-Aspern
- **1988** Ausstellungspavillon an der Traisen, St. Pölten
- **1989–94** Geschäfts- und Bürohaus Schillerpark, Linz
- **1989–94** Büro- und Geschäftshaus Steirerhof, Graz
- **1990–92** Kunsthalle Wien, Karlsplatz
- **1991–94** Neue Welt Schule, Wien-Prater
- **1992–95** Kunsthalle Krems
- **1993–** Bauwerke der Infrastruktur, Donau-City, Wien (in Zusammenarbeit mit Heinz Neumann)
- **1994–95** Österreich-Pavillon zur Buchmesse Frankfurt/Main
- **1995** Teilnahme an der 5. Architektur-Biennale, Venedig
- **1996** Masterplan Wohnbebauung »neues bauen am horn«, Weimar
- **1996–99** Lauder Chabad-Schule, Wien-Augarten
- **1998–2000** Innenausstattung Seminarzentrum Schweizer Rück, Zürich-Rüschlikon (in Zusammenarbeit mit Hermann Czech)
- **2000** Teilnahme an der 7. Architektur-Biennale, Venedig

Marcel Meili
1953 geboren in Küsnacht/Zürich
1973-80 Studium an der ETH Zürich bei Aldo Rossi und Mario Campi | Diplom bei Prof. Dolf Schnebli, Zürich | 1980 Mitarbeit bei Prof. Dolf Schnebli
1980-82 Wissenschaftlicher Mitarbeiter am Institut für Geschichte und Theorie der Architektur an der ETH Zürich | daneben Arbeit als freier Architekt und Zusammenarbeit mit Markus Peter
1983-85 Mitarbeiter im Büro Dolf Schnebli
1985-87 Assistent am Lehrstuhl Prof. Campi an der ETH Zürich | daneben Arbeit als freier Architekt und Zusammenarbeit mit Markus Peter
1986 Dozent an der internationalen Sommerakademie Berlin
seit 1987 eigenes Büro zusammen mit Markus Peter in Zürich
1988-91 Dozent an der Höheren Schule für Gestaltung, Zürich
1989 Dozent an der Sommerakademie Karlsruhe
1990-91 Gastdozent GSD, Harvard University, Cambridge, Mass.
1992-94 Vorsitz im Gestaltungsbeirat der Stadt Feldkirch, Österreich
1993-95 Gastdozent an der ETH Zürich
seit 1999 Professor für Architektur an der ETH Zürich

Werke | Auswahl
siehe rechts bei Markus Peter

Markus Peter
1957 geboren in Zürich; Lehre als Tiefbauzeichner
1980-81 Studium an der FU Berlin | Gasthörer an der Abteilung Philosophie
1981-84 Studium Arch. HTL Tech. Winterthur
1984 Diplom
1985-86 Arch. Büro Prof. Schnebli, Zürich Mitarbeit am Zentrum Ruopingen, LU
1986-88 Assistent bei Prof. Mario Campi, ETH Zürich | daneben freie Arbeit als Architekt und Zusammenarbeit mit Marcel Meili
seit 1987 eigenes Büro zusammen mit Marcel Meili in Zürich
1990 Dozent an der Internationalen Sommerakademie Karlsruhe (Entwurf)
1993-95 Gastdozent ETH Zürich

Meili, Peter Architekten
Werke | Auswahl
1993-95 Holzbrücke Murau, mit Jürg Conzett
1995-98 Kino Riff Raff, Zürich, mit Astrid Staufer und Thomas Hasler
1995-97 Perronhallen hauptbahnhof Zürich, mit Kaschka Knapkiewicz und Axel Fickert
1997-99 Schweizerische Hochschule für die Holzwirtschaft, Biel, mit Zeno Vogel
1995-2001 Swiss Re Rüschlikon, Centre for Global Dialogue

Elisabeth von Samsonow

Geboren 1956 | Philosophin und Bildhauerin | Professorin an der Akademie der bildenden Künste in Wien

Publikationen | Auswahl

- *Die Erneuerung des Sichtbaren. Die philosophische Begründung naturwissenschaftlicher Wahrheit bei Johannes Kepler* (1987)
- *Giordano Bruno* | hg. von E. Samsonow (1996)
- *Telenoia: Kritik der virtuellen Bilder*, hg. v. E. Samsonow und Éric Alliez | Wien (1999)
- *Hyperplastik. Kunst und Konzepte der Wahrnehmung in Zeiten der mental imagery* | hg. v. E. Samsonow und Éric Alliez | Wien (2000)
- *Fenster im Papier. Die Kollision von Architektur und Schrift oder die Gedächtnisrevolution der Renaissance* (2001)

Beiträge | Auswahl

- »Deus sine natura: Theopathie in der Fabrica«, in: *Puppe. Monster. Tod: kulturelle Transformationsprozesse der Bio- und Informationstechnologien* | hg. von Johanna Riegler (1999)
- »O Stern und Blume, Geist und Kleid« | in: *Wolfgang Laib* | KUB, König: Köln (1999)
- »Zurückbiegen (Reflexion) und Umwerfen (Subversion) – Denk- und Handlungstraining für Selbstverhältnisse und andere Beziehungen« | in: *Kunst und Demokratie* | hg. v. Irmgard Bohounovsky-Bärnthaler | Ritter: Klagenfurt (1999)
- »Keramische Erregungsquanten« | in: *Helmut Federle* | KUB, König: Köln (1999)

Margherita Spiluttini

1947 geboren | freischaffende Fotografin | seit 1981 Bild-Autorin zahlreicher Publikationen über zeitgenössische Baukunst | Beteiligung an nationalen und internationalen Ausstellungen | Die sachliche Brillanz und Poetik ihrer Arbeit wurde mehrfach mit nationalen und internationalen Preisen gewürdigt

Günther Vogt

1957 geboren in Balzers, Liechtenstein | Lehre an der Gartenbauschule Oeschberg | Studium der Landschaftsarchitektur am Interkantonalen Technikum Rapperswil

1987 Mitarbeiter bei Stöckli, Kienast & Koeppel, Landschaftsarchitekten

1995 Mitinhaber von Kienast Vogt Partner, Landschaftsarchitekten

2000 Inhaber von Vogt Landschaftsarchitekten

Gilbert Bretterbauer

Born in Vienna in 1957 |graduated from a secondary technical school in Vienna that prepares pupils for the textile industry |compulsory service in the Austrian army |graduate of the University of Applied Arts, Vienna |co-operation with Galerie Peter Pakesch |two-year stay in Japan (Mombusho scholarship) |taught at the University of Applied Arts, Vienna |one-year stay in Los Angeles |MAK Schindler scholarship Los Angeles |Lectured at the Art Center Pasadena, California, lives and works in Vienna and Los Angeles

Hermann Czech

Born in Vienna |studied under Konrad Wachsmann and Ernst A. Plischke | 1985 Architectural Award of the City of Vienna | 1985–86 guest professor at the University of Applied Arts, Vienna | 1988–89 and 1993–94 guest professor at Harvard University, Cambridge, Mass.

Selected works

1967	design for an underground network for Vienna (with F. Kurrent, J. Spalt, H. Potyka, O. Steinmann)
1974	competition entry, Danube Island, Vienna
1980	participation in the Venice Architectural Biennial
1984	remodelling of Palais Schwarzenberg, Vienna
1984	von hier aus, exhibition design, Düsseldorf
1989	residential building Petrusgasse, Vienna
1989	Wunderblock, exhibition design, Vienna
1991	participation in the Venice Architectural Biennial
1994	housing project in Perchtoldsdorf near Vienna
1994	Rosa Jochmann School, Vienna–Simmering
1995	glazing in of the loggia of the Vienna State Opera
1996	XIX Triennale di Milano, exhibition design
1997	one-man exhibition, Architectural Museum, Basel
1997	one-man exhibition, Architekturforum Tirol, Innsbruck
1997	remodelling of the headquarters of Bank Austria
2000	participation in the Venice Architectural Biennial

Numerous critical and theoretical publications on architecture

Günther Förg

Born in Füssen, Germany, in 1952 | lives in Areuse near Neuchâtel, Switzerland | 1992–98 professor at the Staatliche Hochschule für Gestaltung at Karlsruhe | since 1999 professor at the Academy of Fine Arts in Munich | 1996 Wolfgang Hahn Award, Cologne

Selected one-man exhibitions

- 1985 Stedelijk Museum Amsterdam (with Jeff Wall)
- 1986 Kunsthalle Bern
- 1987 Museum Haus Lange, Krefeld
- 1988 Haags Gemeentemuseum, Den Haag
- 1989 San Francisco Museum of Modern Art
  Milwaukee Art Museum
  Castello di Rivoli – Museo d'arte contemporanea Rivoli (near Turin)
- 1989-90 Museum Boymans-van Beuningen, Rotterdam
- 1990 The Renaissance Society at the University of Chicago
  Museum van Hedendaagse Kunst, Ghent
- 1990-91 Museum Fridericianum Kassel
  Vienna Secession
- 1991 Tokyo Museum of Contemporary Art, Tokyo
  Musée d'art moderne de la Ville de Paris
- 1992 Dallas Museum of Art
- 1994 Kunstmuseum Bonn
  Kunsthalle Winterthur
- 1995 Stedelijk Museum Amsterdam
- 1995-96 Kunstverein Hannover
- 1996-97 Museum Ludwig Cologne
- 1997 Haus für konkrete und konstruktive Kunst, Zürich
- 2000 Kunsthaus Bregenz, Austria

Otto Kapfinger

Born in 1949 | freelance architecture scholar and journalist | 1970–78 member of the experimental group Missing Link | 1981-90 architecture critic for the daily newspaper "Die Presse" | 1979–90 editor of the journal »UmBau« | 1997 | 98 visiting professor at the University of Design in Linz | curator of numerous exhibitions and publications on architecture of the 20th century in Austria.

Dieter Kienast

Born in Zürich in 1945 | Gardener's apprenticeship in Zürich | Studied landscape architecture at the Gesamthochschule Kassel, Germany

- 1978 Doctorate with a dissertation about plant sociology | Co-owner of Stöckli, Kienast & Koeppel, Landscape Architects
- 1980-91 Professor of landscape architecture at the Interkantonales Technikum Rapperswil, Switzerland
- 1992-97 Professor of landscape architecture at the University of Karlsruhe
- 1997-98 Professor at the ETH Zürich, Department of Architecture
- 1995-98 Co-owner of Kienast Vogt Partner, Landscape Architects

died in 1998

Adolf Krischanitz

Born in Schwarzach im Pongau, Austria, in 1946 | 1955-72 studied architecture in Vienna | since 1979 freelance architect in Vienna | 1991 Architectural Award of the City of Vienna | 1991-93 President of the Vienna Secession | since 1992 Professor for Design and Urban Renewal, Hochschule der Künste, Berlin

Selected works

- 1987-89 single-family house in Salmannsdorf, Vienna
- 1987-89 housing project Pilotengasse, Vienna-Aspern
- 1988 exhibition pavilion along the Traisen River, St. Pölten
- 1989-94 business and office building Schillerpark, Linz
- 1989-94 office and business building Steirerhof, Graz
- 1990-92 Kunsthalle Vienna, Karlsplatz
- 1991-94 Neue Welt School, Vienna-Prater
- 1992-95 Kunsthalle Krems
- 1993- infrastructural buildings, Donau-City, Vienna (together with Heinz Neumann)
- 1994-95 Austrian pavilion for the Frankfurt Book Fair, Frankfurt/Main
- 1995 participation in the 5th Venice Architectural Biennal
- 1996 master-plan for the housing project "neues bauen am horn", Weimar
- 1996-99 Lauder Chabad School, Vienna-Augarten
- 1998-2000 interior of Training Centre of Swiss re, Zürich-Rüschlikon (together with Hermann Czech)
- 2000 participation in the 7th Venice Architectural Biennal

Marcel Meili

- **1953** born in Küsnacht, Zürich
- **1973–80** studied at the ETH Zürich under Aldo Rossi and Mario Campi | Diploma under Professor Dolf Schnebli, Zürich
- **1980** work for Professor Dolf Schnebli
- **1980–82** Assistant at the Institute for the History and Theory of Architecture at the ETH Zürich | alongside his work as a freelance architect and his co-operation with Markus Peter
- **1983–85** staff member in Dolf Schnebli's architectural office
- **1985–87** Assistant to Professor Campi at the ETH Zürich | alongside his work as a freelance architect and his co-operation with Markus Peter
- **1986** Lecturer at the International Summer Academy Berlin
- **since 1987** he has had his own architectural office in Zürich together with Markus Peter
- **1988–91** Lecturer at the Höhere Schule für Gestaltung, Zürich
- **1989** Lecturer at the Summer Academy Karlsruhe
- **1990–91** Guest lecturer, Graduate School for Design, Harvard University, Cambridge, Mass.
- **1992–94** Chairman of the Advisory Committee on Design of the City of Feldkirch (Austria)
- **1993–95** Guest lecturer at the ETH Zürich
- **since 1999** Professor of Architecture at the ETH Zürich

Works | Selection

see right (Markus Peter)

Markus Peter

- **1957** born in Zürich | apprenticeship as a civil engineering draughtsman
- **1980–81** studied at Freie Universität Berlin audited classes in philosophy
- **1981–84** studied architecture at the Technical Institute of Wintherthur | Diploma in 1984
- **1985–86** work at the architectural office of Professor Schnebli, Zürich | Cooperation in Zentrum Ruopingen, Luzerne
- **1986–88** Assistant to Professor Mario Campi, ETH Zürich | alongside his work as a freelance architect and his cooperation with Marcel Meili
- **since 1987** he has had his own architectural office in Zürich together with Marcel Meili
- **1990** Lecturer in Design at the International Summer Academy Karlsruhe
- **1993–95** Guest lecturer at ETH Zürich

Meili, Peter Architects
Works | Selection

- **1993–95** Wooden bridge, Murau, with Jürg Conzett
- **1995–98** Riff Raff Cinema, Zürich, with Astrid Staufer and Thomas Holzer
- **1995–97** New Roof Addition, Zürich Main Railway Station, with Kaschka Knapiewicz and Axel Fickert
- **1997–99** Swiss School of Engineering for the Wood Industry, Biel, with Zeno Vogel
- **1995–2001** Swiss Re Rüschlikon, Centre for Global Dialogue

Elisabeth von Samsonow

Born in 1956 | Philosopher and sculptor | Professor at the Academy of Fine Arts in Vienna

Selected publications | Books

- *Die Erneuerung des Sichtbaren. Die philosophische Begründung naturwissenschaftlicher Wahrheit bei Johannes Kepler* (1987)
- *Giordano Bruno* | ed. by E. Samsonow (1996)
- *Telenoia: Kritik der virtuellen Bilder* | ed. by E. Samsonow and Éric Alliez | Vienna (1999)
- *Hyperplastik. Kunst und Konzepte der Wahrnehmung in Zeiten der mental imagery* | ed. by E. Samsonow and Éric Alliez | Vienna (2000)
- *Fenster im Papier. Die Kollision von Architektur und Schrift oder die Gedächtnisrevolution der Renaissance* (2001)

Articles

- "Deus sine natura: Theopathie in der Fabrica" | in: Puppe. *Monster. Tod: kulturelle Transformationsprozesse der Bio- und Informationstechnologien* | ed. by Johanna Riegler (1999)
- "O Stern und Blume, Geist und Kleid" | in: *Wolfgang Laib* | KUB, König: Cologne (1999)
- "Zurückbiegen (Reflexion) und Umwerfen (Subversion) – Denk- und Handlungstraining für Selbstverhältnisse und andere Beziehungen" | in: *Kunst und Demokratie* | ed. by Irmgard Bohounovsky-Bärnthaler, Ritter: Klagenfurt (1999)
- "Keramische Erregungsquanten", in: *Helmut Federle* | KUB, König: Cologne (1999)

Margherita Spiluttini

Born in 1947 | freelance photographer | since 1981 her photographs have graced the pages of countless publications on contemporary architecture, has participated in national and international exhibitions. The sober brilliance and poetry of her work have earned her many national and international awards.

Günther Vogt

Born in Balzers, Liechtenstein, in 1957 | Apprenticeship and study at the Horticulture school Oeschberg | Studied landscape architecture at the Interkantonales Technikum Rapperswil, Switzerland

- 1987 employed at Stöckli, Kienast & Koeppel, Landscape Architects
- 1995 co-owner of Kienast Vogt Partner, Landscape Architects
- since 2000 owner of Vogt Landscape Architects

Die Deutsche Bibliothek – CIP Einheitsaufnahme
Ein Titeldatensatz für diese
Publikation ist bei Der Deutschen
Bibliothek erhältlich

Die Deutsche Bibliothek – CIP Cataloguing-in-Publication-Data
A catalogue record for this
publication is available from
Die Deutsche Bibliothek

ISBN 3-7757-1022-1

Herausgeber Publisher
Kunsthaus Bregenz
archiv kunst architektur

Copyright
© 2001 Kunsthaus Bregenz und
Autoren | by Kunsthaus Bregenz
and the authors

Konzeption Conception
Otto Kern | Edelbert Köb
Clemens Schedler

Redaktion Editorial work
Edelbert Köb

Übersetzungen Translation
Maria E. Clay | Kimi Lum

Endlektorat Copy-editing
Claudia Mazanek

Gestaltung Graphic design
Clemens Schedler
Büro für konkrete Gestaltung | Wien

Bildrechte Photo copyright
Margherita Spiluttini | Wien

Druck Printer
Agens-Werk Geyer + Reisser | Wien

Schrift Typeface
Helvetica Neue

Reproduktion Reproductions
Agens-Werk Geyer + Reisser | Wien
Bildbearbeitung | Image treatment:
Boris Bonev

Papier Paper
Kern | Body:
Magnomatt Satin, 170 g/m²
Umschlag | Cover:
Emotion, schlicht weiß, 240 g/m²

Auflage Edition
2000 Exemplare im September 2001
2000 copies in September 2001

Hatje Cantz Verlag
Senefeldstraße 12
D-73760 Ostfildern | Ruit
Phone: (+49-711) 440 50
Fax: (+49-711) 440 52 20
Web: www.hatje.de

Kunsthaus Bregenz
Karl Tizian Platz
A-6900 Bregenz
Phone: (+43-5574) 485 94-0
Fax: (+43-5574) 485 94-8
Web: www.kunsthaus-bregenz.at

Printed in Austria